James d'Alwis

A Descriptive Catalogue of Sanskrit, Pali, and Sinhalese - Literary Works of Ceylon

Vol. I

James d'Alwis

A Descriptive Catalogue of Sanskrit, Pali, and Sinhalese - Literary Works of Ceylon
Vol. I

ISBN/EAN: 9783337230319

Printed in Europe, USA, Canada, Australia, Japan

Cover: Foto ©Thomas Meinert / pixelio.de

More available books at **www.hansebooks.com**

A DESCRIPTIVE CATALOGUE OF SANSKRIT, PALI, & SINHALESE LITERARY WORKS OF CEYLON.

BY

JAMES D'ALWIS,

M. R. A. S.,

ADVOCATE OF THE SUPREME COURT;
AUTHOR OF THE SIDATSANGARA'; AN INTRODUCTION TO SINHALESE GRAMMAR;
INTRODUCTION TO KACHCHA'YANA'S PA'LI GRAMMAR;
THE ATTANAGALUVANSA; CONTRIBUTIONS TO
ORIENTAL LITERATURE, ETC., ETC.

IN THREE VOLUMES.

VOL. I.

COLOMBO:
WILLIAM SKEEN, GOVERNMENT PRINTER, CEYLON.

1870.

TO

SIR HERCULES GEORGE ROBERT ROBINSON,

K. C. M. G.,

GOVERNOR AND COMMANDER-IN-CHIEF OF THE ISLAND OF CEYLON.

SIR,

IT is my pleasing duty to inscribe this work to you, for the compilation of which you did me the honor to appoint me, and for the prosecution of which you have placed at my disposal much of the assistance of which I was in need.

I shall not speak of my own work in terms of approbation,—it is for the public to decide on its merits; nor is it within my province to enhance its value by any allusion to the trouble it has entailed on me,—for that too may be judged of by others: but, apart from the mode in which the work has been executed, permit me to say that, from its very design, it will open to the reading public a means of obtaining rare and valuable information. If the orient pearls for which Ceylon has been famed from all antiquity, are still highly prized amongst the nations of the world, the intellectual pearls which Oriental scholars of many nations will be enabled to gather from Lanka's Store-house of Literature, which you have founded, and the key to which is here presented, will not, I hope, be esteemed as less precious or valuable.

Confident that nothing will more enduringly bind the memory of Your Excellency to the present and future generations of the native Siṇhalese, than "THE SANSKRIT, PÁLI, AND SIṆHALESE LIBRARY" which you have established, it is to me a source of sincere pleasure that I have been enabled to complete, at least, one volume of the Descriptive Catalogue during your Government; and I indulge the hope that, as an Index of the Library, it will set before the world a correct, though feeble, "description" of the now fading, but still rich, literature of the Country, over the Government of which you have presided for the last five years, with great credit to yourself, and lasting benefit to all classes of the people.

I have the honor to be,

Your Excellency's

Most obedient and faithful Servant,

JAS. ALWIS.

Nai-Villa,

28th June, 1870.

CONTENTS.

APPENDIX.

PREFACE.

"That Ceylon is one of the principal seats of Buddhism, that Buddhism is one of the most important religions of mankind, that the Buddhist priests possess a sacred literature which dates from several centuries before the Christian era,—all this is perfectly well known. But it is less well known that though, since the beginning of this century, Ceylon has been an English colony, hardly anything has been done by the English Government to collect these interesting relics of an ancient literature, to deposit them in our public libraries, and thus to render them accessible to Oriental scholars; while the French Government—nay, it would seem an individual French gentleman—has, during the last six years, accomplished all that could be desired."*

Such was the reproach cast on the English Government by the Saturday Review of the 28th of July, 1866. Three years had scarcely elapsed from that date before Sir Hercules Robinson, the Governor of Ceylon, alive to the importance of the subject, has

* "Du Bouddhisme et de sa Littérature à Ceylan et en Birmanis. Collection de M. Grimblot, Vice-Consul de France à Ceylon. Par M. Barthélemy Saint-Hilaire. Extrait du 'Journal des Savants,' 1866.

taken the necessary steps to establish a Public Library of Oriental works, accessible, upon certain terms, both to the inhabitants of this Island, and to those Oriental scholars in Europe, who, I believe, will frequently avail themselves of it.

The history of this work may be briefly stated in the language of official correspondence.

On the 7th of December, 1868, Mr. H. S. O. Russell, the Government Agent of the Northern Province, after alluding to the measures which were then being taken in India for the discovery and preservation of the Records of ancient Sanskrit Literature, suggested to the Governor "that possibly some not unimportant contribution to the catalogue of MS. works in the Sanskrit language, might result from an inspection of the library shelves of Pansalas in Ceylon."* On the receipt of this letter, it was placed in the hands of Mr. L. De Zoysa, Chief Translator to Government, and a well-read Oriental scholar, for his observations, which will be found embodied in the following

"MEMORANDUM.

Mr. Dickson having requested me to offer any observations I may wish to make in regard to Mr. Russell's proposal respecting the discovery and preservation of the records of Ancient Sanskrit Literature, I venture to submit the following remarks for consideration :—

* Government Gazette.

I do not think it probable that the inspection of the library shelves of the Pansalas of Ceylon, is likely to add any Sanskrit manuscripts of any importance, to the Catalogue that is being prepared in India; nearly, if not all, the Sanskrit manuscripts extant in this country, being importations from India.

But if some such scheme as that adopted by the Indian Government be applied not only to the Sanskrit, but also to the Páli and Siŋhalese manuscripts in this country, there is every reason to believe that many important historical and other works which are not now accessible to the learned, may be brought to light. Several destructions of literary records of Ceylon in ancient times, are recorded in the Maha Wanso, and other historical works; and the number of important original works now extant in the country is not very great. In almost every Siŋhalese, or Páli work on History, Grammar, General Literature, &c., now extant, references are made to more ancient works on those subjects, but which either exist no longer, or are not generally accessible. It is however, the general belief, that many valuable and important manuscripts which are unknown to the learned in Kandy, or the Low Country, do exist in some of the Buddhist Pansalas, and other places in the outlying Districts of the Kandyan Provinces, especially in those of the North-Western Province, whence some manuscripts of great value, and formerly not known in the country, have been recently added to the list of works now generally known. Amongst these may be mentioned an ancient Siŋhalese copy of 'Winayartha Samuchchaya,' containing a summary of the *Winaya Pitaka* (Laws of the Buddhist Priesthood), written in a very chaste style, contrasting most favorably with the bombastic style of modern Siŋhalese writings; and a history of Relics of Buddha, containing interesting information respecting parts of the Island, which are now comparatively unknown.

Should the proposed inspection of the Buddhist Libraries of Ceylon bring to light any works on history not known at present, the interest that may be excited by such discoveries, and the benefits to be derived thereby, will not be confined to Ceylon, but will be shared by the learned in India and Europe. It is now generally believed that the ancient historical records of the Siŋhalese are far more valuable and authentic than those of other Indian Nations. The Maha Wanso, (History of Ceylon), translated into English by the late Hon'ble George Turnour of Ceylon, has been pronounced by high authority, to be "the most valuable historical record we possess in relation to ancient India."

I may also be permitted to add, that most of the Buddhist Priests in the interior parts of the Kandyan Provinces, in whose charge the Potgulas (Libraries) are preserved, are very illiterate and ignorant, and do not know what manuscripts exist in their Pansalas, and it is therefore essentially necessary that *all* the manuscripts in their possession, should be inspected by competent persons, who take an interest in the work, and catalogued in the manner proposed by the Indian authorities.

Respectfully submitted,

L. De Zoysa,

Chief Trans. to Govt.

Colonial Secretary's Office,
Colombo, 12th January, 1869."

When the above correspondence, together with an endorsement* of approval by Mr. John F. Dickson,

* "I fully agree with the Chief Translator that it would be desirable, in the interests of learning and historical research, to make

Assistant Colonial Secretary, was laid before Lieutenant-General S. Hodgson, the Officer then administering the Government of Ceylon, he issued a Circular* to Government Agents of Provinces, indicating "the possibility of accurate catalogues of MSS. in the Pansalas being obtained," and inquiring what steps could be taken for ascertaining the contents of the libraries of the various Pansalas, "with a view to the discovery of any interesting or unknown MSS., Páli and Siṇhalese as well as Sanskrit." Whilst the Native Headmen were in correspondence with Buddhist priests, and were actually preparing lists of MSS. (which have been since forwarded to me) in accordance with the above official requisition, Mr. John Murdoch, the Agent of the Christian Vernacular Education Society, with that praiseworthy anxiety which he has ever evinced in the promotion of Religion, Literature, and Science, addressed the following letter to Government.

"I have the honor to submit to His Excellency the Governor, a copy of a classified Catalogue of printed Tracts and Books in Siṇhalese.

While the above Catalogue will be useful for some purposes, Oriental scholars wish information respecting the

---

enquiry in Ceylon for unknown Páli and Siṇhalese, as well as for Sanskrit manuscripts, and I beg to submit this paper for the favorable consideration of the Colonial Secretary.

JOHN F. DICKSON."

* See Gazette; letter 4th Feb., 1869.

numerous works which still exist only in manuscript, in the possession of temples or individuals, scattered over the Island. The obtaining of a complete list of the books extant in Siŋhalese and Páli can be obtained only through the aid of Government. Such an enquiry, embracing the whole Island, would form an important department of the work of the Archæological Commission. To conduct it successfully, requires a competent scholar, familiar with the literature of the country, and whose other engagements permit him to devote the requisite time to the investigation. Fortunately the right man is available,—James De Alwis, Esq., has written the best account of Siŋhalese literature which has been published, and is well known to Oriental scholars, from his works on Grammar and Buddhism. I have reason to believe that his services would be gladly rendered for such an object.

In the first instance, it would simply be necessary to print a classified Catalogue of the Manuscripts. A statement explanatory of the object in view, should be published in the *Government Gazette.* Copies should be forwarded through the Government Agents to all the Buddhist Temples and the Native Headmen. The Commissioner might send them to any other parties likely to afford assistance.

The following information should be obtained regarding each work :--

1. Where found.*
2. The Title, with the name of the Author, if known.

---

* Since a collection of MSS. is now being made, it is not necessary to state this though the fact will be noticed in the case of rare MSS. preserved in certain old Temples, and which the priests are reluctant to part with.

3. The size: number of leaves, with the length and number of lines in each page. If incomplete, should be mentioned.*

4. The subject.

The replies should be forwarded to the Commissioner. A classified catalogue, according to the arrangement suggested by Messrs. Winter, Jones and Watt of the British Museum, might then be made out and printed. The number of MSS. existing of each work, so far as indicated by the replies, might be mentioned.

Copies of the catalogue might be forwarded to Oriental scholars, and books which they considered valuable might be collected. In some cases the owners would be sufficiently patriotic to give them up for such a purpose. When necessary, MSS. might be purchased or copied.

The result of the researches of the late Mr. Turnour lead to the hope that some important works might thus be brought to light. It has already been proved that the historical literature of the Siṇhalese is the most valuable in the East. Should the enquiry shew that nothing further of importance existed, even this would be of some consequence. In a broader view, however, the investigation would certainly be interesting as an index to the national mind.

The expense would be very trifling, and the catalogue would be prized by Oriental Scholars throughout the world. Lists of books in the languages of India are in progress; but

---

* I have attended to this as a rule, but have departed from it only in such cases as where the size of the ola did not give an accurate idea of the extent of writing, or where the bulk was ascertainable from the mention of the number of anushtab verses, banavaras, gathas, stanzas, etc.

Ceylon is the only Buddhistical country, except the south of Burmah, under the British Government. A class of works is found here not now procurable in India.

May I be permitted also to suggest, that all printers should be required to supply at least one copy for payment of each work published. The Director of Public Instruction might append a short notice of the Native Press to his Annual Report. It is true that the publications at present are comparatively few in number and insignificant in character. Still, they are more numerous than might be expected, considering that only a very few years have elapsed since the first press was owned by a native.

JOHN MURDOCH.

Colombo, 15th June, 1869."

The above led to the following notification in the Ceylon Government *Gazette* of 17th July, 1869.

"The following papers suggesting that enquiry be made in the interest of learning and historical research, as to the Páli, Siŋhalese and Sanskrit MSS. to be found in the Pansalas of Ceylon, are published for general information; and it is notified that Mr. James D'Alwis having consented to collect the desired information, all Government Officers are hereby required to afford him all the information and assistance in their power.

By His Excellency's Command,

HENRY T. IRVING,
Colonial Secretary.

Colonial Secretary's Office,
Colombo, 12th July, 1869."

The above was followed by an official communication from the Colonial Secretary addressed to me, dated the 15th July, 1869.

"I am directed by the Governor to inform you, that the Government gladly avails itself of the services which you have been so public-spirited as to place at its disposal for the purpose of ascertaining what valuable and unknown MSS. are to be found in Ceylon."

As the Catalogue proposed by Mr. Murdoch would, according to the above requirement, be necessarily limited to "valuable and unknown MSS."; and since "valuable" was a relative term, and the value attached to a work might vary according to the peculiar ideas of each individual, it was not without some deliberation that I resolved upon the plan of the work. I clearly perceived that, even if I examined every book in every Pansala in Ceylon, and yet found no MS. that I considered either "valuable or unknown," my labours for months, and perhaps, for years, would be in vain. On the other hand, if I selected a few MSS., and pronounced them "valuable or unknown," some one might differ from me in opinion, and pronounce them both "valueless and known."

It was moreover stated by several educated Natives, as well as Europeans, in Ceylon, that "a simple list of books with their titles and authors' names, and a specification of the subject on which they treated, would lead to no important results," and that what they desired to have was "information respecting the works"—information which "it was desirable to obtain without reading an entire book." I therefore determined to make a Descriptive Catalogue of all the MSS. which had their origin in Ceylon, and wrote the following letter to Government:—

"I purpose to write a descriptive Catalogue of all the Sanskrit, Páli, and Siŋhalese books composed, and now extant in Ceylon, and to print it in sheets as I proceed, and finally to make an Alphabetical Index to the whole work. This I find to be the object aimed at, not only in the Indian papers, but in Mr. Murdoch's letter published in the *Government Gazette.* A simple notice of only what I may consider 'valuable or unknown MSS.,' as required by your letter, may not, I fear, secure the desired information, nor lessen my trouble and labour, except in the mere writing out of a description of each work. Besides, the many works extant in this Island, though not possessing an interest to any one particular class of readers, may yet be of service to Oriental students in general. I shall therefore be glad to be informed, whether the plan of the work which I propose to adopt meets with His Excellency's approval."

Not content with a simple examination of libraries, and the publication of a Catalogue, I took the liberty, at the same time, of suggesting the formation of a Library, and with what success the correspondence which follows the subjoined proposal will sufficiently explain.

"In the interest of Learning, Science, and Historical research, I beg to submit for His Excellency's consideration, the desirability of forming a Library of Páli, Sanskrit, and Siŋhalese works. In some of the Temples which I have already visited, there are to be found duplicate and triplicate copies of valuable MSS., and it may not be impossible to purchase them, through the agency of Government Officials, for a sum considerably below their cost price; and, it is also probable, when it is known that the object of Government is to preserve their records in the interest of the Siŋhalese nation, as well as of Science and Learning, that many persons will be disposed to give up some of their duplicate copies without charge. The expense too of getting copies made of such of the works as may not be procured, as above indicated, will not be great. If His Excellency should deem such a collection desirable, it may not be difficult to procure from Burma a complete set of all the works on Buddhism, which are identical with those in Ceylon, except in the particular character used, which is the Burmese.

"Whether, however, a collection of MSS. is made at once, or the scheme be postponed for a future period, it is very desirable to procure from Burma a list of all the books, which the people of that country have from time to time obtained from Ceylon. It is believed,—and tradition supports the belief,—that amongst those books are some of our most valuable works, which are either rare at present or not extant in Ceylon. And I may here mention, on the authority of the late Mr. George Turnour, that the success of his translation of the *Mahawansa* was attributable, chiefly, to a rare correct copy of the Gloss, which that gentleman obtained through Nadoris de Silva, Mudaliyar, from the Burman Empire."

From the COLONIAL SECRETARY to Mr. J. ALWIS.

Colombo, 25th September, 1869.

I have laid before the Governor your letter of the 15th instant.

I am desired to inform you, in reply, that the plan of the work which you propose to adopt, as explained in the 3rd paragraph of your letter, meets entirely with His Excellency's approval, and that the necessary instructions will be given to place the Government Printing Office at your disposal.

* * * * * *

As regards your proposal to form a Library of Páli, Sanskrit, and Siŋhalese Works, I am desired to state that His Excellency would be glad to receive from you a detailed statement of the steps necessary for carrying out such an object, and its probable cost, both at starting and afterwards annually.

The Government Agents and Assistant Agents will be instructed to furnish you with the particulars you require, respecting number, situation, &c., of the Monasteries or Pansalas.

From Mr. JAMES ALWIS to the COLONIAL SECRETARY.

8th December, 1869.

* * * * * *

I have carefully considered the subject of forming a Páli, Sanskrit, and Siŋhalese Library; and I beg to state briefly my views, as to the steps necessary for carrying out such a laudable object.

By far the most valuable and the most voluminous works, which are comprised under the head of Tepiṭaka and their Commentaries, may be procured for a sum not exceeding £500. For their revision, I propose that the sum of £100 be laid out.

The learned High Priest of Adam's Peak is now engaged with a Committee of learned Priests in the work of revision; and I beg to recommend that the same Committee be engaged to furnish to Government, which they are willing to do, a complete set of the books above-mentioned for a given price, which can be ascertained and fixed upon hereafter.

All the other Páli, Sanskrit, and Sinhalese books in this Island, of which I shall furnish a List, need not cost more than £600; and copies of them may be purchased or procured through the instrumentality of the Government Agent of Galle and his Assistants in the Southern Province—the only part of this Island where Ola-writing is carried to perfection, and where qualified copyists are to be found.

In my previous letter I indicated that books might be procured in different ways; and I am still not without hope, that many MSS. may be obtained without charge; but these are details which may be left to the parties employed by Government for the collection of books.

A Library, thus formed at a cost of £1,200, may be attached to the Government Record Office. Three large rooms (say 20 × 25 feet each) will contain all the necessary shelves, which may be constructed of sheet iron, containing a cell for each book, with a lid, whereon the name of the book may be marked. The furniture, so far as I can judge, need not cost £300; and thus the entire expense of getting up a Library will be no more than £1,500.

When once the Library has been established, the expense of upkeep will be very trifling. The servants of the Record Office alone will be sufficient to do the needful in respect of the preservation of the books. The Library may be open to the Public, subject to Rules which the Government may deem proper to prescribe; and the only Officer who, so far as I can foresee, will be required to carry out such Rules, is a Librarian, whose salary need not be more than £100 per annum.

I beg again to press on the attention of Government the great desirability of forming such a Library, and the manifold and lasting advantages which will accrue thereby to the Siŋhalese Nation and the English Community, not to speak of the benefits which will be derived therefrom by Scholars in Europe, and by distinguished Travellers who visit Ceylon.

From the COLONIAL SECRETARY to Mr. JAMES ALWIS.

Colombo, 4th January, 1870.

Having laid before the Governor and the Executive Council your letter of the 8th ultimo, submitting suggestions for the establishment of a Páli, Sanskrit, and Siŋhalese Library, I am desired to inform you that the project meets with the entire approval of the Government, and that His Excellency will be prepared to apply to the Legislative Council for the necessary funds to carry it into effect.

It is His Excellency's wish that you should take a leading part in the formation of the Library, and he would be glad if you would from time to time furnish Lists of the Books which you think should be procured, naming what you consider a fair price for them, and suggesting in each case the best agency for conducting the negotiations.

The object of this Preface is not so much to give information on the establishment of a Library, as to explain the plan of the Descriptive Catalogue. Yet, as the one is inseparably connected with the other, I may briefly allude to the steps which are being taken for the formation of "the Government Oriental Library of Ceylon."

The Legislative Council of Ceylon has voted the funds necessary for immediate expenditure; and Committees composed of influential priests and laymen, under the presidency of Government Agents, have been appointed by the Government in the Sabaragamuwa District, in Galle, and in Mátara, to secure in the first instance, what I am glad to find Professor Max Müller in his letter on the subject to the Secretary of State for the Colonies,* calls—"the important" viz., "the sacred literature of Buddhism." I believe these Committees are actively engaged in the work of transcription assigned to them, and I trust the time will not be long before the existence of a Public Oriental Library in Ceylon will be a fact. The Government have also secured the benefit of a revision of a portion of the canonical works of Buddhism, made by a body of learned priests under the presidency of the learned High Priest of Adam's Peak, in the monastic establishments of Sabaragamuwa. The only want hitherto felt for rendering this copy as accurate as possible, was that of a complete copy of the Burmese Code, which had been taken away many centuries ago from this Island; but I believe there is every probability of this being soon obtained from the king of Burma. It is not possible to purchase *all* the MSS., but where the writing presents undoubted evidences of high antiquity, it would be desirable, as remarked by Professor Max Müller, "that the original MSS. should be bought and preserved;"

---

* See Appendix A.

and I see no objection to his proposal "to preserve carefully-made copies (of them) in Ceylon, and to transfer the originals to England," where they would be (not only) in safer keeping than elsewhere, but would be more thoroughly examined and published than in Ceylon.

Application has also been made to the authorities at Burma; and a copy of the Tepiṭaka consisting of 42 vols. is on its way to Ceylon; and it is not unlikely that a similar application to the king of Siam will secure to the Colony the benefit of the version extant in that country. The advantages to be derived from an intercomparison of these versions with our own cannot be overrated.

Such are briefly the facts connected with the proposed Library: and, though its establishment, (which may be looked upon as an accomplished fact), has in a great measure rendered an alteration in the original design of the Descriptive Catalogue necessary; yet, since it was impossible to frame a classified Catalogue until the very last MS. had been examined, and it would be difficult to say when that would be possible; and since much valuable time, which could be devoted to printing, would, in the meantime, be lost; I resolved, as desired by Mr. Murdoch, to afford "information to Oriental scholars respecting the numerous works which still exist," and to publish a description of each book as it presented itself, without reference to any alphabetical order of names, or to the subjects which it treated upon,—purposing, however, when this has been done, to frame a "classified Index," which should serve all the purposes of the Catalogue originally designed, and which might moreover be regarded as the official Catalogue of the Government in connection with the Library it has established.

The following sheets are issued as a specimen of the Descriptive Catalogue, preparatory to the official Classified Catalogue, the framing of which, with the assistance of the former, will be comparatively easy, and can be completed at the same time as the Library.

A few words may here be necessary in explanation of the plan of my work.

With a view to concentrate as much information as could be collected into one book from different sources, —information which is much sought for by European inhabitants of Ceylon, and by natives, as well as by Oriental scholars in Europe,—I have availed myself of my own previous labours, as well as of those of other writers, after due acknowledgment. Where a work appeared to possess more than ordinary interest, *e. g.*, Tepiṭaka or Dípávansa, I have, within legal bounds, either noticed or embodied all the translations hitherto made and scattered in various periodicals; and have, whenever possible, given a brief analysis of the unpublished portions.

Though exception has been taken by some to the course thus pursued, I see no valid objection to it, except on the score of delay and bulk. As for "delay," there can be none, since, the materials are already at hand, and have scarcely taken any time in the printing;

and as to "bulk," that is a matter more for my consideration, than that of others. It has also been urged, that it was "useless to include in this what was in everybody's hands." Now, though this might be said of my remarks under the title of Attanagaluwansa, which previously formed part of the Preface attached to my Translation of that work; yet I may remark that the Attanagaluwansa* has not had the circulation which some have supposed, and that, as remarked by European friends in Ceylon, whose opinions are entitled to weight, "if the object of the 'Descriptive Catalogue' is to concentrate all the information regarding a particular work, including the subject on which it treats, twenty-eight pages devoted for such a purpose is an advantage rather than the reverse." As regards the observations under the title of Kachcháyana, a cursory perusal of them will shew the cause which rendered them necessary. They are intended more to correct a previous erroneous identification of the author by myself, than for any display.

The space which I intend to devote to a proper elucidation of different important topics connected with the Tepiṭaka may, I trust, be not deemed too great. No one has yet examined the entire text of the Páli, much less its huge Comment. The time

---

* This work has not yet been completed; and the Text is still in the press. Only a few copies of the Translation have been forwarded to England, and to some friends on the Continent of Europe.

indeed is far distant before such an examination can be accomplished. In the meantime, great misapprehensions exist as to the real words of Buddha, his doctrines, the authenticity of the Páli version, the supposed admixtures into it by his pupils, the date when it was consigned to writing, the age of its language, etc., etc. It is therefore my intention, in the article devoted to the consideration of Tepiṭaka, briefly to notice many of the above points, and to refer to facts and circumstances which may perhaps appear new to many. My views may be incorrect, my inferences wrong, and my readings inaccurate; and yet those very errors will, I am persuaded, lead to investigations which—as in the case of Kachcháyana's Páli Grammar—may result in the ascertainment of facts previously unknown, or discoveries interesting to the students of science.

As to the only other titles under which lengthy extracts have been admitted, viz., the Mahawansa and Dípáwansa, the course is justified by the interest which attaches to the extracts, and the scarcity of the works from which those extracts have been made. Except in these instances, and few others, I have not thought proper to elaborate particulars beyond describing the work, ascertaining the name of the author, fixing his age, and presenting the reader with a specimen of each writer, with a translation such as I was able to produce according to my humble ability, aided and directed by an accomplished Pandit "whose critical acumen" has been already acknowledged by learned European Scholars.

It is perhaps needless for me to say, that, with all the attention I have bestowed, there still appear errors of both omission and commission; and that all my translations from the Sanskrit and Páli may be wanting in critical accuracy. If however the island abounded —which it does not—with Oriental scholars, and with linguists both able and ready to render assistance,* the case might have been different. But without a single European who has mastered the Páli or Sanskrit, with but few Native scholars possessing a fair acquaintance with English, Páli and Siṇhalese—and those generally inaccessible to me either for consultation or advice—I have had to struggle through all difficulties single-handed, so far as the translations into English were concerned. Under such circumstances it is perhaps not too much to ask for the indulgence of the public.

I have anticipated Professor Max Müller, as was done by the Hon. Mr. Turnour before the publication of the Mahawansa, in the adoption of the Roman alphabet, very nearly in accordance with the system sanctioned by Government in the Minute which is published in the Appendix. Great care has been taken, as further suggested by the learned Professor, "that the extracts are given correctly,"† and to render the translations as "literal" as possible.

---

* See remarks in Introduction to Kachcháyana, page cxxxiii.

† The system of printing Páli and other Asiatic languages in the Roman character is quite new to the country. Neither copyists nor compositors are yet familiar with it. The consequent

In my notes and observations on the Buddhist literature and religion,* I have endeavoured, as suggested by the same Professor in his Introduction to Dhammapada, " to adopt Sanskrit throughout as the *lingua franca*," and I have departed from this principle in those instances only where I have been treating of particular doctrines, or expressions in a particular book : in which case I have adopted Sanskrit, Páli, or Siṇhalese words as they occurred in each: and this appears to me the only mode† in which a great many difficulties may be obviated.

I estimate that the entire work, with the Indices, will not exceed 800 pages, and therefore purpose to divide the whole into three volumes. Though this specimen contains but 230 pages, I have MSS. on hand which will cover 200 pages more. In addition to these, I have in a state of progress several articles, which will occupy, when completed, at the least, 300 pages.

I do not indeed expect that my observations, though carefully worded, and adapted for a document such as this Catalogue is, will be received by the learned Oriental Scholars of Europe with universal approbation; but whether they be correct or not, I have no

---

correction of " copy," and the subsequent alterations in the course of printing are manifold. Under such circumstances, it is not to be wondered at that the writer's vigilance has not detected errors such as " nara " and " ńnara " at page 4.

* See my Review of Dhammapada.

† A departure has been sometimes rendered necessary owing to the want of the required type.

doubt they will be appreciated by many, as affording topics of great interest for consideration and future investigation. Any remarks which they may be pleased to forward to me directly, or through the Government, will, I beg to assure them, be accepted thankfully, and shall receive my best and most careful attention.

In conclusion, whilst acknowledging the invaluable assistance I have received from the publications of Weber, Turnour, Gogerly, Hardy, Fausböll, Max Müller, Childers, and Kuhn, I beg to offer my warmest thanks to Mr. Skeen for his kind and valuable assistance in carrying this work through the press, and to the Rev. J. Scott, the Chairman of the Wesleyan Mission in Ceylon, for placing at my service the whole of the valuable Páli library of the late Rev. D. J. Gogerly, of which I have largely availed myself in the examination of several questions of great interest.

JAS. ALWIS.

A
DESCRIPTIVE CATALOGUE.

A

DESCRIPTIVE CATALOGUE

OF

LITERARY WORKS

IN

CEYLON.

ABHIDHA'NAPADI'PIKA'

is the only ancient Páli Dictionary in Ceylon, or, so far as it is known, any where else. It is of the highest authority, and holds the same place in Páli, which Amarakoṣa does in Sanskrit literature. Indeed it may be called a twin-sister of the Sanskrit Vocabulary. They are both composed exactly in the same style and plan, (if indeed one is not a transcript of the other), and are intended to help those who study the Bauddha sacred works. The name, too, adopted for the Páli work is one by which Amara's Sanskrit Vocabulary had already been known, viz., *Abhidhána* (Nouns), for the purpose of throwing 'light' (*padípiká*) on which, this work is professedly undertaken.

It was printed in 1824 by the Rev. B. Clough of the Wesleyan Mission, with a translation into English but he omitted to give both the *Introduction* and the *Conclusion* of the book,—an omission which led Oriental scholars to express various conjectures as to the date of the Dictionary, until the Translator of a portion of Kachcháyana's Páli Grammar published them in 1863.* As affording a specimen of the work, and a description of the Vocabulary under notice, the following is transferred from the work last named.

1. Tathágato yo karuná karo karo
'Payátamossajja sukhap padan padan
Aká paratthan kalisam bhave bhave
Namámi tan kevala duk-karan karan

2. Apújayun yam muni kunjará jará
'Rujádimuttá yahi'muttare tare
Ṭhitá tivaṭṭambu nidhin nará'nará
Tarinsu tan dhamama' maghá pahan' pahan

3. Gatam munindo' rasasúnutan nutan
Supuññakhettan bhuvane'sutan sutan
Ganam'pi páni kata sanvaran varan
Sadá guno' ghena nirantar'an taran

4. Náma lingesu kossallan
'Attha nichchhaya káranan
Yato mahabbalan Buddha
Vachano páṭa vatthinan.

---

* See Alwis's Kachcháyana's Grammar, p. vi. *et seq.* We learn on the authority of Professor Weber of Berlin, that "Westergaard, too, (Catal. p. 586,) communicates only the verse in which the author's name is contained."

5. Námalingán' yato Buddha
Bhásitassá' rahá n'ahan
Dassayanto pakásissam
'Abhidhána' padípikan

6. Bhíyo rúpan tará sáha
'Chariyena cha katthachi
Kvachá' hachcha vidhánena
Ñeyyan thípun napunsakan.

7. Abhinna lingínan yeva
Dvando cha lingaváchaká
Gáthá pádanta majjhaṭṭhá
Pubban yantya'pare paran.

8. Pumitthiyan padan dvísu
Sabba linge cha tís'viti
Abhidhánan tará rambhe
Ñeyyan t'vanta mathádi cha.

9. Bhíyo payoga'mágamma
Sogate ágame kvachi
Nighaṇḍu yuttin ch'ániya
Náma lingan kathíyati.

'I adore *Tathágata,* who is a mine of compassion, and who, having renounced the beatific *nibban* within his reach, conferred happiness on others, performing all the difficult-to-be accomplished acts in metampsychosis, the fountain of sin.

'I (adore) the sin-scaring *Dhamma,* to which holy sages, devoid of decrepitude and disease, have paid reverence; and by conformance to which the high and the mean, both (amongst) men and other beings,* have crossed the tri-annular† ocean (of metampsychosis.)

'And ever (do I adore) the supreme *priesthood*, (like unto a merit-(producing)-field, who have become the legitimate sons‡ of Buddha; and who receive reverence—are illustrious in the (three) worlds—preserve the *sanvara*, § like life itself—and ever practise an abundance of virtues.

'Since an intimate acquaintance with *nouns*, and (their) *genders*, is essential to the (ascertainment of) the correct significations (of words), and is a powerful help to those desirous of mastering the word of Buddha;

'I shall publish the Abhidhánapadípiká,¶ illustrating *nouns* and (their) *genders*, according to their application in the language of (the discourses of) Buddha.

'The masculine, feminine, and neuter are to be distinguished, chiefly, from their different forms; sometimes from the association of words (context); and sometimes by specific rule.

'[In this work] *dvanda* compounds will consist (of nouns) of the same gender. When words which

---

* 'Nara and ánara'—human and non-human.

† The 'tivaṭṭambu-nidi.'—The ocean, encompassed with three circles, is here used for 'metampsychosis;' and the three barriers are 'Kamma,' action which begets merit and demerit; 'Kleṣa' evil, trouble, pain or sorrow; and 'Vipáka' the rewards of merit and demerit.

‡ *Sons*—a term applied to disciples.

§ That is, 'Preserve the *Síla* or precepts.'

¶ Lit.—'Lamp of Nouns.'

denote the gender occur at the end or the middle of a line in a verse, (such words) refer to the (names at the) beginning (of that line); (but where they are placed at) the commencement, (they refer to) the remaining words (of the same line.)

'Know that the term *dvísu* denotes both masculine and feminine; that *tísu* signifies all the genders; and that words ending in *tu* or (preceded by) *atha*, &c., are given to express the commencement of a series of names.

'Nouns and (their) genders are (here) illustrated, according to their application, chiefly in the Buddhist works, and sometimes after the usage adopted in Lexicons.'

The above is the Introduction to the Abhidhánapadípiká; and it cannot be conceived why it was omitted in the translation of that work by Mr. Tolfrey, or was left out by his publisher, the Rev. B. Clough. At the conclusion of the same book are also nine stanzas, which are likewise left out in the publication above mentioned; and which, since they enable us to fix the date of the work, are here subjoined:—

1 Sagga kaṇḍo cha bhú kaṇḍo
Tathá sámañña kaṇḍakan
Kaṇḍattayanvitá esá
Abhidhánappadípiká.

2 Tidive mahiyan bhujagá vasathe
Sakalattha samavhaya dípani'yan
Iha yo kusalo matimá sanaro
Paṭu hoti mahámunino vachane.

3 Parakkama bhujo náma
Bhúpálo guṇa bhúsano
Lankáya' mási tejassì
Jayì kesari vikkamo.

4 Vibhinnan chiran bhikkhu sanghan nikáya
Tayasmin cha káresi sammá samagge
Sadchan'va nichchá 'daro dígha kálan
Mahaggheli rakkhesi yo pachchayehi.

5 Yena Lanká vihárehi
Gámá'ráma purîhicha
Kittiyáviya sambádhí
Katá khettehi vápihí.

6 Yassá' sádháraṇan patvá
'Nuggahan sabba kámadan
Aham'pi gantha kàrattam
Patto vibudha gocharan.

7 Kárite tena pássáda
Gopurádi vibhúsite
Sagga kaṇḍe'va tattoyá
Sayasmin paṭibimbite.

8 Mahá Jetavaná khyamhi
Viháre sádhu sammate
Sarogáma samúhamhi
Vasatà santa vuttiná.

9 Saddhammaṭṭhiti kámena
Moggallánena dhímatá
Thereṇa rachitá yesá
Abhidhánappadípiká.

'The Abhidhánapadípiká consists of three sections—on Heavenly, Earthly, and General subjects.

'It interprets the names of all objects in Heaven, Earth, and the Nága regions. A sensible person who excels in this, will master the words of the great sage.

'There was in Lanka a Monarch named Parakkamabáhu—celebrated, successful, endowed with virtues, and valorous as a lion.

'He in the right manner (in the legitimate mode) reconciled* the *Bhikkhus* and *Sanghas* of the three *Nikáyas*;† and, with unceasing love, long extended his protection to (them) as to his own body, with valuable objects of maintenance.‡

'He established to profusion in Lanka, in the same manner that it was filled with his renown,§ monasteries,¶ villages,‖ parks,** cities,†† fields‡‡ and tanks.§§

---

* 'He reformed the religion.'—Upham, vol. i. p. 299.

† "Association or Congregation performing the same duties."

‡ 'Pachchaya'—Objects of maintenance, which are four, viz., 'chívara,' garments; 'piṇḍapáta,' food; 'senásana,' sleeping objects; 'gilána pachchaya,' that which is necessary for the sick—medicines.

§ See Ceylon Almanac for 1834.

¶ "He built the viharas in the city of Anurádhapura."—*ib.* at p. 190.

‖ "The King also made several hundreds of houses and many streets arranged with shops."—*Mahawansa.*

** "He formed many pleasant and delightful gardens."—*Mah.* C. B. A. S. J., p. 148.

†† "He built three more cities."—*Upham's Mahawansa*, p. 277.

‡‡ "He formed paddy fields."—*Mah.* C. B. A. S. J., vol. vii., p. 141.

§§ "The King also repaired many ancient tanks."—*Mahawansa, ib.* p. 149.

'I, the special object of his wish-conferring patronage, have also acquired the privilege of authorship peculiar to the learned.

'Desirous of perpetuating the *Saddhamma*, the Abhidhánapadípiká was composed by the erudite Moggallána thera—

'Of mild deportment, dwelling amongst the *Sarogáma** fraternity (who were) received by the virtuous with approbation; and (residing) in the Monastery called the *Mahá Jetavana*;—

'[A monastic establishment] adorned with the temples, ornamented porches, &c., which were built by him (the aforesaid king) as it were a portion of Heaven reflected in his tank.'

Here we have sufficient data to fix the date of the Abhidhánapadípiká. It was composed by a thera named Moggallána, who had been patronized by king Parakkama. His acts, which are here related, can only be identified with those of "the heroic and invincible royal warrior, gloriously endowed with might, majesty, and wisdom; and radiant with benignant virtues,"† "the most martial, enterprising and glorious of the Siṇhalese Sovereigns,"‡ who, according to history, was Parakkamabáhu of Polonnoruwa. He ascended the throne in 1153 A. D.; and when we notice that that sovereign, who reigned for thirty-three years, turned his

---

* This is a Pali translation of the Siṇhalese proper name *Velgam.*

† Inscription in Ceylon Almanac for 1834.

‡ Mahawansa, p. lxvi.

attention to the internal improvements which are here mentioned, in the latter part of his reign, and after he had brought his local and foreign wars to a termination; we may assign to the Abhidhánapadípiká a date at the latter end of the second half of the twelfth century. This, therefore, is posterior to the Amarakoṣa,* which may be placed about the middle or end of the fifth century after Christ. To shew their correspondence the three following introductory stanzas are here introduced from the last named work.

'The masculine, feminine, and neuter (genders) are to be known chiefly by their different forms; sometimes by the association of words; and sometimes by specific rule.

'Here with a view to distinct elucidation (nouns of) different unspecified genders are not rendered into *dvandva* compounds. Neither are they, without order, jumbled together; nor indeed expressed by 'eka ṣesha.'†

---

* Professor H. H. Wilson thus notices the date of this writer in the Preface to his Sanskrit Dictionary; "Amera Sinha may therefore be left, agreeably to tradition, to the beginning of the Christian era; or as connected with other traditionary notices of names and events, which, I shall proceed to describe, he may be brought down to a later date, and placed about the middle or end of the fifth century after Christ."

† 'Eka ṣesha': 'one left out,' *i. e.*, the omission of one to designate the same by another, which has been mentioned; or, conversely, the expression of one name to designate another omitted name of the same genus or family; as Aṣvinu 'the two Aṣvin,' in the dual, designate 'the Physicians of heaven, and twin sons of the sun, or children of the constellation Aṣviní,' who are separately named Násatya and Dasra.

'The term *tríshu* (denotes) the three genders; and *dvayoh* the male and female. (Where a certain) gender is expressly negatived, the remaining ones (are meant); and, where words ending in *tu* (occur, or) *atha*, &c., they do not refer to the preceding (words).'

As already intimated the work is divided into three parts; the first treats on *celestial*, the second on *terrestrial*, and the third on *miscellaneous*, objects. Each part is sub-divided into several sections; but the whole book may be regarded as a Dictionary of Synonymes, except the 3rd and 4th sections of part third, the former alone being devoted to homonymous terms, and the latter to indeclinable particles. The entire work contains 1212 *gáthás* of, chiefly, 32 syllables, though occasionally we meet with longer metres. Some MSS. which my Pandit has examined, contained two or three stanzas which are omitted in the printed editions.*

In addition to the Translation and the Text of the Abhidhánapadípiká, published by Clough, a second edition of the same was printed in 1865, by a Buddhist priest named Subhúti. Both these editions, as well as the original, are deficient, for want of an Alphabetical Index,—a deficiency which the late Rev. D. J. Gogerly endeavoured to supply; but his Dictionary has not

* After the above description it is unnecessary to state the space which this work occupies in Ola MSS., as they vary, according to the size of the leaves on which they are written. A copy in my possession, with four stanzas to the page, contains 152 leaves.

been published. It is however now being revised by the Rev. J. Coles of the Church Missionary Society, and will, it is hoped, be published in the early part of next year.

Attanagaluvansa.

Amongst the many historical works extant in Ceylon, is the Pali work above indicated, written in very ancient times upon the authority of 'old historians and ancient legends.'

According to the established usage of all eastern nations, it opens with an adoration, which is the usual Buddhistical one, and proceeds to an invocation, between which and that in the *Sáhitya Darpana* there seems to be much agreement. Although this book is entitled the *Attanagaluvihárovansa*, 'the history of the Temple of Attanagalla'; yet, as a prelude to that which is the chief subject matter of the work, the writer devotes several chapters to depict the history of Srí Sanghabodhi, whose decapitation at the place abovementioned led to the erection of a Temple which still exists; and who was the only one from amongst the Sovereigns of Ceylon to whom the historian has devoted an entirely separate work.

He was one of three Princes, connected with each other, of the Lambakanna (Lamini, Siṇh.) race, who had their domains at Mahiyangana in Bintenna, a place still known by that name. Sanghabodhi's father

Sela-Abhaya is alone mentioned here, but in a rock-inscription at Mihintala,* his parents are *both* named—the father as Abaya-Sela (the same names inverted), and the mother as Devugon.

In the Attanagaluvansa Selabhaya is simply called a 'Khattiya' (prince); but he was, probably a provincial chieftain or sub-king. For, both the inscription above-mentioned and the Siṇhalese version of the Attanagaluvansa, designate him 'monarch.'

It would seem from the history under notice, and from the particulars given in the Mahavansa that Sanghabodhi and his associates Sanghatissa and Goṭhábhaya, repaired to Anurádhapura, and soon became established in high favor at the Court of the reigning prince (Wijaya Indu A. D. 241,) obtaining from him the highest offices of the state, and enjoying his unlimited confidence. They were not, however, long in subjection to Wijaya Indu; for scarcely a year expired from the time they had entered into his service, when Sanghatissa, procuring Goṭhábhaya to assassinate his benefactor, ascended the throne.

Sanghabodhi, it would appear from the Attanagaluvansa, (vide cap. iii. § 6), was no party to this foul deed; and the general character given of him in the Dipavansa, as 'a good and pious prince,'† goes to support that statement. Yet such a belief is inconsistent with the version of the transaction in the Mahavansa,

* For the original see Sidatsangará, p. xxxvi.

† Sanghabodhi'ti námena Rájá ási susilavá;
Dve vassáneva so rájà rajjan káresi Khattiyo.

which, in the language of Mr. Turnour's translation, p. 229, runs as follows:

'These three persons, on their reaching the capital, were most graciously received by the monarch Wijaya in whose court they were established, and employed in offices of state. Conspiring together, they put to death the rája Wijayo in his own palace; and two of them raised (the third) Sanghatisso, who was at the head of the army, to the throne.'

Sanghatissa reigned only four years, at the termination of which he was poisoned by the people, who could no longer bear the oppression of the exactions made during his royal excursions to the Eastern Provinces.

Upon the death of Sanghatissa, Goṭhábhaya, who was destined (according to the prediction of a blind sage) to reign longer than his two associates, requested Sanghabodhi to assume the reigns of Government. But he declined this high honor; and his denunciation of principalities, dominions, and powers, as recorded by the historian in a beautiful speech, is couched in oriental imagery, and exhibits a thorough knowledge of man and his depraved nature,—a fact however, not borne out by his subsequent conduct. Sanghabodhi was soon prevailed upon by the priesthood to accept the pressing invitation of the people. The historian here dwells on the principles of good Government, as having been enunciated by the prince's preceptor, Nanda, to whose previous discourse on the duties of Man, and the necessity for the early formation of right principles, nearly an entire chapter is devoted.

The policy however of Sanghabodhi's government was characterized by great weakness. After he was crowned, he continued to evince, as he had done before, greater devotion to the interests of religion than to the affairs of the state. This from

'A man on earth devoted to the skies,'

was scarcely unexpected. He mixed not with the world, and could not therefore distinguish the *local* from the *natural* man. He was too much absorbed in religious affairs, to enable him "to track the silent march of human affairs, and to seize with happy intuition on those great laws which regulate the prosperity of empires." His meditations did not permit him to reconcile principles to circumstances, or to devise measures in anticipation of the effects which state-affairs had upon "the entangled relations and awkward complexity of real life."

Buddhism, moreover, manifested an antagonism to good Government. The principles of the former conflicted with those of the latter. The exercise of those duties which a state policy demanded, threatened the destruction of all religious merit. The enthusiasm and rigid piety of so great an adherent of Buddha as Sanghabodhi, permitted not a departure from the duties prescribed by his religion,—even where the majesty of the law demanded the infliction of punishment. And the consequence was, as may be easily expected, that, having forgotten 'the highest virtue of a king, (which) is the protection of his subjects,'* the old

---

* Manu, vii. § 144.

existing Ordinances for the repression of crime, the promotion of the comforts of the poor, and the security of their person and property, became disregarded.

"When the malefactors were brought to the prison of the capital," says the historian, "as the king's vows precluded the possibility of their being executed, they were secretly released at night after condemnation, and the corpses, furnished by the usual casualties of a populous city, were exhibited at the place of execution, on gibbets and impaling poles, as the victims of violated laws." Thus, says the historian, a pious king not only successfully repressed crime, but also gave the criminal time and opportunity to reform.

The contrary however was indeed the result. Crime increased in the same proportion that Sanghabodhi neglected to punish the offender. "The whole frame of society was disorganized." The whole country became the scene of plunder, and a prey to lawless banditti who infested its environs, encouraged by the unbounded charities of the reigning prince. Nor was this all. A famine and a pestilence soon made their appearance; and to the sufferings of the people from these causes, the historian adds those arising from the ravages of a cannibal, who, in the usual phraseology of Oriental exaggeration, he describes as a monstrous "demon" of extraordinary appearance and magnitude.

Such a state of things could not continue for any length of time. Goṭhábhaya, impatient to become a king, and availing himself of the weakness of his friend, and the feebleness of his Government, plotted his destruction. He collected an army from amongst the marauders that pillaged the country, and prepared for war.

In the mean time the commotion of an insurrection reached the king's ears; and he instantly left the city in disguise, abdicating the throne in favor of him who had been instrumental in placing him on it. But Goṭhábhaya was disliked by the people. Suspecting therefore the stability of his power so long as the people's favorite was suffered to remain in the country, he offered a reward for Sanghabodhi's head. At this time the latter was enjoying the solitude of an hermitage in Attanagalla in the Sína Korale of the Western Province, with the contemplation of exercising those religious duties, especially the Dána páramítá (which includes the sacrifice of life,) in expectation of attaining to a Buddhaship.

Mr. Turnour, who was probably indebted to the Rájavaliya for the matter in the following passage, (see Ceylon Almanac for 1834, p. 175) says, "Many heads, obtained by murder and assassination, had been produced before the usurper (Goṭhábhaya,) by persons who successively forfeited their own heads for the imposition they had attempted to practise. Siri Sangabo hearing of these enormities, resolved to put an end to them by sacrificing his own life. In this frame of mind he met with a peasant who had fled from his home, horrified at the suggestion of his wife, of destroying the king. He revealed his distress to his disguised sovereign. In order that the reward might be secured to this man, the king avowed himself, and with his own hand severed his head from his body." But the Attanagaluvansa omits the matters stated in the early part of this extract, and contradicts those given in its conclusion, especially as to the visit of the peasant having been originated by the suggestion of his wife; and as to the pre-knowledge of Sanghabodhi regarding the high reward which had been set on his head. All that the Attanagaluvansa authorizes us to state, is, that the king accidentally met a poor peasant travelling by his hermitage; and, whilst partaking with him his meal, heard the proceedings of his *soi-disant* friend. Heartily glad at the opportunity thus presented of carrying his designs into effect, viz., of 'propitiating' his own life, the destruction of which he prohibited in others, he requested the peasant to accept his head. The latter indignantly protested against being considered an assassin, or one capable of murder; and declined the offer. But he was soon prevailed upon; and the result was, that the king himself severed his head from his body, and presented it to the traveller. On its being taken before Goṭhábhaya it sprang up (as predicted by Sanghabodhi) into the air, and proclaimed to the suspecting king, that 'it *was* the identical head of king Sanghabodhi.'

The history then proceeds to narrate the events connected with the death of Sanghabodhi's queen in the same forest in which the king's corpse was found; and the cremation of the royal couple with that pomp and grandeur to which their high station entitled them. Then follows a narrative of the erection of monumental and religious edifices by Goṭhábhaya, upon the spot where Sanghabodhi had perished; and the history concludes with the high munificent attentions which they had received from successive Sovereigns by way of maintaining the TEMPLE OF ATTANAGALLA, from whence the appellation of this little history is derived.

The reader is doubtless aware of the locality indicated by the name of Attanagalla. It is a village in the Síná Kóralé, in the Western Province, and its delightful scenery, as it presents itself in passing from the Maritime Province into the Kandyan country, is but imperfectly described in the record before us. "There," says Forbes,* "the Imbul and Muruta trees, covered with scarlet and pink flowers, or the blaze of white blossoms on the Nágaha trees, form a beautiful variety to the heavy green of continuous forests; and cocoanut-trees are only seen in plume-like tufts near villages, of which they are the valuable ornament and certain index."

In the seventh chapter of the work under notice is found a graphic description of the Forest as it stood many centuries ago. The picture is indeed not overdrawn. When, some years ago, I visited this part of the country, my eyes rested on a scene which I could not soon or easily forget. Its greatest attraction was the stately Forest. Whilst I stood amazed at the pro-

* Eleven Years in Ceylon, vol. i. p. 88.

digious height to which the trees had grown, straight from the ground, the eye lingered with delight on the "pillared shades," thick with their dense green foliage, and laden

—"with their pendent fruits and flowers."

The Figs and the Palms which grew up together reminded me of the Cocoa-nut and the Bread-fruit which rose, as it were, in love's embrace in the south-west coast of Ceylon. The Talipot, the Ná, the Śapan, the Hedawaka, the Ketakála, the Del, the Milila, the Godapara, (not to mention other timber-trees enumerated in the text), were all here seen side-by-side with the Katu-imbul, the Goraka, the Veralu, the Kaju, the Erabadu, etc., etc. There were also climbing plants in endless variety. The Póțá, the Kirindi, the Kiritilla, and the Kiri-anguna* entwined themselves round the trunks as they clambered up in search of light. The ferns and the orchids, which thrived luxuriantly in the hollows of old trees, waving their brilliant foliage, seemed as if they were the cultivation of some nymph of the forest. Nothing could exceed the beauty of the flowing tresses of the Hedayá, of

---

* Speaking of this plant [*Gymnema lactiferum*] Sir Emerson Tennent, says "it is a creeper......used medicinally by the Natives, but *never as an article of food.*"—History of Ceylon, vol. i. p. 102. This is an error. It is a pot-herb commonly used by all classes of the Sinhalese. There are few places in the Western Province where it is not cultivated. The Temple premises contain a beautiful creeper; and the writer sees, just as he is now writing, another in his own town residence.

which two species were met within the cold and mossy clefts of trees that never saw the light of the sun. Under the shade grew the Vana-Rája. Revelling in the rich and luxurious vegetable mould, which lay several feet thick, this dwarf "King of the Forest" spread out its leaves, "the most exquisitely formed in the vegetable kingdom, and whose colour resembles dark velvet approaching to black, and reticulated over all the surface with veins of ruddy gold."* It is difficult to realize the beauty of the distant landscape along the streams and marshes of the forest. The graceful Bambu was surrounded by the magnificent Asoka. The pale azure of the Sal, which deeply contrasted with the burnished green of the delicately tinted foliage of the Siambalá on the hillocks, and both with the deep emerald brushwood below,—waved over the Gloriosa Superba (Niagalá), whose matchless flowers festooned the adjacent heaps of verdure; whilst the Muruta overshadowed the Bándurá, which grew luxuriantly beneath the pink-clad branches of the former. Nothing, again, could surpass either the splendour of the flowers, or the beauty of the leaves. Some of the latter by themselves exhibited the hues of the former. The scarlet shoots of the Ná, for instance, vied in beauty with the gorgeous flowers of the Kaṭu-imbul, the pink clusters of the Muruta with the ripe leaves of the

---

* Sir James E. Tennent, from whom I quote the above description, calls it "a terrestrial orchid (the *Anœctochilus setaceus.*)"—See his History of Ceylon, vol. i. p. 103.

Koṭṭambá, the pale yellow Champac with the tawny Veralu, and the snow-white blossoms of the Idda with the tender buds of the Mussenda.*

Such were the charms with which the Forest was invested six-and-twenty years ago, as I beheld it at the confluence of the Levangam and the Halgam becks, which converging into one rivulet, take a westerly direction near this forest, from whence it is called the Attanagalu Oya. My second visit was not many months ago, and it is not surprising to observe that the physical change which has progressed throughout many districts of the Island has also affected this part of the country. The stately jungle has partially disappeared before the kẹtta-cutting of Native cultivation; extensive Cocoa-nut plantations, one of which may be seen immediately adjoining the premises of the Temple, have displaced the timber trees; creepers of the sweet-potato have taken the place of the flower-trees of the marshes; large plantations of the Mauritius and West Indian Pines are met with, together with those of the Rambutan and the Mango; houses and botiques have sprung up here and there; and the Moorish botique-keeper and the itinerant tradesman

---

* This creeper (*Mussenda frendosa*) produces cream-white leaves, a colour very rare in the vegetable kingdom. Their beauty as seen over green verdure, and close upon the *Gloriosa superba*, is enchanting, and surpasses anything I have seen in the jungles which line the principal roads of this (Western) Province. The flower is also very pretty, and being similar in shape and size to the ear-rings of the Siṃhalese, their little children wear it in their ears.

occupy the paths which were once infested by wild beasts. The elephants have altogether disappeared; and but for a solitary tame beast, the property of Mr. Christopher Dias, the Mudliyar of the district, who has turned him to good account, the sight of one would be a novelty to the rising generation of these parts. The paths themselves, which were "narrow, crooked, and winding," are no longer impassable and covered over with the stretching arms of the surrounding jungle. A beautiful road, which commences at or near the 27th mile-post of the great trunk road to Kandy, intersects this part of the country. This beautiful line, called the "Pasyála and Haṉwęlla road," which was opened in 1850 by the indefatigable and zealous Mudliyar already named, passes between the Temple and the Oya of Attanagalla, and terminates at the Héwágam Kóralé, at a distance of twenty miles. As you proceed towards the south, and reach the 4th mile-post on this road, you see on your left the site of the Nivan Pokuna, or 'the Pond of Repose,' into which the queen of Siri Sanghabodhi fell in her wearisome rambles in search of her royal husband. The progress of sixteen centuries has converted this pond into a corn field; yet from its high embankments it still gives indication of its original character. A few yards farther take the traveller to the Temple* grounds of Attanagalla,

* Of all the numerous writers on Ceylon and its Antiquities, none have made the most distant allusion to this ancient Temple, except Turnour and Forbes. But even they never visited it,

situated on the right hand side of the road. These are by no means extensive, and their limited area, as compared with the vast extent indicated in the Attanagaluvansa, induced me to inquire what had become of the large domains attached to this monastery by ostentatious kings of old, as detailed in the history before us. It appears, from the information received in the course of my enquiries, that during the times of the Portuguese, the priests as well as the people of this part of the Island, had deserted their homes, and that the lands owned by them had been taken by that Government; and that although the priests laid claim to the extensive temple property which had been granted to them under Siṇhalese sovereigns, yet they could only succeed in resuming possession of the monastery and the lands immediately surrounding it, which, according to a recent Government survey, do

although it was not farther than 28 miles from Colombo. The former in his remarks on Siṇhalese Inscriptions, (see Ceylon Almanac for 1834,) notices that Sanghabodhi's head was buried with great pomp at Attanagalla, over which the usurper raised a Dágoba, which is still standing. The latter, in his Eleven Years in Ceylon, at p. 168, after alluding to the delightful scenery of Attanagalla, says:—"At the Attanagalla Oya, the road approaches one of the low ranges of hills which diverge in all directions from the mountainous centre of the Island; and four miles off to the right is situated the Rock of Attanagalla, surmounted by religious buildings. The principal of these were erected about A. D. 248 by Goloo Abba, to the memory of King Siri Sangabo, who had abandoned his throne and retired in disguise to this place, where he was killed by a peasant in order to obtain the reward offered."

not exceed 26 acres. Entering this garden, which is fully planted with a variety of fruit trees, chiefly Cocoa-nuts and other Palms, and many of the trees mentioned in cap. vii. of the History, amongst which the Sal, the Kumbuk, and the Náwá are the most prominent, we reached a rocky hill about 80 feet higher than the surrounding country. Ascending a flight of steps, about 25 feet high, of fine granite slabs, and passing through large heaps of granite, the remains of carved works and ancient buildings, we entered the lower terrace of the temple. Here is to be seen the foundation of the five-storied structure originally erected by Upatissa (cap. x. § 3), and subsequently rebuilt and altered by Moggallána into one of three stories.

At present, it is a square building, 54 × 44 feet, with four neat porches, facing the cardinal points. Of the ancient granite pillars, upon which the original structure of five-stories was built, and of which upwards of one hundred existed 26 years ago, there are only 16 now left, each nine feet high On the south of this hill is a large irregular building, probably patched up from time to time, but containing ample evidence of its former splendour. This is used as a residence of one of the two fraternities of priests, amongst whom the establishment is now divided, Walpola Indrajóti being the chief over both. Leaving this, and proceeding westward, the traveller has again to ascend a flight of 73 steps, 36 feet in height. Here nothing attracts his attention more prominently than the granite slabs that lie scattered on either side, exhibiting faint traces of the skill of the Siṃhalese sculptor. Inscriptions are also found, but they are so defaced and decayed that one cannot learn from them anything beyond the fact that they once bore some Déva Nágara characters. When once you get upon the topmost terrace, the most remarkable of the buildings is the "Rotunda," built by Goṭhábhaya. (cap. ix. § 6). This is 158 feet in circumference, and is most substantially built, with a broad foundation rising about 3½ feet from the ground, of entirely large slabs of hewn granite. It has four porches for entrances; and the roof, which contains two stories covered with flat tiles, rests upon two rows of granite pillars,—the top story in the centre on eight granite pillars, occupying an area of about 250 feet, and the lower story upon 16 similar pillars, which are fixed close to the round wall. Both the roof as well as the walls are beautifully painted in the style peculiar to Buddhists, embellished with statues, pictures of the Devas, etc., The Thûpa which was originally built by Goṭhábhaya, (cap. ix. § 7), and subsequently restored by Parakkama, after its destruction by our intestine foes (cap. xi. § 3), and of which so much has been written in the history before us, occupies the centre. It is a neat structure of bricks, surmounted with a silver-gilt pinnacle, and reaches the roof which is intended as a canopy for the same. (cap. ix. § 7.)

Outside these pillars and facing the four doors, are four images of Buddha, in a sitting posture, enclosed in neat glass cases. One of the statues is of granite;

but the head, which was destroyed by some fanatics, has been since restored. In close proximity to this sacred building is the rocky pool, near which Sanghabodhi met the poor traveller; (cap. viii. § 1). Its sides are found scarped and polished, and the crevices and holes neatly filled up with granite. It contains a plantation of the Lotus; and our attendant, the High Priest of the Temple, pointed out to us a healthy bush of corn, which he would have us believe never ceased to live. 'This, Sir,' said he, with great self-satisfaction, 'is the plant produced from the Má-ví-rice, thrown by Siri Sangabo at the time he partook of the traveller's hospitality. This never ceases to exist, when one withers, another shoots up.' 'Yes, of course,' said I, promptly, 'if you don't reap the corn it is sure to drop down and shoot again.' The Priest would not understand the solution of the mystery, nor did he seem to relish the explanation. I was not therefore over-anxious to ridicule a notion, perhaps honestly entertained, by one who paid me much attention, and who treated me with great courtesy. I therefore changed the subject of our conversation, and he took us to another side and pointed out to us an outline of a head and two feet—emblems engraved on the rock. 'This,' he declared, 'was the identical spot where the old king cut off his head. These marks were of course made in subsequent times to preserve the tradition respecting the spot.' We then inspected a large granite slab 2 × 8 feet, standing in the centre of the compound and containing traces of an inscription, defaced by atmospheric influences. This is probably the one erected by Patirája and mentioned in the Mahavansa. After an unsuccessful attempt to decipher even a word of this inscription, we proceeded to the Bauddha-house, which is close to the rocky pool. Here too desolation and ruin reigned supreme: the figures and images were all partially broken,—and even the granite images of Buddha mentioned at cap. xi. § 10, had wholly disappeared.

We next inspected a little Dévála, a very modern structure. There was nothing remarkable about it, except some drawings on its walls, which were pointed out to us as the portraits of Sir Edward Barnes, and the late Abraham De Saram, Esq., Second Maha Mudliyar —representations, which, though rude and unfaithful, yet exhibited the genuine feeling of gratitude, respect, and esteem felt for two of the greatest statesmen of the times in which the Temple was repaired.

Casting a glance at the stately Bô which occupies a corner of the terrace, and which was stated to have been a branch of the sacred Bô at Anurádhapura, we descended a flight of steps on the south of this elevation, and proceeded to the adjacent rocks, which, tradition affirms, King Sanghabodhi selected for his hermitage. They consisted of two large granite boulders, one over-hanging the other and the ground below, so as to render it a secure habitation, free from sun and rain. It almost realized to the mind Shakspeare's description of the

—'hallow'd, gloomy cave, with moss o'ergrown,
The temple join'd of Nature's pumice stone.'

Though not so large as the rocks of Aluvihára at Mátalé, and though, as in the latter, no

> ———'antique images by priests were kept,
> And wooden deities securely slept;'

yet there was the sameness of appearance in the formation of a cave by the overhanging brow of a granite boulder which had been precipitated from the rocks above. Except this, there was little to see here beyond the sleeping apartments of another section of priests belonging to the establishment, and the surrounding vegetation, consisting chiefly of the Kaneru, planted for the sake of its flowers. We then proceeded to partake of the kind hospitality of the Mudliyar of the district; but, before quitting the premises, there was one other spot which I desired to see, it was the Vidhavá Vana (see Note 4, cap. ix.) The surprise of the priests was great, when I asked them to show me this place. They seemed to wonder how I had known the name; and from this and other circumstances, I concluded that they were not conversant with the Attanagaluvansa.

They took me a little distance and pointed in the direction of a paddy field called Kanavenduma, bearing in the vernacular Siṇhalese the same sense as the name given to it in the Páli work, and its Siṇhalese translation. This is the spot, as the reader is aware, where the Queen of Sanghabodhi rested; and on inquiry, with a view to test the accuracy of the descriptions in the history before us, I ascertained that during heavy rains the surrounding country still exhibited white sandy spots, on one of which, close upon a "blooming shrubbery," the Queen is stated to have spent the night before her death.—Cap. ix. § 1.

To return to Attanagaluvansa. It will be observed, that in t no dates are given either as to the number of years which Sanghabodhi reigned, or the year on which he ascended the throne. According to the Mahavansa, he was crowned in A. D. 246, and he reigned only two years. The Dipávansa bears out Mahanáma, in the following stanza—

Sanghabodhi'ti námena rájá ási su-sílavá
Dve vassáneva só rájá rajjan káresi khattiyo.

That is to say: 'There was a highly religious king named Sanghabodhi: the same, who was a Khattiya reigned only two years.' There is nothing, therefore, in the Attanagaluvansa to induce us to doubt the correctness of Mahanáma's figures. On the contrary there is much in it which confirms the facts given in the Mahavansa. Yet, it would seem from one of the Mihintala inscriptions, that the reign of Sanghabodhi had extended to more than sixteen years.*

Next to the historical and political considerations which are suggested by the Attanagaluvansa, the religion which it presents to the reader in one of its most engaging phases,—indeed in that in which its greatest superiority is boasted of, and maintained by its adherents, viz., its moral code, may not be devoid of interest.

---

* For a reconciliation of these conflicting statements, see Attanagaluvansa, p. ci. *et seq.*

Not less interesting is it in other respects. 'The objects,' says Professor H. H. Wilson, 'for which an ancient dialect may be studied, are its philology and its literature, or the arts and sciences, the notions and manners, the history and belief of the people by whom it was spoken.'* Many of these objects may indeed be attained to no mean degree by a study of this historical novel. It is reckoned by our learned Pandits as one of the best Páli works which can engage the attention of the beginner. Though more artificial than the style of the Piṭakas, it is by no means inferior to many other works such as Buddhaghosa's Atthakathá, Milindappanna, etc. It even excels in its diction the Mahavansa, the Dípávansa, the Rasaváhíní, etc. Its language is generally intelligible, and, altogether, elegant. It is the first Páli work which is read in many of the Buddhist Monasteries of this Island, with a view to illustrate grammatical forms; and there is scarcely a book more calculated to assist the Páli scholar, or one which better delineates the manners and feelings of the Siŋhalese, or more largely draws its illustrations from the Institutions, Usages, Arts, and Sciences which prevailed among them in ancient times. Here is a specimen from cap. vii. §§ 1—3.

CAP. VII.

Atha kadáchi Vassádhikatánan devatánan pamádena avaggaho páturahosi.—

---

* Pr. Wilson's Hindu Plays, vol. i. p. ix.

Nidágha vegena raví patápí
Uṇhábhi tatto pavano kharo cha
Jaráture'vá 'sisirá dharácha
Pivinsu te sabbadhi sabbama'mbun.

Antobhu sunhena vipachchamána
Sanissananbho bharite'va cháṭí
Tibbátapakkanta vanantaráji
Rutákulá kháyati chírikánan.

Vassánakále'pi pabhá karassa
Patápasantápita m'antalikkhan
Samáchitan paṇḍara váridehí
Sachandanálepa m'ivá'ti rochi.

'At this time, through the neglect of the divinities presiding over rain, there was a drought. By reason thereof a scorching sun, a hot burning atmosphere, and a dry earth,—these three, like those affected by fever, had imbibed all the moisture in all parts. The beautiful forest scorched by the sun, and filled with the cry of crickets, seemed as it were a bason filled with hissing water, boiling with great heat. The (expanse of the) sky, hot with the burning sun, was brightened, even in the rainy season, with masses of white clouds, as if it were anointed with (the powder of the) Sandal.'

With a view, however, to render this work interesting to the general reader, as well as to the Oriental scholar, the writer has lately published a translation of this work into English, the text itself is at the same time printed in the Siṇhalese character.*

It may be here convenient to determine the date of this work. Tradition affirms that it was written in the reign of Parakkama III., the celebrated patron of men and letters in the 13th century, (1266—1301 A. D.) Both internal and external evidence support this belief. Its style is not incompatible with that of other works of the same date. The events, too, which it records are brought down to the end of this prince's reign; and it is remarkable that the writer, after recording the various works which Parakkama had executed in connection with the Temple of Attanagalla, abruptly concludes the history, by expressing a fond hope that the annals of Attanagalla from thenceforth might be continued by future historians.

"If hereafter any pious (persons), by way of repairing that which is dilapidated, or adding any thing new to it, or of making a provision of offerings (for it), such as fields, etc., shall maintain this temple, let them record in continuation their names as well as their acts."

Although the above is not conclusive proof of this work having been written at the date to which the events it records are brought down, yet it may be

* This is the more to be regretted, as an earnest hope is entertained by Professor Weber, in his elaborate Review of Kachcháyana's Páli Grammar printed in his *Bibliographische Anzeigen*, that the Translator should 'use only the Roman character,' since 'the Siṇhalese letters are difficult to read and cause needless trouble.'

safely inferred that a work which implies the prior existence of Parakkama III., was written during, or subsequent to, the reign of that prince; and how far posterior may be conjectured from another fact, namely, that the self-same work was translated into the Siṇhalese during the reign of Buvanekabáhu in 1304 Saka, or 1382 A. D., answering, according to the chronological tables of Mr. Turnour, to the 4th year of the reign of Buvanekabáhu IV. of Gampola.

The Anomadassi mentioned in the Siṇhalese version is also named in the original Páli version; and the following extract from the Mahawansa contains the reasons for the belief generally entertained that he was identical with the priest of that name, to whom the Temple of Attanagalla was bestowed by Parakkama Báhu.

Tato gantvána so Hattha-vanagalla Vihárakan
Raññá vutta niyámena katvá bahu dhanabbayan
Kárápetvána pásádan tunga singan tibhúmakan
Anomadassi námassa mahá sámissa dhímato
Tan datvána tato tassa mahárája niyogato
Dánavaṭṭampi kappetvá Silá lekhanakárayí.

'He (Patirájadeva), having gone from thence (Adam's Peak) to the monastery of Hattha-vanagalla, and having, pursuant to the orders of the King, expended large sums of money, built a lofty mansion of three stories. Offering it to the erudite and venerable Lord named Anomadassí, and establishing, according to royal command, a continuous bestowal of alms for him, he put up a stone Inscription.'*

According to the above record and the tenor of other passages in the Mahawansa, the Attanagaluvansa must have been written, as is generally believed, by a pupil of Anomadassí during the latter part of the reign of Parakkama, when that monarch had retired from the active labours of his life by entrusting the Government to Wijayabáhu.

Professor Weber of Berlin in a Review† of this work, says: "If this Temple-legend be compared with similar works of the kind—the so-called Máhâtûrya found amongst the Brahmans,—a difference greatly in favour of the Buddhist legend will become apparent. Instead of the wonderful tales of gods and heroes of the Puranas, we here possess a sober narrative, which indeed, though not altogether free from some conflicting mythical exaggeration [who could expect such a thing!] is nevertheless very evidently, and possibly faithfully, related to the truth."‡

Having noticed the Páli work, a brief notice of its

SINHALESE VERSION

may not be out of place here. It was written in 1301, A. D., and the modesty of the writer has prevented the publication of his name. His language however

---

* This Tablet is the one referred to ante, p. 27.

† Literarisches Centralblott. July 13, 1867.

‡ The printed edition contains 43 octavo pages, and the Ola M.S. in the Temple at Pelmadulla has 36 pages of 1½ feet in length, with 7 lines to a page, closely written.

would authorize the inference that he was a Buddhist priest. The following Introduction will serve as a specimen of his language:—

Svastippraṣasta pravara dvijakula kamalavana rájirájahaṇsáya mánavú Akshara Likhita Gaṇita Gándharva Nakshattra Chhandas Nighaṇḍu Alaṇkára Sálihotra Yantra Tantra Mantra Jyótigñána Itihása Puránádi sakalakalávanṭa kalánidhihu vẹnivú Sútrábhi-dharma vinaya saṇkhyáta Tripiṭaka buddha vachanayehi anómadarṣivú Anómadarsíuam saṇgha rájadhurandaravú mahá-svámihu visiṇ méhayanaladuva itihása kathávahá púrva-likhitayada úsṣrayakoṭa púrvayehi Mághadhika bhásháven rachanákaranalada Attanagaluvihára-vaṇsakkhyáta Prabandhaya ṣrí ṣaka varshayen ekvádahas tunsiya sivu vasak pirunusanda, trisiṇhaládhíṣvara navaratnádhipati Bhuvanaikabáhu Naréndrayáhaṭa aggrámáttyavú sraddhá buddhi sampanna ratnattraya saranaparáyana asarana-sarana saranágata vajra paṇjara anavarata dánahétuppraṇchíkrita vividha vibhava saṇchíkrita Vaṇchí purappravara pavitra púrva gótraika kálapprabhúta chandra súrya manḍala yugaláyamánavú Srílankádhíṣvara Alakéṣvaranam mantríṣvarayánanhá mema mantríṣvarayánanṭa sahódaravú—'*Paranárí sahódara*'—yanádí anékapprakára virudávali ẹti svártha parártha karaṇa pravíṇa ishṭártha praṣavaya kirímen arthíjana manóratha púraṇayehi atyarthayen arthívú Arthanáyakanam Mantríṣvarayánan há dedenágé karuná kaṭáksha nirikshanayen susan rakshita madhuratara kusalaphala bharita taruṇa vriksháyamánavú paraṣattru kuṇjara nikara nirákaraṇayehi pravína siṇháyamánavú Ṣatru Siṇha Kunjarábhi dhána sénáná-yaka pradhánîhú visin ṣótrujanayágé sukháva-bódhaya piṇisa svakíya Siṇhala bháshávèn pravartitavuvahot yehekẹyi árádhitava ṣástrárambhayehi ishṭa déva-tá'rádhanáva sandahá púrva kattrínvisin varṇitavú *snehuttaráya hadayá mala mallikáya*—yanádí prathama gáthávehi paṭam artha kathanaya karamu.

'Patronized by the glance-of-support of two descend-ants of the ancient, illustrious, and pure family of the city of Vanchi,* like unto the sun and moon manifested at one and the same time, viz., (one) named Alakéṣvara—the Prime minister of Buvanékabáhu king of the three-divisioned Siṇhala, and lord over the nine treasures,†—a Chieftain of Lanká, who is possessed of faith and wisdom, and is dependent entirely on the protection of the three gems;‡ who helps the weak, and is a mine [cage] of diamond to the needy; and, who, by reason of his unceasing munificence, has accu-mulated and increased great wealth:—and [the other] his brother, Minister Arthanáyaka, the object of the hymns of praise, such as 'Paranárí Sahodara'‡‡ etc.,

---

* This is not known, and cannot now be identified. Probably it was a renowned city in India.

† All precious gems found in the island were anciently the property of the sovereign, and hence the allusion to his being "the lord over the treasures," (lit. 'gems'), of which there are nine kinds.

‡ "Buddha," "the Priesthood" and "the sacred writings" are meant by "the three gems."

‡‡ Lit. 'A brother to others' wives,' etc.

who is unceasing in doing himself and others good, and who ever longs to satisfy the desires of mendicants by giving away the desired objects:—and, invited by the Chief General of the Forces named Sátru Siṇha Kunjara, who is like unto a young tree laden with the fruits of his delectable* fortune, and an experienced lion to subdue the elephants of foreign enemies; and who intimated the propriety of perpetuating [the Páli Attanagaluvansa] in the native Siṇhalese language, with a view to render it easy of comprehension to the (learner) student:—we, at the lapse of 1304 years after the Saka era, paraphrase, commencing from *Snehuttaráya hadayá malu mallikáya*, &c., the first gáthá uttered by its author, in adoration of the deity of his own Faith in his literary introduction to the Attanagalu-Vihâravansa, which was in aforetime composed in the Mágadhí language upon the basis of ancient writings and traditions, and under the auspices of His Lordship Sanga Rája Anómadassi, a very Royal-Hansa to a mass of Lotuses† of the supremely venerable Brahaman race, and who (as his name signifies) is 'highly educated' in the Tripiṭaka word of Buddha, consisting of the

---

* I have used this word as the nearest that can be employed to express the original, which conveys the quality of the 'fruit' as well as of 'fortune';—one 'sweet' and the other 'pleasing.'

† Lit. 'Lotus-massy-line.' This may not be a correct English expression. It is however an elegant Oriental metaphor. As the Hansas or cranes are supposed to dwell in lotus fields, here the writer compares the object of his praise to a 'Hansa,' and his lineage to a "long-row of Lotuses growing in masses."

Sútra Vinaya and Abhidharma (sections), and which (moreover), like unto Kalánidhi* (moon) is accomplished in all practical and mechanical arts and sciences (such as) Akshara, Likhita, Ganita, Gándharva, Nakshattra, Chhandas, Nighanḍu, Alankára, Sálihotra, Yantra, Tantra, Mantra, Jyótigñána, Itihása, Purána,† etc.

The language of this translation will give the reader but a very imperfect idea of the elegance of the style of the original. The collocation of the different parts of the above, which, contains but one sentence, and which in the Siṃhalese may be pronounced to be exceedingly beautiful, is however such as to render its translation into English very difficult. Just before each name there are a number of complimentary epithets and metaphors adjectively used, which, as the reader will perceive, when rendered into English,

---

* This word is Kalínidi in my copy. It is probably Kalá-nidi or 'moon.' As the moon is supposed to be filled with ambrosia, so the object of the writer's comparison is said to be accomplished in the (kalá) arts and sciences.

† Akshara may be translated 'letters,' Likhita 'writing,' Ganita 'calculations or arithmetic,' Gándharva 'music, dancing,' Naksattra 'science of asterisms or astrology,' Chhandas 'prosody,' Nighanḍu 'philology,' Alankára 'rhetoric,' Sálihotra 'Ferriery,' Yantra 'science of diagrams' for equinoxes, etc., Tantra 'science of medicine, etc.' [This is used to signify different arts—such as Nyàya 'philosophy,' Yóga 'meditation,' jugglery, etc.] Mantra 'charms,' Jyótigñána 'astronomy,' Itihása 'ancient legends—such as Mahá Bhárata, etc.' Purána 'ancient history.'

suspends the sense between the several members of that sentence.

Though the translator calls it a 'paraphrase'; yet the work is a free translation, with but few errors, and those of not much consequence. This translation is also now being printed with the original, and will soon be published. The M.S. ola copy contains 72½ pages of 15 inches × 2⅛, with 7 lines to a page.

KACHCHA'YANA-PA'LI GRAMMAR,

is a very ancient Páli Grammar, and is held by Buddhists in the same high estimation that Pánini is by the Brahmans. It is to be found in nearly all the Buddhist Monasteries in Ceylon, although the learned translator of the Mahawansa states, in his Introduction, that it is no longer extant in this island.

The writer of this notice has lately published a translation of a portion of this Grammar; and the Rev. F. Mason of the Baptist Mission has made a compendium of the entire work, on the model of European Grammars.

This Grammar is divided into eight books. The first treats on "Combination," the second on "Declension," the third on "Syntax," the fourth on "Compounds," the fifth on (Tadhita) "nominal Derivatives," the sixth on "Verbs," the seventh on (Kitaka) "verbal derivatives," and the eighth on "Unnádi Affixes."

These are found subdivided into Chapters or Sections. But, all the aphorisms do not exceed six hundred and eighty seven.* The following extract embraces the writer's introductory remarks, together with the first Section of his Grammar:—

Seṭṭhan tiloka mahitan abhivandi yaggan
Buddhan cha dhamma' mamalau gana' mutta mancha
Satthussa tassa vachanattha varan suboddhun
Vakkhámi sutta hita' mettha su Sandhikappan.

Seyyan Jinerita nayena budhá labhanti
Tanchá'pi tassa vachanattha subodhanena
Atthan cha akkhara padesu amoha bhává
Seyyatthiko pada'mato vividhan suneyya.

'Having reverentially bowed down to the supreme chief Buddha adored by the three worlds, and also to the pure dhamma, and the illustrious priesthood; I now celebrate† the (pure) Sandhikappa in accordance with the Suttas, to the end that the deep import of that teacher's words may be easily comprehended.'

'The wise attain to supreme (bliss) by conforming (themselves) to the teachings of Buddha. That (is the

---

* Sattá sítuttará Suttá
chha satá' sun pamánato=687 Suttans.

† *Vakkhámi* "I utter"—The true import of this word, taken in connection with the allegation that 'Kachcháyana published (pakásesi) his Grammar in the midst of the priesthood,' may lead to the inference that it had at first only a memorial existence. This Introduction may therefore belong, consistently with tradition, to the compiler who reduced the aphorisms into writing.

result) of a correct acquaintance with the import of his word. The sense, too, (is learnt) by a [non-ignorance] knowledge of characters and words. Wherefore, let him who aims at that highest felicity hear the various verbal forms.'

Lib. I. Section 1.

1. Attho akkhara saññáto.

The sense is known by letters.

2. Akkhará pádayo eka chattáḷísan.

The letters, *a* &c., are forty one.*

3. Tatth'odantá sará aṭṭha.

Of these the eight ending with *o* are vowels.

4. Lahumattá tayo rassá.

The three light-measured (are) short.

5. Aññe díghá.

The others, (are) long.

6. Sesá byanjaná.

The rest are consonants.

7. Vaggá panchapanchàso mantá.

Each (set of) five to the end of *m* (constitutes) a class.

8. An iti niggahítan.

This *n* † is a dependent.

---

* Moggalláyana disputes the correctness of this Suttan, and says, that the Páli alphabet contains forty-three characters, including the short *e* (epsilon) and *o* (omicron.) The Siṇhalese Alphabet, which is nearly as old as the Siṇhalese nation, also omits these. This is evidence of that language being derived from the Páli.

† The *anusvára*.

Para samaññá payoge.*

Other's names in composition.

10. Pubbam'adho-ṭhitam' assarau sarena viyojaye.

Let the last † consonant in the first (word) be separated from (its inherent) vowel.‡

Such is the sententious brevity with which the Rules in Kachcháyana's Grammar are expressed. The author adopts three modes of explaining them. First, Vuttiyá or Vártikas, comments to supply the deficiencies in the Suttas, and to render them clear; secondly, examples; and thirdly, explanatory notes on some of the principal grammatical terms, in the shape of questions and answers. To these again are occasionally added, a note to mark the exceptions to the Rule. In the examples, mention is made of several of the places and towns which were rendered sacred by the abode of Gotama, such as Sávatti, Patáli,

---

* Names or technical terms.

† *Adho-ṭhitam* "that which stands below [after such separation.]" The word below must however be understood to mean preceding; for in composition, which Eastern writers regard as a tree from bottom to top, the first-written character is considered as being at the bottom or below the rest.

‡ There is some confusion, as remarked by Professor Weber, in the translation of this Sutta in my Introduction (p. xvii.) It is here rendered plainer—'Let the last consonant in the first (word) be separated from (its inherent) vowel.' *e. g.* Take *loka* and *agga.* Here *ka* is the last consonant in the first word. When *k* is separated from its inherent vowel, say we get *lok—a+agga.* Then by the rule *sará sare lopam* we obtain *lok-agga*; and by the rule *naye param yutte,—lok'agga.*

Báránasí, &c. There is also much correspondence between the Páninya Sutras and those given in Kachcháyana. *e. g*:—

1. Apádáno panchamí—*Pánini* III. 4, 52.
   Apádáne panchamí--Kachcháyana.

So likewise :—

2. Bhúvádayo dhátavah. I. 3, 1.
   Bhúvádayo dhátavo.
3. Káládhvano ratyanta sanyoge. II. 3, 5.
   Káladdhána machchanta sanyoge.
4. Kartari krit. III. 4, 6.
   Kattari kit.
5. Asmadyuttamah. I. 4, 107.
   Amhe uttamo.

Again, the text of Páninі is altered to meet the exigencies of the Páli Grammar, thus;

6. Tiñas tríṇi tríṇi praṭhama madhyamottamáh
   Dve dve paṭhama majjhimuttama purisá. [I. 4, 101.

Tradition with one voice represents that the whole of the aphorisms were written by one and the same person; viz., Sáriputta Mahá Kachcháyana.

From their language, the aphorisms appear to have been written in very ancient times.

In the commentary on the Rúpasiddhi, we find the following distinct and important particulars regarding Kachcháyana.

"Kachcháyano signifies the son of Kachcho. The said Kachcho was the first individual (who assumed that name as a patronymic) in that family. All who are descended from that stock are, by birth, Kachcháyaná.

"(If I am asked) who is this Kachcháyano? Whence his name Kachcháyano? (I answer), It is he who was selected for the important office (of compiling the first Páli Grammar, by Buddho himself; who said on that occasion): 'Bikkhus, from amongst my sanctified disciples, who are capable of elucidating in detail that which is expressed in the abstract, the most eminent is this Mahákachcháyano.'

"Bhagavá (Buddho) seated in the midst of the four classes of devotees, of which his congregation was composed (viz., priests and priestesses, male and female ascetics:)—opening his sacred mouth, like unto a flower expanding under the genial influence of Surio's rays, and pouring forth a stream of eloquence like unto that of Brahmo—said: 'My disciples! the profoundly wise Sáriputto is competent to spread abroad the tidings of the wisdom (contained in my religion) by his having proclaimed of me that, —'To define the bounds of his omniscience by a standard of measure, let the grains of sand in the Ganges be counted; let the water in the great ocean be measured; let the particles of matter in the great earth be numbered'; as well as by his various other discourses.

"It has also been admitted that, excepting the saviour of the world, there are no others in existence whose wisdom is equal to one-sixteenth part of the profundity of Sáriputto. By the Achárayos also the wisdom of Sáriputto has been celebrated. Moreover, while the other great disciples also, who had overcome the dominion of sin and attained the four gifts of sanctification were yet living; he (Buddho) allotted, from amongst those who were capable of illustrating the word of Thathágato, this important task to me,—in the same manner that a Chakkawatti rája confers on an eldest son, who is capable of sustaining the weight of empire, the office of Parináyako. I must therefore render unto Thathágato a service equivalent to the honor conferred. Bhagavá has assigned to me a most worthy commission. Let me place implicit faith in whatever Bhagavá has vouchsafed to propound.

"This being achieved, men of various nations and tongues, rejecting the dialects which had become confused by its disorderly mixture with the Sanscrit and other languages, will, with facility acquire, by conformity to the rules of grammar propounded by Tathágato, the knowledge of the word of Buddho: 'Thus the Thero Mahá Kachcháyano, who is here (in this work) called simply Kachcháyano, setting forth his qualification; pursuant to the declaration of Buddho, that 'sense is represented by letters,' composed the grammatical work called Niruttipitako."* Mahavansa, p. xxvii.

Before I notice some of the objections urged against the above tradition, it may perhaps be convenient to

* "Another name for the Rúpasiddhi."—In the above note Turnour identifies Rúpasiddhi with Niruttipitaka. But, it would seem that the latter is an original work of Mahá Kachcháyana, different from his Grammar, and different also from his theological work entitled the Nettipakarana. See Kachcháyana Vannaná.

refer to the various other Páli writers who have given it the sanction of their high authority.

Kachcháyana commences his work, as we have already seen, with Atthó akkhara saññàto; and it has already been shewn from the passage quoted by Turnour, that that Suttan was declared by Buddha himself. This is more clearly stated as follows in the Sutta Niddesa.

Atthó akkhara saññáto-ti ádi máha; idan suttan kena vuttan? Bhagawatá vuttan. Kadà vuttanti—Yama Uppala námaká dve Brahmaná khaya-vaya kammaṭṭhánan gahetvá gachchhantá Nadí-tíre Khaya-vayanti kammaṭṭháne kariyamáne eko udake machchan ganhitun charantan bakan disvá, udaka bakoti vicharati. Eko ghaṭe patan disvá ghaṭa paṭo ti vicharati. Tadá Bhagavá obhásan munchitvá attho akkhara saññáto-ti vákyan ṭhapesi. Tesan cha Kammaṭṭhánan patiṭṭhahi. Tasmá Bhagavatá vuttanti vuchchati. Taññatvá mahá Kachcháno Bhagavantan yáchitvá Himavantan gantvá Mano-silá talc dakkhina disábhágan sísan katvá puratthima disábhimukho hutvá attho akkhara saññáto-tiádikan Kachcháyana pakaranan rachi.

'It is said that 'sense is represented by letters,' &c. By whom was this suttan declared? It was laid down by Bhagavá. (To explain) when it was declared:—Two Brahman (Priests) Yama and Uppala, having learnt (from Gotama) the khaya-vaya branches of Kammatthánan,* went away; and, whilst engaged in

* Such studies as Abstract Meditation, &c., preparatory to the attainment of the paths leading to Nibban.

abstract meditation, repeating 'khaya-vaya' on the banks of the Nadí, one of them saw a crane proceeding to catch a fish in the water, and began muttering* udako bako, 'water-crane.' The other, seeing a ghaṭe-paṭan, 'a cloth in a pot,' began muttering ghaṭa-paṭo. At this time Bhagavá by means of a light which he issued, declared the sentence, Attho akkhara saññato—'The sense is represented by letters.' Their Kammaṭṭhánan was also effectual. Wherefore it is said that this Suttan was declared by Bhagavá. When Mahá Kachcáhyana learnt this, he proceeded with Bhagavá's permission to Himavanta. Reclining in the Mano-silá region with his head towards the south, and facing the east, he composed the Kachcháyana-pakarana, consisting of (the Suttans) attho akkhara saññáto, &c.'

In the atthakathá to the Anguttara Nikáya, Mahá Kachcháyana is spoken of;† and the Tíká to the same work contains further particulars, which are embodied in the following extract from

THE KACHCHA'YANA VANNANA'.

A'chariyá pana lakkhana vutti udáharana sankhátan iman Kachcháyana gandha pakaranan Kachcháyanattherena eva katanti vadanti. Tena ahá eka nipáta Anguttara tíkáyan 'Mahá Kachcháyanatthero pubba patthaná vasena Kachchyána pakaranan, Mahá Nirutti pakaranan, Netti pakaranan, cháti pakaranattayan sangha majjhe pakásesi.

---

* Or rather pondering on what he had observed.

† Vide extract there-from *infra*.

'Teachers say that this Kachcháyana gandha pakarana, which numbers lakkhana (Rules), vutti (supplementary notes), and Udháharana (Examples), was composed by Kachcháyana thera himself. Wherefore the Tíká to the Anguttara of the Ekanipáta says, 'the thera Mahá Kachcháyana, according to his previous aspirations, published in the midst of the priesthood the three compositions, viz. Kachcháyana Pakarana, Mahá Nirutti Pakarana, and Netti Pakarana.'

The literary qualifications of the théra Kachcháyana, seem to have been indeed such as to warrant the belief that he devoted his time to the elucidation of the language of Dhamma. He was, as is abundantly proved in the Páli works, a distinguished member of the Buddhist fraternity. He is also mentioned in the Tibetan Buddhistical Annals, as one of the disciples of Gotama; and it is expressly stated of him, that 'he recited the Sútra on emancipation in the vulgar dialect.' By 'the vulgar dialect,' Mons. De Korési doubtless meant the language to which Colebrooke had previously given that appellation—the Mágadhí. Gotama himself states that of all his pupils Mahá Kachchàyana was the most competent to elucidate his Dhamma. In the very language of the sage, which is here quoted from the Ekanipáta of the Angutta Nikáya, —Etanaggan Bikkhawé mama sávakánan bikkúnan sankhittena bhásitassa vitthárena atthan vibhajantánan, yadidan Mahá Kachcháno—'Priests, he who is Mahá Kachcháyana is the chief of all the bikkhus, my pupils, who can minutely elucidate the sense of what is concisely expressed.' That this supremacy refers both to the literary, and the theological attainments of Kachcháyana appears from the following comment, which we extract from the Atthakathá to the Anguttara Nikáya.

Aññe kira Tatágatassa sankhepa vachanan attha vasena vá púritun sakkonti vyañjana vasena vá; ayan pana thero ubhayenápi sakkoti: tasma aggo-ti vutto.

'Some are able to amplify the concise words of Tathágata either by means of letters, or by [shewing] their sense. But this thera can do so in both ways. He is therefore called the chief.'

In the Nyása or the Mukha-matta-dípaní, which is supposed to be the earliest commentary on Kachcháyana's Páli Grammar, and is, as may be proved, older than the Rúpasiddhi, the author of this Grammar is not only identified with the Kachcháyana thera, whose 'intellectual supremacy was extolled by Buddha', but his memory is thus respected by an 'obeisance.'

> Kachcháyanan cha muni vannita buddhi-massa
> Kachcháyanassa mukha matta mahan karissan
> Paramparú gata vinichchaya nichchayan cha.

'Also (bowing down to) Kachcháyana, whose intellectual attainments had been complimented by Buddha, I shall comment upon the positive conclusions (Rules), which have been handed down by tradition as the very oral (teachings)* of this Kachcháyana.'

---

* Mukhamatta 'the very (word of) mouth,' a term which does not necessarily imply the absence of writing.

With reference to the name Kachcháyana in the above extract, the following passage occurs in the Nirutti-sára-Manjusa, wherein also the writer acknowledges the consummate scholarship of the Grammarian.

Kasi Kammadina vyapárena kachchati dippatíti Kachcho, thera pita tassa apachchan putto Kachcháyano Neruttukánan pabhava bhúto pabhinna paṭi sambhido etadagga ṭháne ṭhapito khinásavatthere tan pana natvana.

'By reason of the occupation of ploughing, &c. [comes] Kachchati 'he shines.' Thence, Kachcho, (the name of) the théra's father. His son is Kachcháyana —a théra, who was an arahanta, who was placed in the highest position, who had attained the paṭisambhidá,* and who was the first cause (source) of all Neruttiká, [Grammarians or] philologers.'

Although it is stated† that Kachcháyana was resident at Avanti, the pachchanta or 'the foreign regions'‡, it is however expressly stated that this Grammar was

---

* See Sivupilisimbiyá in Clough's Dictionary. Turnour has defined this to be 'the attainment of the four gifts of sanctification.'

† In the Chammakkhandaka section of the Maha Vagga.

‡ Mr. Muir, in his Sanskrit texts, says that "the people whom Yaska designates Prachyas, or men of the East, must have been the Kitakas or the Magadhas, or the Angas, or the Vangas."—p. 371. In the Buddhist annals, however, the word Pachchanta is used to designate all the countries beyond the Majjhima desa, which is thus defined in the Maha Vagga: 'Here the Pachchanta are these countries. On the east [of Majjhima] is the market

written in the Himavanta; and, from the mention of the principal towns celebrated by the presence and abode of Gotama, and especially that which had risen from a small village to the importance of a populous city in the time of the sage, I mean Pátaliputta,* it may be inferred the writer took for his examples such of the names as were then of recent celebrity.

It must also be borne in mind, that although tradition in one voice ascribes the authorship of the Páli Suttans in the Sandhikappa to Sáriputta Mahá Kachcháyana, yet that writers are divided in their belief as to the Vutti having been written by that distinguished hierarch of the Buddhist Church, as stated in the

---

town called Kajangala, and on the west Maha Sala. Beyond them is the great country of Pachchanta, and this side of it is the Majjha. On the south-east is the river called Salalavati. Beyond it is the Pachchanta country, and this side of it the Majjha. On the south is the town called Setakanni. Beyond it is the Pachchanta country, and this side of it is the Majjha. On the west is the Brahman village called Thuna. Beyond it is the Pachchanta country, and this side of it the Majjha. And on the north is the mountain called Usuraddhaja. Beyond it is the Pachchanta country, and this side of it is the Majjha.' For the original of this see Childers' *Khuddaka pátha*, p. 20.

* It is stated in the Buddhist annals (see the first Banavára of the Parinibban Suttan) that this city, which in modern times has received the name of Patna, was built during the lifetime of Gotama, for the purpose of checking the Vajjians; and it is also stated that at the time it was built by Sunidha and Vassakara, two ministers of the reigning prince Ajátassatta, Gotama predicted its future opulence and grandeur, as well as its partial destruction by fire and water.

KACHCHA'YANA BHEDA TI'KA'.

The following extract from it contains the tradition as to who were the authors of the supplementary notes and examples in Kachcháyana's Grammar.

Taná'ha Kachcháyana Dípaniyan.

Sandhimhi eka paññásan
námamhi dvi satan bhave,
Aṭṭhá rasádhi kanchena
kárake pancha tálisan;
Samáse aṭṭha visan'cha
dvásaṭṭhi Taddhite matan,
Aṭṭhá rasa satákkhyáte
kite sutta satan bhave;
Unnádimhi cha paññásan
ñeyyan sutta pabhedato;—
Sabban sampinḍa mànantu
cha sata sattati dvecha'...ti.

Imáni sutta sankhyáni ñyáse ágata sutta sankhyáhi nasamenti; kasmáti che? pakkhepa suttan gahetv ganantá dasádhika sata sata suttáni honti. Imáni suttáni Mahá Kachcháyanena katáni; vutti cha Sanghanandi sankhátena Mahá Kachcháyanen'eva katá—payogo Brahmadattena kato...ti. Vuttan ch'etan.

"Kachcháyana kato yogo
vuttí cha Sanghanandino,
Payogo Brahmadattena
ñyáso Vimalabuddhiná"...ti.

'It is said in the Kachcháyana Dípaní—that the distribution of Suttáni may be regarded (as follows, viz. that) there are fifty one (Suttáni) in the (book which treats on) Combination; two hundred and eighteen on Nouns; forty-five on Syntax; twenty-eight on Compounds; sixty-two on Nominal Derivatives; one hundred and eighteen on Verbs; one hundred on Verbal Derivatives; and fifty on Unnádi. The aggregate (number is) six hundred and seventy-two.

'These numbers of aphorisms do not correspond with the numbers appearing in the Nyása. To explain wherefore: By the computation of the interpolated aphorisms there are seven hundred and ten aphorisms. These aphorisms were composed by Mahá Kachchá-yana. The Vutti were made by Mahá Kachcháyana himself, (who was also) called Sanghanandi;—and the illustrations by Brahmadatta. So it is expressly stated—that

'The aphorisms were made by Kachcháyana
The Vutti by Sanghanandi*—
The illustrations by Brahmadatta—
And the ñyása by Vimalabuddhi.'

To sum up all the evidence on the subject: In the first place, tradition asserts that the writer was Kachcháyana, one of Gotama Buddha's disciples. 2. It is

---

* It will be observed, that the writer's statement, that Sanghanandi was identical with Mahá Kachcháyana, is not borne out by the authority quoted. From the distinct mention of different names for the authors of different parts, viz., the Grammar, its supplements, its notes, and its principal comment, the Nyása; it would seem that Sanghanandi (also called Sankhanandi) was a person different from Mahá Kachcháyana.

written in a very ancient style—that of the algebraic aphorisms of Pánini. 3. The Rules laid down are adapted to a language, which was certainly more refined than the Mágadhi of the third Ecumenical Convocation, and therefore as the writer himself states, to the language of Buddha.* 4. The allusions to places, etc., in the examples are those which were rendered sacred by the abode of Gotama.

Such are the facts and circumstances connected with the age and authorship of this Grammar, on which, without a thorough examination of the entire work, and unwilling to believe that so many writers have stated that which was not the fact, I was induced to uphold Tradition, and to support the same in my Introduction. But I was not over sanguine as to the correctness of my views. Even then I expressed the belief that future researches might enable me to adduce more satisfactory proof, which would tend materially to qualify the inferences and conclusions I had drawn. Later researches, I am happy to say, have considerably shaken them.

Professor Weber of Berlin in his Review† of my work, above referred to, has also expressed "his disbelief in the identity of the author of this Grammar with

---

* See my Notes in the Appendix to the Introduction of Kachcháyana.

† See the Journal of German Oriental Society, vol. xix. p. 649. This Essay was translated into English and published in Pamphlet form by Williams and Norgate; and wherever reference is made to the Review in this work, it will be to the English Translation.

Sáriputta, on the ground of his extensive acquaintance with previous works on Grammar; of the highly systematic arrangement he has adopted; and of the want, in the older documents of the language, of the complete attano-pada forms which he recognises."

Now, "the extensive acquaintance with previous works on Grammar" proves scarcely anything; since the age of many of them, for instance Pánini, is not yet settled, and which I am still inclined to believe was ante-Buddhistical. Neither is lucid and systematic arrangement, especially in view of similar evidence of arrangement in the canonical works of Buddhism, an argument against this work, containing what one of the writers already quoted, says, 'the Rules which have been traditionally handed down as the very oral (teaching) of [Sáriputta] Kachcháyana.' Again, the paucity of attano-pada forms in the Buddhistical works signifies little or nothing in view of the fact that such forms are unquestionably found in the Tepiṭaka,* and that the Grammarian could never have intended to exhibit entirely obsolete forms. And it is very remarkable that the Grammar notices the fact of their gradual displacement by parassa-pada.

But the learned Professor's conclusion may, however, be upheld on other grounds: and I am glad of the opportunity which the publication of this Catalogue affords me, not only to confirm those views, but also to set myself aright with the literary public by qualifying some of the opinions which I have previously expressed.

---

* See examples given under the title of Tepiṭaka.

i. As remarked by the learned Professor I do not, any more than he does, place implicit reliance on Tradition, unless indeed the same is supported, and not contradicted, by collateral circumstances. Now, supposing for the sake of argument, that this work was written—contrary to the testimony which tradition furnishes—in this island, and after the age of Asoka, let us see if that supposition militates against inferences drawn in favour of my previous position.

ii. "It is written in an ancient style." Though this is a circumstance quite worthy of consideration along with other facts; yet by itself it throws no weight in the scale: since compositions of an undoubtedly modern date, *e. g.* Rúpasiddhi, etc., are found written in a similar style. The same remarks apply to the

iii ground in support of my previous position—"that the Rules laid down are adapted to the language of the Piṭakas." Before, however, dismissing this part of the evidence, I may point out that the paucity of attano-pada forms, as remarked by Dr. Weber, in "the sacred literature," does not militate against the belief I once entertained; and that the Grammar only shews what the sacred texts clearly prove, that when the latter came into existence, whether mentally or as a written composition, the attano-pada forms were being gradually superseded by *parassa pada*. Attanopadáni parassapadattam. *Kach.* vi. 4. 37. But these forms, though sparingly, are to be found in the text-books of Buddhism.

iv. 'From the mention of names rendered sacred by the abode of Gotama' no inferences can be drawn; since, as I have recently found, the name of "Devánanpiya Tissa" (a king of Ceylon, the ally of Asoka, 307 B.C.) occurs in the following extract from

BOOK II. SEC. V.

Sutta—KISMA' VO.

Vutti—Kimichche tasmá vappachchayohoti Sattamyatthe.

Example—Kva gato'si tvan Devánan Piyatissa.

S—'Va' from 'Kin.'

V—To this 'kin' is (added) the affix 'va' in a locative sense.

E—O Devánan-piya Tissa! where was it that thou hast gone?

It may however be urged on the other side, that though the Vutti and the Examples were, as a second tradition clearly states, by Sanghanandi and Brahmadatta; yet the Suttas themselves might have been by Mahá Kachcháyana, to whom tradition without exception points at. In this view of the question it has also been pointed out to me by a friend, that the majority of writers on the subject attribute the *Suttas alone* to Mahá Kachcháyana. For instance, it is said, in the Sutta Niddesa (*see ante, p.* 47) that he "composed the *Kachcháyana-pakarana,* consisting of (the Suttans) *attho akkhara Saññáto etc.*"

Hence it is quite clear, that upon the recent researches to which I have adverted, Kachcháyana can only be looked upon as the author *of the Suttas*. This too appears to be very doubtful, according to the new lights which have been thrown upon this investigation, and to which I shall now proceed to advert.

1. A close and careful study of the oldest works on Buddhism has satisfied me of the correctness of my Pandit's remark, that the existence of the introductory stanzas in the Vasantatilaka metre justifies us to place this Grammar at a period long subsequent to the age of Sáriputta Mahá Kachcháyana. It may be confidently asserted, that there are no such metres in the text books of Buddhism. An examination of all the poetic portions of the Piṭakaṭṭáya thoroughly establishes the fact, that at the time it came into existence, no such Sanskrit metres were known. See *post*, under the head of *Tepiṭaka*. But it is suggested, that "though in point of fact the prefatory stanzas have been introduced by the compiler, yet the Suttas might have been, according to tradition, the work of Kachcháyana." Neither does this appear to have been the case; for the Mukhamattadípani, the oldest comment on this Grammar, refers to the words of the introductory stanzas as the very words of the Grammarian.

I must not omit to state that Sáriputta Mahá Kachcháyana is also mentioned in a Burman work called the *Múlamule*, as the author of a Páli Grammar. The Rev. Francis Mason, in an article in the American Oriental Journal, vol. iv. p. 107, writes: "The *Mulamule* opens with the statement that, when Gautama, soon after he attained the Buddhahood, preached to his followers in Páli, they found it difficult to understand him; but one of them, the great Kachcháyana, prepared a Páli Grammar, which enabled them to understand his language with facility."

This tradition is substantially the same that is current in Ceylon; and the fact here stated renders no assistance whatever in the investigation before us; since the mere existence of Kachcháyana's Grammar in Burma proves nothing. The best available evidence as to the introduction of Páli books and character into that country points at Ceylon; and the earliest period at which the same were taken to Pegu from Ceylon, was, according to the statement of P. Carpanus, on the authority of a Burman History called the Mahárazoen, by Buddhagosa in the 940th year of their era, answering to 307. A. D.* This, according to the authentic chronology of the Mahawansa, could not have been earlier than 432 A. D. Be that however as it may. We have clear evidence, as we shall hereafter shew, that Buddhagosa did not see Kachcháyana's Grammar: and it is thence clear that the work of Kachcháyana, like the tradition as to its authorship, has been carried from Ceylon to Burma.

Allowing our conclusions to be thus far correct, there is indeed another view of the whole question. It is this—that, though, as we have already seen, the Grammar which goes by the designation of *Kachcháyana's Páli Grammar*, and which is also extant in

---

* See Essai sur le Páli, by Burnouf and Lassen, p. 62.

Burma, was not entirely the work of Sáriputta Mahá Kachcháyana, yet there is nothing in the evidence which we have examined to preclude, but many things to warrant, the belief—that a Grammar in point of fact was composed by him, and that it is either now entirely lost; or, having been partially deranged, was at a subsequent date reproduced by some one with the aid of Pánini and other Sanskrit Grammars, by adopting their terminology.

Indeed I have already shewn* that some of the technical terms adopted in Kachcháyana were borrowed from Sanskrit writers.

Book 1. Cap. 1. § 9.

Para samaññá' payoge. Vutti—Yá cha pana Sakkata gandhesu Samaññá ghosá ti vá aghosá ti vá tá payoge sati etthá'pi yujjante. 'In composition other's terminology. Vutti--Such (grammatical) terms as are called ghosá (Sonants) or aghosá (Surds) in Sanskrit gandhas (or literary works) are here adopted as exigency may require.'

I have also shewn that though some of the aphorisms in Kachcháyana, like portions of its terminology, were the same in Pánini, yet others greatly differed; *e. g.* Panchamí and Sattamí, for the 'Benedictive' and 'Potential' Moods, were not found as a 'fifth' and 'seventh' division of the Verb in any Grammar that I have examined. The Bálavatára explains—

---

* See Introduction to Kachcháyana, pp. xxv. et xl.

Panchamí Sattamí tyáyan pubbáchariya saññá—that 'Panchamí and Sattamí were the terminology of former teachers;' and the Mahá Sadda-níti states that those terms were in accordance with Sanskrit Grammars such as the Kátantra.

I have not however had the good fortune of consulting the work to which reference is here made. M. Kuhn, who has only had the benefit of examining a few fragments which Theodore Aufrecht published of the doctrine of the Kátantrics in his Catalogue of Sanskrit works in the Bodleian Library No. 374, has the following observations appended to his translation of Kachcháyana's section on Káraka, which has just* been received in Ceylon:—

"It is not surprising that D'Alwis, p. xli., was excited at such agreement with the opinion that Pánini was before the eyes of Kachcháyana while composing his work. He grants, however, that this agreement may be explained too, in another way. And, indeed by a certain grammarian of the Páli language, I mean the author of the Grammar Mahásaddaniti, in D'Alwis's work, p. xl., we are referred to the Kátantric School, for the terms used by Kachcháyana, which were 'in accordance with Sanskrit Grammars such as the Kátantra.' Weber in his Review of D'Alwis's book, p. 564., has justly observed, that D'Alwis has incorrectly rejected this assertion. His words are: 'This passing remark of a scholiast can but seem to us as a

* April, 1870.

plain and simple statement, and although we need not naturally take it up for present use as ready money, it may nevertheless serve at all events as a welcome support for future investigations.'

"And, in fact, that this opinion is not plainly alien from the truth, appears most perspicuously from those few fragments, which Theodore Aufrecht published, of the doctrine of the Kátantrics, in his Catalogue of Sanskrit works in the Bodleian Library, No. 374. For the prefaces of both works (D'Alwis p. xvii., Weber, in the place already cited, p. 657.—Aufrecht p. 168) and the rules that are read in the beginning of every book alike exhibit a certain likeness. These are the rules:

Kat. Aufr. p. 169. Samás. 1. nâmnâm samáso yuktârtah.
Samás. 2. taststhâ lopyâ vibaktayah.
Taddh. 1. vâṇṇ apatye.
A'khy. 1. atha parasmaipadâni.
A'khy. 2. nava parâṇy âtmanepade.
A'khy. 3. trîni trîni prathamamadhyamottamáh.

Kacc. Samâs. 1. nâmânam samâso yuttattho.
Samâs. 2. tesam vibhattiyo lopâ ca.
Taddh. 1.ván apacce.
Akhy. 1. atha pubbâni vibhattinam cha parassapadani.
Akhy. 2. parâny attanopadáni.
Akhy. 3. dve dve pathamamajjimuttamapurisâ.

"Now, though these rules, which are similar to each other, of the Kátantrics and of Kachcháyana, differ greatly from the rules of Pánini and his followers, yet Kátantra Nam 1. Dhâtuvibhaktivarjam arthaval lingam (compare Pân. 1, 2, 45: arthavad adhâtur apratyayah prátipadikam) is of almost greater importance; whence it is evidently perceptible that, amongst the Kátantrics and in Kachcháyana's Grammar, the word linga had the same signification, namely the notion of a nominal theme (see what we have discussed above on the rule Karak. 15.) That even Vopadeva had the same notion of the word linga before his eyes, in forming the noun of the theme li, is handed down to us by the scholiast on Vopad. 1, 12; but Vopadeva made use of many books belonging to the Grammar of the Kátantrics. (Westergaard. Radices prœf. p. iv.) Finally, it seems proper to remark, that in Durgasinha's commentary to the Kátantric Grammar, (in the place already cited, p. 369,) the arrangement of the krit suffixes is attributed to one Kachcháyana.

Vrikshâdivad amî rûḍhâh Kritinâlamkritáh kritah
Kâtyâyanena te sṛishṭáh vibuddhipratibuddhaye.*

"The Kátantric Grammar 'does not labour under the studied brevity and obscurity of Panini and his school,' and when the great number of its appendices (pariçishṭa) is considered, you will scarcely doubt of its being composed for the use of beginners. Excellently therefore do the perspicuity and the method of

* Colebrooke names a certain Vararuchi also amongst the commentators of the Kátantric Grammars, misc. ess. ii, 45. Weber Zeitschr. d. deutschen morgenl. Gesellschaft viii. 851.

Kachcháyana's work agree with that Grammar, giving a sketch only and being less ample; points in which the 3rd book also departs widely from Pánini's Grammar; and, if the author has followed the Kátantrics, he could have also drawn from their compendium those articles which are common to Pánini and himself; and assuredly the Kátantrics have, by no means, rejected the method of the Páninians in the exposition of the uṇâdi particles. However this may be, it is already apparent that Kachcháyana's work has the semblance of a very great affinity with the Kátantric Grammars.

"It is quite evident that there are, in this third book, two kinds of examples which are drawn from Brahmadatta. And the first kind is that which is mostly used* in Sanskrit Grammars, such as the commentary to Kac. 2: himavatá pabhavanti pañca mahânadiyo, and the scholium to Pán. I, 4, 31: himavato gangâ prabhavati. Kach. 3: yavâ patisedhenti gâvo, and Pân. I 4, 27, yavebhyo gâm vârayati. Kach. 4, upajjhâyâ antaradâyati sisso; and Pân. I, 4, 28, upâdhyâyâd antardhatte. Kach. 5, satasmâ bandho naro; and Pân. II, 3, 24, catâd baddhah. The proper names devadatta and yajñadatta are set by each other in the same manner. Kach. 6 and Pân. I, 4, 52, 55.

* It will do to cite the Scholia to Pánini's work. It is well known that the learned men who in the beginning of the present century commented at Calcutta, on Pánini's Sútra, drew from more ancient sources. Many examples are found also in Siddhántakaum.

Kach. 7 alam mallo mallassa, and Pân. II, 3, 16, alam mallo mallâya. Kach. 8, tilesu telam, and Pân. I, 4, 45, tileshu tailam (see what was expounded above concerning âkâse sakunâ yanti) Kach. 8, gangâyam ghoso, and Pân. I, 4, 42, gangâyâm ghoshah. Kach. 9, dâtena lunâti, and Pân. I, 4, 42. II, 3, 18 dâtrena lunâti. Kach. 14, kamsapâtiyâ bhuñjati, and Pân. II, 3, 64: dvih kâmsapâtryám bhunkte, Kach. 20, kena hetunâ vasati, and Pân. II, 3, 26, annasya hetor vasati Kach. 25, sotthi pajânam, and Pân. 2, 3, 16, svasti prajâbhyah, Kach. 28, Kaṭam karoti, and Pân. I, 4, 49, II, 3, 2, the same. Kach. 29, mâsam adhîte, and Pân. II, 3, 5, the same. The examples which are adduced from the scholia to [Pân. I. 4, 52, appear to have been of some little authority even in the text of Kachcháyana's 31st Rule; compare çî çâyayati, and sî sâyati; adhi-i adhyâpayati and the synonym paṭh pâṭhayati. Kah. 34, gonânâm sâmi, gonesu sâmî &c., and Pân. II, 3, 39, gavâm svâmî, goshu svâmî. Kach. 35, kanhâ gâvînam (gâvîsu) sampannakkhîratamâ and Pân. II, 3, 41, gavâm (goshu) kṛishṇâ bahukshîrâ. Kach. 36, rudato dârakassa (rudantasmiṇ dârake) pabbaji, and Pân. II, 3, 38, rudatah (rudati) prâvrajît. Kach. 41, dîpî cammesu haññate, kuñjaro dantesu haññate, and the Vartt. to Pân. II, 3, 36, carmaṇi dvîpinam hanti, dantayor hanti kunjaram. Kach. 44, gosu duyhamânesu gato, duddhâsu âgato and Pân. II, 3, 37, goshu duhyamânesu gatah, dugdhâsv âgatah. Kach, 44, upa nikkhe kahâpanam, and Pân. I, 4, 87, upa nishke kârshâpaṇam.

Kach. 44, adhi Brahmadatte pancâlâ, and Pân. I, 4, 97, II, 3, 9 adhi Brahmadatte pancâlâh.

"The second kind of examples is what are added by the author, who was devoted to Buddha's doctrine, from the sacred books, as comment to Kach. 7, saggassa gamanena vâ from the Dhamapa. str. 178. Kach. 17, manasâ ce paduṭṭhena, and manasâ ce pasannena from Dhammap, str. 1 and 2. Kach. 26, pâpâ cittam nivâraye from Dhammap, str. 116. abbhâ mutto va candimâ from Dhammap. 172, 382 Kach. 33, pâpasmim ramati mano from Dhammap str. 116. Kach. 40, sabbe tasanti daṇḍassa, sabbe bhâyanti maccuno from Dhammap, str. 129 &c., &c.

"I have been able to use only a single copy, in order to learn the constitution of the entire text, namely a copy written with a style in the writing of "Cambodia," and supplied with emendations added by another hand. I have collated another copy concerning the sûtras, containing all the sûtras of Kachcháyana. The former copy is most negligently written with respect to orthography, so that I judged it unnecessary to notice a variation merely orthographical; but in this still very doubtful matter I have mostly followed Fausböll."*

Coincidences like the above lead *per se* to no important results as to the age of Kachcháyana; yet they are, when taken with other circumstances, not without

---

* Translated from "Specimen of Kachcháyana" by Ernestus Kuhn, pp. 19—22.

value as exhibiting, if nothing farther, than, as Kuhn says, "a semblance of a very great affinity between Kachcháyana's work and the Kátantric Grammars."

Failing in all my endeavours to fix the age of the work under notice, I have resorted to the only practicable mode, suggested by Professor H. H. Wilson, of examining what I may call positive and negative evidence furnished by subsequent writers.* Anxious, therefore to find out the oldest book which refers to Kachcháyana or his terminology, I was, in the course of my investigations, naturally led to an examination of Buddhagosa's Atthakatḥá; and I am glad to say my trouble has not been altogether fruitless. Indeed it has led to one important result, viz., to shake the confidence which I had previously placed on Tradition, and to establish the fact, that the work under notice was not known to the Siṇhalese between the age of Buddhagosa and that of the Ṭíkás to the Atthakathá. Now, if this Grammar was written by the eminent disciple of Buddha, to whom it is attributed by tradition, it is very reasonable to believe that it, like the Páli language, found its way into Ceylon soon after the introduction of Buddhism into it, and upon the arrival of Mahinda. In that case, too, Buddhagosa

---

* "The comparative age of various compositions is in many cases ascertainable by the references which the writers make to their predecessors; and the absence of the notice of a celebrated work where mention of it is likely to be found, is a very strong presumption of its not being in existence."—*Preface to the Sanskrit Dictionary*, p. xxv.

must have found it here on his arrival, if indeed he had not been already familiar with it; and nothing is more reasonable than to find that in his comments on the Piṭakaṭṭáya—especially when we consider that he had to translate from the Siṇhalese into the very language from which the Siṇhalese version itself was produced,—he had, in the interpretation of terms, referred to the very personage whom Buddha had so much complimented, or had frequently quoted or alluded to his Grammar, or, at least, had adopted the technical terms given in his Grammar. Such would have also been precisely the result, though Mahinda had not brought the work into Ceylon, yet, if it was the work of Mahá Kachcháyana in India. But it is strange to find, that, far from any allusion being made to the author of this Grammar, and far from the Grammar itself being in any way cited, there is not even an agreement between the terminology of Buddhagosa and Kachcháyana.

Some of the terms used by the former are thus collected in the following stanza, which we quote from Sutta-Niddesa.

Pachchatta' mupa yo gancha
Karanan Sampadániyan
Nissakka Sámi vachanan
Bhumma'málapanaṭṭhamaṇ.

And they may be thus tabularized:—

Buddhagosa.		*Kachcháyana.*		*Siṇhalese.**		*Signification.*
Pachchattaṇ	...	Paṭhamá	...	Pera	...	Nominative.

* See Sidatsangará, § 26, et seq.

Buddhagosa.		*Kachcháyana.*		*Sinhalese.*		*Signification.*
Upayogan	...	Dutíyá	...	Kam	...	Accusative.
Karanan	...	Tatíyá	...	Katu	...	Auxiliary.
				Karana*	...	Instrumental.
Sampadána	...	Chatutthí	...	Sapadan	...	Dative.
Nissakka	...	Panchamí	...	Avadi	...	Ablative.
Sámi	...	Chhatṭhí	...	Sabanda	...	Genitive.
Bhumma	...	Sattamí	...	Adara	...	Locative.
A'lapana	...	A'lapana	...	Alap	...	Vocative.

So reasonable is the inference which we drew before, "that if Kachcháyana was pre-Buddhagosic, that he would have adopted his terminology,"—that we find in the *Ṭíkás*, or 'paraphrases' to the Atthakathá, not only the terminology of Kachcháyana, but that of Buddhagosa—indicating, as clearly as any matter of this kind can be shewn, that this Grammar came into existence between the age of the Atthakathá and that of the *Ṭíkás*.

To this it is no argument to say, that it is possible that Buddhagosa simply translated into the Páli the words adopted in the Siṇhalese Atthakathá, as the words Karana, Sampadána, and A'lapana clearly shew their agreement with the Siṇhalese Grammatical terms Karana, Sapadan, and Alap for the same cases; for, if a portion of the terminology of Buddhagosa was that which Mahindá's Siṇhalese version contained,

* The Siṇhalese divide the Karanan into two, the instrumental (Katu) and the auxiliary (Karana). See Sidatsangará, p. 30, note (†).

and therefore the terminology of the Siṇhalese Atthakathá, originally made at the first dawn of Buddhism, it is inexplicable, on the supposition that this Grammar was by Sáriputta, that Buddhagosa did not, in some parts at least of his Translation, adopt the terminology of the eminent disciple of Buddha, but departed so widely from it as to employ the technical terms of Sanskrit Grammarians.

NETTI-PAKARANA.

Another work which is ascribed to Sáriputta Mahá Kachcháyana is the one above indicated. From an examination of its style it would seem to be the work of a person different from the author of the Grammar; but the difference of the subjects, and therefore of their treatment, might have led to the difference of style as already pointed out by me elsewhere.* It is, what it professes to be, a very full and complete commentary on the Texts of Buddhism. It combines a Commentary with a Dictionary. It quotes passages said to have been uttered by Buddha himself. The metres of the Gáthás are clearly Prákrit. And, from the interpolations of certain notes, which make reference to some of the distinguished members of the Buddhist Convocations, and which are also to be found in all the MSS. which I have consulted, I am the more inclined to the belief, that this "extensive dogmatical

---

* See Introduction to Kachcháyana, p. xxiii.

and exegetical commentary on a metrical text containing questions and answers, diffuse and prolix, as is the case in works of this kind,"* was written by Mahá Kachcháyana. Professor Weber adds in a note—"It is probably on account of this text that the whole work has been ascribed to Sáriputta, and it is indeed just possible that at least part of the text may be by him. For it appears from king Asoka's letter to the Bhabra Convocation, that even at that period the *question of Upatissa* (upatisapasina) *i e.*, of Sáriputra, formed part of the sacred texts.—See 'Indische Studien,' iii. 172."

The book from which the following specimen is extracted contains 108 olas; each two feet long, with nine lines written on each page.

Tattha katamo vichayoháro? 'yan puchchhitancha vissajjitancha' ádi gáthá. Ayan vichayoháro kin vichinati? Padan vichinati, pañhan vichinati, vissajjanan vichinati, pubbáparan vichinati, assádan vichinati, ádínavan vichinati, nissaranan vichinati, phalan vichinati, upáyan vichinati, ánattin vichinati, anugítin vichinati, sabbe nava suttante vichinati. Yathá kin bhave? Yathá áyasmá Ajito Páráyane bhagavantan pañhan puchchhati—

"Kenassu nivuto loko [ichchá yasmá Ajito]†
Kenassu nappakásati
Kissábhilepanan brúsi
Kinsutassa mahabbhayan..." ti

* Weber's Review of Alwis' Introduction to Kachcháyana, p. 29.

† This passage within brackets is stated by the commentator to have been interpolated in one of the Buddhist Convocations.

Imáni chattári pádani puchchhi táni. Socha kho eko pañho, kasmá? eka vatthupariggaho. Evanhi áha —'kenassu nivuto loko'-ti—lokádhiṭṭhánan puchchhati: 'kenassu nappakásatí' ti—lokassa appakásanau puchchhati: 'kissábhi lepanan brúsi' ti—lokassa abhilepanan puchchhati: 'kinsutassa mahabbhayan'ti—tasseva lokassa mahabbhayan puchchhati. Loko tividho,—kilesa loko, bhava loko, indriya loko. Tattha vissajjaná

"Avijjá [ya] nivuto loko [Ajitáti bhagavá]
Vivichchhá* nappakásati
Jappábhi lepanan brúmi
Dukkham'assa mahabbhayan..." ti

Imáni chattári padáni imehi chatuhi padehi vissajjitáni—Paṭhamau paṭhamena, dutiyan dutiyena, tatiyan tatiyena, chatutthan chatutthena.

'Kenassu nivuto loko'ti—pañhe 'avijjá nivuto loko'ti—vissajjaná. Nívaranenahi nivuto loko, avijjánívaranáhi sabbe sattá yatháha bhagavá. "Sabba sattánan bhikkhave sabba pánánan sabba bhútánan pariyáyato ekam'eva nívaranan vadámi, yadidan—avijjá; avijjánívaraná-hi sabbe sattá, sabbaso cha bhikkhave avijjáya nirodhá chágá paṭinissaggá, natthi sattánan nívaranan ti vadámi"—tenacha paṭhamassa padassa vissajjaná yuttá.

'Kenassu nappakásatí'ti—pañhe vivichchhá,† nappakásatí'ti vissajjaná; yo puggalo nívaranehi nivuto so

---

* After this word, I find "pamádá." It is, I believe, the interpolation of a note.

† "Pamádá" also occurs here.

vivichchhati, vivichchhánáma vuchchati vichikichchhá —So vichikichchhanto nábhi saddahati, anabhisaddahanto viriyan nárabhati akusalánan dhammánan paháháya kusalánan dhammánan sachchhi kiriyáya, so idha pamáda'manuyutto viharati; pamatto sukke dhamme na upádiyati; tassa te anupádiyamáná nappakásanti—yathá'ha bhagavá—

"Dúre santo pakásenti
Himavanto va pabbato;
Asantettha na dissanti
Ratti khittá yathá sará;
Te gunehi pakásenti
Kittiyá cha yasena cha"...ti.

Tena cha dutiya padassa vissajjaná yuttá.

Kiss'ábhi lepanan brúsi'-ti pañhe 'japp'ábhi lepanan brúmí'...ti vissajjaná; jappánáma vuchcha-ti tanhá; sá kathan abhilimpati yathá'ha bhagavá—

"Ratto atthan na já náti
Ratto dhamman na passati;
Andhan taman tadá hoti
Yan rágo sahate naran"...ti

Sá'yan tanhá ásattibahulassa puggalassa evan abhijappáti karitvá; tattha loko abhilitto náma bhavati—tena cha tatiyassa padassa vissajjaná yuttá.

'Kinsu tassa mahabbhayan'ti pañhe 'dukkham'assa mahabbhayan'ti vissajjaná. Duvidhan dukkhan káyikan cha chetasikan cha, yan káyikan idan dukkhan, yan chetasikan idan domanassan, sabbe sattá hi dukkhassa ubbijjanti, natthi bhayan dukkhena sama saman kuto vá pana tassa uttaritaran. Tisso dkkhatá—

dukkha-dhukkhatá, vipari náma dukkhatá sankhára dukkha-tá ti, tattha loko odhiso kadáchi karahachi dukkha dukkhatáya muchchati, tathá viparináma dukkatáya; tan kissa hetu honti loke appábádhá'pi dígháyuká'pi. Sankhàra dukkha táya pana loko anupádisesáya nibbánadhátuyá muchchati, tasmá sankhára dukkhatá dukkhan lokassá ti katvá 'dukkham'assa mahabbhayan'ti—tenacha chatutthassa padassa vissajjaná yuttá. Tená'ha bhagavá 'avijjá nivuto loko...'ti.

'Of the foregoing what is vichayahâro? [See] the gáthá—'Yan puchchhitan cha vissjjitan cha' etc. What does this vichayahâro investigate? It investigates parts of speech [words]. It investigates questions. It investigates answers. It investigates what precedes, and follows [the context]. It investigates happy [results]. It investigates ill-effects. It investigates [their] non-existence. It investigates consequences. It investigates means. It investigates canons. It investigates parallel passages. It investigates all the nine-bodied suttans. What is it? Just as in the question propounded of Bhagavá by the venerable Ajita in the section [entitled] Páráyana—*

'Say by what has the world been shrouded?
Wherefore is it not manifested?
Whereby is its attachment?
What is its great fear?'

'These four sentences were thus propounded [by Ajita]. They comprise one question. Wherefore?

* A section of Sutta Nipáta.

[Because] they take in one matter. He has stated it thus: By [the first sentence] kenassu nivuto loko, he investigates the abiding cause of the world [living beings]; by [the second] kenassu nappakásati he investigates its non-manifestation; by [the third] kissábhi lèpanan brúsi, he investigates its allurements; and by [the fourth] kinsutassa mahabbhayan, he investigates its very dreadful horror. The [loka] world is threefold, viz., world of kilesa,* world of [bhava], or existence; and the sensible [indriya], world. The explanation of the question [is as follows:]

'I say the world is shrouded by Ignorance;
'By doubt is it not manifested;
'By desire is its attachment;
'And its horror [proceeds] from Affliction.

'The four sentences [first quoted] are explained by the four sentences [last quoted]. *i. e.*, the first [of the former] by the first [of the latter], the second by the second, the third by the third, and the fourth by the fourth.

'The world is shrouded by Ignorance'—is the explanation of the question, 'by what has the world been shrouded?' Yes, it is shrouded by an obstacle; yes, all beings are clothed with the obstacle of Ignorance. So it is declared by Bhagavá: 'Priests, I declare that all beings, all lives, all existences, have inherently a particular obstacle, viz., Ignorance;—yes, all beings are beclouded by ignorance. Priests,

* Evil in thoughts, desires, or affections.

I declare that by completely destroying, abandoning, (and) forsaking Ignorance, (existing) beings have no impediment.' Hence the explanation of the first sentence is satisfactory.

'By doubt is it not manifested'—is the explanation of the question, 'by what has (the world) been shrouded?' He, who is impeded with an obstacle, doubts. By the (obsolete) term vivichchhá (in the text) vichikichchhá (doubt) is expressed. [Thus] a person who doubts, is devoid of pure faith. He who is devoid of pure faith, exerts not, to destroy demerit, and to acquire merit. He (thus) lives clothed with procrastination. He who procrastinates, fails to practise good deeds [religious and abstract meditation.] He who does not practise them, is not manifested.* So it has been declared by Bhagavá, that 'The righteous are manifested far-and-wide like the Himalaya mountain; (but) the wicked are here unperceived, like darts shot at night. The former are manifested by (their) virtues, fame and renown.' Hence the explanation of the second sentence is satisfactory.

'By desire, I say, is its attachment'—is the explanation of the question, 'whereby is its attachment?' By the (obsolete) term jappá (in the text) tanhá (or) lust is conveyed. How she forms an attachment is thus stated by Bhagavá:—'He who is actuated by lust, knows not causes (of things); he who is actuated

* I have rendered this passage rather freely, without reference to words.

by lust perceives not what is right. Whenever lust enslaves [lit. bears] a man, then is there a thick darkness.' Thus the aforesaid lust in an inordinately lustful person becomes (as if it were) a glutinous [substance.] In it the world becomes adhesive. Hence the explanation of the third sentence is satisfactory.

'Affliction* is its dreadful horror'—is the explanation of the question, 'what is its great fear?' Affliction is two-fold; that which appertains to the body, and that which appertains to the mind. That which appertains to the body is pain, and that which appertains to the mind is sorrow. All beings dread affliction. There is no dread equal to that of Affliction (dukkha.) Where indeed is a greater than that? Affliction in the abstract is three-fold—inherent misery (dukkha-dhukkhatá), vicissitudinary misery (viparináma dukkhatá), and all-pervading misery (sankhára dukkhatá),'† Hence a being, sometimes, in the course (of transmigration) becomes free from inherent misery.‡ So likewise, from vicissitudinary misery.§ From what causes? [From] his being free from disease, and also (by the enjoyment of) longevity. A being also becomes free from all-pervading misery by means of (final)

* In the sense of the word "trouble," in the passage "Man is born unto trouble."—Job v. 7.

† Sankhára—'appertaining to all states of existence,' 'that which comes to existence, exists, and dies away.'

‡ *e. g.* 'Brahmans'—says the Commentator.

§ 'Those who are born in the *arúpa* or the incorporeal world.'

birthless nibbána. Hence, treating the affliction of a being as all-pervading misery, (the reply was), 'Its dreadful horror [proceeds] from Affliction.' Hence the explanation of the fourth sentence is satisfactory. Wherefore Bhagavá has declared:—

Avijjá nivuto loko, &c.

'I say, the world is shrouded by Ignorance;—by doubt is it not manifested;—by (reason of) desire is its attachment;—and its dreadful horror [proceeds] from Affliction.'*

BA'LA'VATA'RA.

This is the Grammar which is in current use among all Páli students. It is the smallest Grammatical work on the basis of Kachcháyana, and is found compiled nearly in accordance with the principles of Làghu-kavu-mudí. It treats of all grammatical rules as in Kachcháyana, but the arrangement is different, and is as follows:—The first Chapter treats on Sandhi; the second on Náma; the third on Samása; the fourth on Taddhita; the fifth on A'kkhyáta; the sixth on Kitaka, with a few Suttas on Unnádi treated of as Kitaka; and the seventh on Káraka, divided into two sections, one entitled Uttá'nutta, and the other Vibhattibheda.†

---

* This work is complete in 108 palm leaves of 2 feet in length, with 9 lines to the page.

† The matter in these two Sections, especially the treatment of the subjects, corresponds with cap. ix. and x. in the Sidatsangará.

It begins with the following gáthá:—

Buddhan ti dhá'bhivanditvá buddhambujavilochanan
Bálávatáran bhásissan bálánan buddhi vuddhiyá

'Having made a three-membered obeisance unto Buddha, the sight (of whom is as) delightful as the open lily, I shall declare (bhásissan) the Bálávatára for the promotion of the knowledge of the young.'

And it concludes with the following:—

Sátirekchi chatuhi, bhánavárehi niṭṭhito
Bálávatáro janatá buddhi vuddhin karotuhí

'May this Bálávatára, completed (slightly) in excess of four bhánaváras, increase the knowledge of mankind.'

The Rev. B. Clough, of the Wesleyan Mission, published, (in 1824) a translation of this work made by M. W. Tolfrey, Esq. late of the Ceylon Civil Service.* Don Andris De Silva Batuvantudáve, adopting the name of Devarakkhita, which he had assumed when a Buddhist priest, also published the Text in 1869. It contains 77 octavo pages.

Neither the name of the writer, nor the date on which it was composed, is given in the book. It however appears to be an old work, but I cannot ascertain

* Mr. Childers late of the Ceylon Civil Service, in his Prospectus to a Páli-English Dictionary, says: "Practically there are no Grammars of the Páli language. Clough's Páli Grammar is quite unobtainable by the ordinary student; D'Alwis's Introduction is a mere fragment; and Mason's recent work leaves our knowledge of Páli Grammar exactly where it was before." See Trübner's American and Oriental Literary Record for April, 1870.

how much older it is than the Panchikápradípa,* which mentions its earliest and best Siṇhalese commentary, that goes by the name of the Temple in which it was composed, viz.:

GAḍALA'DENI SANNA.

This also appears from its style to be a very ancient book; but the name of the writer and its date are not given. It contains 232 ola pp. of 15 inches in length, with 9 lines to the page.

The author in his comment on sec. 40 of the Báláva-tára, see edition 1869, quotes Pánini and Kátantra, and says, that 'the Sutta karmavat karmaná tullyakriyah in Pánini (iii. 1. 87.) is rendered karmavat karma kartá in the Kátantra.'

There are several other Siṇhalese Commentaries and Translations which I shall hereafter notice. In the meantime I extract the following specimen from the writer's observations on Taddhita.

Shabdayó yógikayaha rúḍhayaha yógarúḍhaya hayi trividha vet. Ehi yógikayó nam pachanádíkriyá sambandhaya pravritti nimitta koṭa ęti páchakádí shabdayaha: rúḍhayó nam lóka prasiddha sajñá mátra pravritti nimitta koṭa ęti ghaṭa paṭá'dí shabdayaha: yóga-rúḍhayó nam kriyádí sambhandayada lóka

* This was written in the 45th year of the reign of Parákrama-bábu VI., answering to A.D. 1455. See some remarks on the subject under the head of Sidat-Sangará.

prasiddha sajñávada pravritti nimittakoṭa ęti pańkajádí shabdayaha. Pańke játan pańkajan, maḍehi upanne Pańkaja namí: pańkaja shabdaya pańkayehi jánana kriyá sambandhayada lóka prasiddhayada apékṣákoṭa pavatinéya: maḍehi upan sesu Hólu ádín ęta, ovun kerehi pańkaja yana lóka prasiddhayak nęti heyin ovun hęra Piyumhima vé. Meseyinma taddhita shabdaya artha prakáshana kriyá sambandhayada vriddha prasiddha sajñávada pravritti nimitta koṭa vanné: artha prakáshana rukkho pachati kattabbo yanádí sesu padayan ętada rukkha yanádín keréhi taddhitaya yana vriddha vyavaháraya k nęti heyin ovun hęra ṇa nikádí pratyántavú váseṭṭha ghátikádín kerehima vé.

'Nouns are of three kinds,—Yógika, Rúḍha, and Yóga-rúḍha. Here the Yógika are nouns (such as) páchika 'a cook,' etc., originating in usage, and signifying an action (such as) pacha 'to cook,' etc. The Rúḍha are nouns such as ghaṭa 'pot,' paṭa 'raiment,' etc., originating in usage, and expressing a previously well-known appellation. Yóga-rúḍhayo are nouns such as Pańkaja 'lotus,' etc., originating in usage, and signifying an action, and also expressing a previously well-known appellation. Pańké játan Pańkajan, 'that which is born in mud is named Pańkajan.' The noun pańkaja, 'lotus,' is used according to usage, and with a view to its action of birth in mud. There are (however) other (species) that are produced in the mud, such as Hólu 'water lily,' etc.; but, since there is no usage to designate them pańkaja, (that word) is only applied to Piyum 'the lotus,' to the exclusion of others.

In the same manner nouns (named) Taddhita 'nominal derivatives,' originate in ancient usage, signifying an action, and expressing a previously well-known name. Though there are expressions, conveying a certain sense, such as rukkho 'tree,' pachati 'he cooks,' kattabbo 'that which should be done,' etc.; yet, since ancient usage has not sanctioned words such as rukkho 'tree,' etc., in the sense of Taddhita, they are excluded, and that name is applied only to nouns such as Vásiṭṭha 'son of Vasittha,' and ghátika 'clarified butter,' etc., ending in affixes na, nika, etc.'*

DHA'TU-MANJUSA'.

Páli, like Siŋhalese Lexicography, is comparatively more recent, and has attained to a less degree of cultivation, than Páli Grammar.† As we have already seen, the Abhidhánapadípiká, is a metrical vocabulary, and contains no verbs. There are indeed several Dhátupáthas, or Lists of Radicals, but they are very

---

* From the trivial errors with which this work abounds,—errors, which cannot be traced to incorrect transcription, and which are also inconsistent with the great learning and research exhibited by the author; and, moreover, from the absence of the usual 'Adoration,' and any remarks of the writer, either at the beginning or at the end of the work, I am inclined to the belief that the writer had died before he fairly completed it.

† Speaking of the Páli, Mr. Childers has the following remark; and so far as it applies to 'Dictionaries' he is quite right. "It has long been felt as something of a reproach that an oriental

defective, both as to arrangement, and the meanings assigned to them. Among them, however, there are none which can claim such decided pre-eminence as belongs to the work under notice.

It is an ancient Páli work. It was composed by a learned Buddhist Priest named Sílavansa, on the basis of the Grammatical System propounded by Kachcháyana. Thence it is also called Kachháyana Dhátu Manjusá. The residence of the author is stated to have been Yakkhaddhi Lena. But there is no proof in support of the conjecture that it refers to Yakdesságala in the district of Kurunẹgala. No date is given in the work; and there is no clue to its discovery. The following is the author's Preface.

Nirutti nikará pára párávárantagan munin
Vanditvá Dhátumanjúsan brúmi pávachananjasan
Sogatágama má'gamma tan tan vyákaraṇáni cha
Páṭhe chá'paṭhitá' pettha dhátvatthá cha pavuchchare
Chhanda hánittha mo'káran dhátvantánan siyá kvachi
Yúnan dígho cha dhátumhá pubbam'attha padan api

'Having bowed unto Buddha, who has crossed the boundless ocean of all philological sciences (treasures), I compose the Dhátu Manjusá, ['Casket of Radicals'], which is a path to the Saddhamma, or the sacred Scriptures.

---

language of singular wealth and beauty, and embodying a literature of surpassing interest, should be destitute both of Grammars (?) and of Dictionaries.'—Trübner's Literary Record," April, 1870.

'Having studied Buddhism, and various Grammars, I have given the Radicals, and their significations, consisting both of what have, and have not, been treated of, in the Páthá or Glossaries.*

'To meet the exigencies of metre, I have in some places [substituted] an *o* at the end of the Radical, and have rendered the final *i* and *u* long. I have also occasionally given the sense before the Radicals.'

The author after embodying about 421 Radicals in 148 stanzas, offers the following explanation as to the plan of the work, to which I may add the fact, that an Alphabetical List is being prepared by the publisher, to facilitate reference:—

Bhú vádí cha rudhádí cha divádí svádayo gaṇá
Kiyádí cha tanádí cha churadí'ti'dha sattadhá
Kriyá vá chitta makkhátu'mekekattho bahú'dito
Payogato'nugantabbá anekatthábi dhátavo
Hitáya manda buddhínan vyattan vaṇṇakkamá lahun
Rachitá Dhátu-manjúsá Sílavansena dhímatá
Saddhamma pankeruha rájahanso
ásiṭṭha dhammaṭ ṭhítí Sílavanso;
Yakkhaddi lenákkhya nivása vásí
yatissaro so yamidan akásí.

'Thus, the seven classes of Radicals are, bhûvádi 'bhû, &c.,' rudhádí 'rudha, &c.,' divádí 'diva, &c.' súvádi 'sú, &c.' kiyâdi 'ki, &c.' tanâdí 'tanu, &c.,' and churâdi 'chura, &c.'

---

* Lit. "Prose collections."

'Radicals have various meanings which must be learnt from (reading) authors. I have, for the most part, given but one signification [of each Radical] to convey the action which (each) expresses.

'The Dhátu Manjusá, rendered clear and easy by means of alphabetical arrangement,* has been composed for the instruction of the uninitiated, by the learned Silávansa,—that Silávansa, a priest, who resides in the [Temple of] Yakkhaddi Lena, with aspirations that Buddhism may continue long, like a Hansa to the lotus-of-Scriptures.'

The following is a specimen of the work:—

G.

6. Aggo (tu) gati koṭille laga saṅge mag'esane
Agí igí rigí ligí vagí gatyattha dhátavo

GH.

7. Silágha katthane jaggha hasane aggha agghane
Sighi ágháyane hoti laghi sosa gatísu cha

Don Andris De Silva Batuvantudáve, Pandit, in publishing this work with a Siṇhalese and an English Translation, has not only prefixed the number of the stanza in which each word in the alphabetical list occurs, but has also prefixed to each Radical the number of the class to which it belongs. He has also added two

* This refers to the alphabetical arrangement in the verses, not the list.

stanzas (the 4th and 5th) by way of supplying an omission occurring in the work. They are the following:—

KH.

Ikkho (tu) dassanan'kesu khí khaye kankha kankhane
Chakkha dasse chikkha váche dikkho'panaya muṇdhisú
Vatá'desesu niyame bhakkhá'da namhi bhikkha cha
Yáche rakkho rakkhanamhi sikkho vijjaggahe tathá.

Although the author has generally given but one meaning to each word; yet, where he has added an 'etc.' to a given signification, the publisher has not failed to add others, for which he is chiefly indebted to the Buddhist scriptures.

I shall conclude this notice with a specimen of the Alphabetical list, p. 22:—

KI'—120.	KI'...vinimaye, dravya ganudenu kirímehi, 'to buy', 'to exchange.'
BHU'— 64.	KI'LA...bhande, bẹndímehi, 'to bind' 'to wedge.'
BHU'— 84.	KI'LA...viháre, kelímehi, 'to play' ['to draw a line.']*
BHU'— 2.	KU...saddekuchchhite, shabdkirímehi, kutsitayehi, 'to sound' 'to contemn.'
BHU'— 2.	KUKA...á'dáne, gẹnmehi, 'to take,' 'to accept.'
BHU'— 8.	KUCHA...sadde, shabdakirímehi, 'to sound.'
TU— 85.	KUCHA...sankochane, hẹkilímehi 'to straiten,' 'to narrow,' 'to contract.'
BHU'—20.	KUṭA—chhedane, kẹpímehi, 'to cut.'

* I believe this means 'to peg,' in the sense of planting sticks on the ground to draw lines for cutting foundations.

THE NA'MA'VALIYA.

It is well known that poetry has from time immemorial been the idol of literary men in the East. At a period when poetry was cultivated by the king as well as the peasant, the recluse in his monastery, and the traveller on the road, the necessity for abridged vocabularies of synonymous and homonymous terms, was quite obvious. To facilitate therefore, reference, and to render one's memory the store-house of information, such vocabularies were invariably composed in easy metre. To this class belongs *Amara-Kosha*, called in Ceylon, after the writer's name, *Amara Sinha*—to which 'has been assigned the first place in Lexicography by the unanimous suffrage of the learned in the East.'

In close imitation of this work is the Námávaliya of the Siṇhalese, composed in 1421, A.D. by Nallaratun, a chieftain of the time of Parákrama Báhu VI. A comparison of the Sanskrit Amara Kosha and the Páli Abhidhánapadípiká with the Námávaliya, will not fail to interest the philologer and the historical student. At the same time that the Siṇhalese words shew an affinity to the Sanskrit family of languages, the student will also perceive the still closer relationship which the former bears to the Páli. Between the Maharashtri, which Lassen has designated the '*dialectus præcipua*,' and the Siṇhalese, there seems to be great connection; and, when we compare the Siṇhalese in its relation, whether verbally or grammatically, with the Prákrit, the conviction forces itself on the mind, that the former is a sister dialect of the latter, which Hemachandra defines to be—[*Prakritih Sanskritam, tatrabhavam tata ágatam vá 'prakritam'*]—'that which has its source in Sanskrit, and is either born with, or sprung from, it.'

In wading through the Lexical works of the East, one peculiarity, which must necessarily strike the student, is, that both in Páli and Siŋhalese, Lexicography is in its infancy. The Abhidhánapadípiká, the best of all Páli Dictionaries, and one certainly superior to all the Dhátupáthas that were ever written, is inferior to Professor Wilson's Sanskrit Dictionary, and even to the Radices Linguæ Sanskritæ of Professor Westergaard of Copenhagen, and the Glossarium Sanskritum of Bopp. A close examination of Námávaliya will exhibit this inferiority, and the comparative superiority of modern Lexicographers, as compared with the ancient writers, who merely put down some thousands of words into metre without order, method, or arrangement. In the number of words too, the superiority of Professor Wilson's Dictionary is greater than the Amara Kosha in the proportion of 60,000 to 12,000.

The rhymes in which the work is composed, though useful in one point of view, are nevertheless calculated to weary the beginner in the ascertainment of the words, which run into one common mass with the observations of the Poet. Námávaliya labours under this and many other disadvantages.

To render therefore, its use easy to all classes, and especially to the European student, the Rev. C. Alwis has published an English Translation* after the plan of Colebrooke's version of the Amara Kosha.

The utility and importance of the Vocabulary are thus noticed by the Translator:—

'Námávaliya, the subject of the following pages, is a work of great authority, and is constantly referred to by Siṇhalese scholars. It holds the same position in Siṇhalese literature, as the Amarakosa vocabulary in the Sanskrit, and Abhidánap-padípika in the Páli, both of which works have been translated and published. It is scarcely necessary to adduce anything by way of demonstrating the utility of offering the Námávaliya to the public in its present shape, beyond the fact that there is hardly a Siṇhalese scholar, who is not in possession of a manuscript copy, or to whom its contents are not familiar.'

However useful this little work may be for various purposes, especially as a ready help to the student in furnishing him with a variety of names, from which he may at pleasure select such as may suit the exigencies of a peculiar metre, yet it cannot be denied that, like the Amara Kosha, it contains but a very small portion of the words of a very copious language. Neither verbs or derivatives are given in it. Except a few epithets which are appropriated as titles of deities, or as names of plants, &c., ordinary compound

* Námávaliya, by Rev. C. Alwis, 1858, octavo, pp. 123.

words, (not to mention *sesquipedalia* and *septipedalia*), are omitted. Technical terms, too, as in most dictionaries, are excluded from this. The catalogue of homonymous words is also defective; and this is not to be wondered at, when we find the same deficiency in the Amara Kosha, which contains only about 12,000 words. But it is to be regretted that neither the original writer, nor his translator has given us the etymology of the words. Nor have we the gender of the nouns, which, as our readers know, it is difficult to distinguish in the Siņhalese; for it does not recognise, as in many modern languages, a philosophical or an intelligible principle, in fixing the genders of nouns.

The writer, after the usual adoration to Buddha, gives the following introductory stanza:—

Lóvęḍa pinisa poranęḍuran metin kala
Nam páliyen mut bęvinudu kavi nokala
Vanapot kara viyat bęvu vana lesa lakala
Pada bęnda kiyam Námávaliya Siņhala.

'Though the names, which ancient teachers employed, for the good of the world, were in prose and not rendered into verse; yet, do I, in rhyme, sing the Siņhalese Námávaliya, so that (persons) may be distinguished in learning, by committing (the same) to memory.'

This work is divided into two parts, the first consisting of synonymous, and the second of homonymous terms. The first is subdivided into thirteen orders of names, consisting:—

1. Of celestial terms, for things above human abodes. Under this head are comprised the names of Buddhas, deities, both religious and mythological, the cardinal points, the heavens, the different phenomena of nature, the various stars, including the personifications of the planetary system, the various distinctions of time, colour and season, the emotions of the mind, &c.

2. Of geographical terms, for objects in and beneath the earth, such as the nága worlds, the hells, darkness, serpents, waters, seas, rivers, fishes, and marine objects, &c., &c.

3. Of terrestrical objects, which enter into the graphic delineation of a landscape in poetry.

4. Of towns, and all the wealth, beauty, and splendour thereof.

5. Of mountains, rocks, stones, &c.

6. Of the vegetable kingdom,—giving the names of trees and flowers and some of the best medicinal herbs known to the Siṃhalese.

7. Of beasts, birds, &c.

8. Of men, and their different relations to each other in a domestic and social point of view; the different distinctions of their growth; the variety of names by which the organs of the body are distinguished; the various objects which are used for the adornment or comfort of the person, &c.

9. Of terms relating to asceticism, which Mr. Alwis has literally translated "Brahaman," the originator of monachism, according to eastern legends.

10. Of kings, and their attendants, pageantry, armies, martial weapons, kingdoms, wars, powers, royal virtues, &c.

11. Of merchants, and the different articles of trade, as anciently carried on.

12. The distinctions of caste and classes, slaves savages, outcasts, &c.

13. Miscellaneous terms not included in the above.

Part second contains a number of homonymous words, placed without any arrangement or order.

Having thus glanced at the contents of Námávaliya, we come to the Index No. 1, which is well got up, containing all the names given in the Námávaliya, arranged alphabetically, and referring by roman figures to the pages in the text, where their English significations are given in foot-notes. The reader will find by casting his eyes over pages 76 to 114 that the Námávaliya contains about 3,500 words.

There is also a second Index given by Mr. Alwis of the English terms in his translation, and referring by figures to their nearest Siŋhalese significations in the text. It will be thus seen that Mr. Alwis has not only given a literal translation of an oriental metrical Vocabulary, but has reduced all the terms contained in it into both an English and a Siŋhalese Dictionary, alphabetically arranged. He says:—

"Of the two indices or alphabetical lists, at the end of the work, the first will serve the purpose of a Siŋhalese and English Dictionary, and the second, as an English and Siŋhalese, as far as the words of the Námávaliya are concerned.*

The Mahawansa.

Of all the Páli works extant in this island, no class possesses a more absorbing interest than the Historical Records of the Siŋhalese. Besides the general archæological interest attached to the writings of the past, there is in these Siŋhalese Historical records much to excite admiration and suggest inquiry,—*admiration* for a people, from whom has originated in the East a desire for historical pursuits;—and *inquiry* into matters of the greatest value to the Antiquarian and Philologer, as well as to the Statesman and the Christian Missionary. It is a remarkable fact that no country in the East possesses so correct a history of its own affairs, and those of India generally, as Ceylon.

The Phœnicians, who had influenced the civilization of a very large portion of the human race by their great inventions and discoveries, by their colonies

---

* Though modern works by Europeans do not come strictly within the plan of this work, I may nevertheless here notice two Siŋhalese Dictionari c One is a school Dictionary: Part First, Siŋhalese aud English; and Part Second English and Siŋhalese, with an Introduction containing (valuable) observations on these languages, designed to assist the student in their acquirement, and an Appendix containing Latin and French phrases in common use, by John Calloway, Wesleyan Missionary, Colombo Wesleyan

established in almost every quarter of the globe, and above all by the extensive commerce which they carried on,—have left nothing behind, except the alphabet which they invented. The Persians, a very interesting and a very ancient race, to whom we naturally look for historic information, have little beyond their Zendavasta, two chapters of which contain some traditions of their own.

The Hindus, a people who had a literature of their own from a period long before the Siṇhalese became a nation, have no historical records; and their scanty "fragmentary historical recollections," which have been embodied in their religious works, such as the Purânas, present themselves in the language of prophecy; and upon their basis no trust-worthy chronological calculations can be made.* In the Vedas again, which are perhaps older than any Ceylonese Buddhist writings, and which are supposed to "furnish the only sure foundation on which a knowledge of ancient and modern India can be built up,"† there is a "lamentable

---

Press, 1821, pp. 156 and xxii. And the other by the Rev. B. Clough, is an English and Siṇhalese Dictionary, and also a Siṇhalese and English Dictionary, 2 vols. 8vo. in 1821, pp. 628 and 852. This work is chiefly valuable for the explanations it gives of Buddhistical phraseology. It is out of print; and a copy, occasionally offered to public competiton, fetches from seven to eight pounds. The Rev. W. Nicholson has also published a small octavo.

* See Pr. Lassen's Indische Alterthumskunde, p. 503.

† Essay on the results of the Vedic Researches by W. D. Whitney, American Oriental Journal, iii. p. 291.

lack of a historic sense, which has ever been one of the most remarkable characteristics of the Indian mind."*

Although our Dravidian neighbours, especially the Tamils, had attained to a very high degree of civilization at the time our first monarch sought for, and obtained, a Pandian princess as his queen; yet hey have no works which can be called historical, and their literature, however ancient, is much inferior to that of the Brahmans.†

The Chinese, who boast of a descent from times remoter than the days of Adam, have no historical writings which can throw the slightest light upon the affairs of the East.

In the country of Maghada, so greatly renowned as the birth-place of Buddhism, and of the still more interesting language (the Páli) in which it was promulgated,—a kingdom, moreover, which dates its origin from the time of the Mahá Bhárat,‡—we have no records of a historical character, beyond religious inscriptions sculptured on stone, and grants of lands engraved on plates of copper. These "unconnected fragments," beyond serving to fix the dates of particular Kings, furnish us at present with neither history, nor matter sufficient to help us to a general chronology. The Bactrian coins, again, afford us little or nothing beyond the kind of information which the monumental

* Ib. p. 310.

† Caldwell's Dravidian Grammar, p. 81.

‡ Elphinstone's History of India, vol. i. p. 260.

inscriptions furnish us. "The only Sanskrit composition yet discovered in all Asia, to which the title of History can with any propriety be applied, is the Rájataranginí;" * a comparatively modern work which was compiled A.D. 1148: but, this again does not bear any comparison either in point of the matter it contains, or in the interest which attaches to the subjects it treats upon, with the Siŋhalese Historical Records. The genuine historic zeal exhibited by the Siŋhalese from the very time they colonized Ceylon, far surpasses that of all other Indian nations.†

The love which the Siŋhalese had for such pursuits, was participated in by their rulers themselves; and, whilst tradition asserts that some of our early Siŋhalese Annals, from which the Mahavansa was compiled, were the works of some of our Monarchs,—history records the facts, that "the national annals were from time to time compiled by royal command;" and that the labours of "the historians were rewarded by the State with grants of lands." The interest which our Sovereigns took in this part of the national literature was indeed so great, that many a traveller and geographer of the middle ages was particularly struck, as "a trait of the native rulers of Ceylon," with the fact of the employment by them of persons to compile the national annals.‡ And, though comparatively

---

* Pr. H. H. Wilson's Introd. to Rájataranginí.

† Lassen's Indis. Alt. vol. ii. pp. 13--15.

‡ Edrisi, clim. 1, § 8, p. 3.

few are the records which the ravages of time, and the devastating hand of sectarian oppression, have left behind;—they, nevertheless, excel in matter and interest, all the Annals of Asia. As "the first actual writing, and the first well-authenticated Inscription in India, are of Buddhist origin,"* so, likewise, the first actual chronicle, as well as the most authentic history, in the whole of the eastern hemisphere, may be traced to a Ceylon-Buddhistic source. "The Mahavansa stands," says Sir James Emerson Tennent,† "at the head of the historical literature of the East, unrivalled by any thing extant in Hindustan, the wildness of whose chronology it controls."

When, for instance, the watchful mind of Sir William Jones seized with avidity the identity of Chandragupta and Sandracottus, and thence discovered the only key for unlocking the history and chronology of Asia, the annals of Ceylon were not without their use in removing the doubts which had been conjured up by antiquarians. When the indefatigable labours of a Prinsep enabled him to decipher the rock inscriptions of Piyadási or Dévanampiya, the discovery could not with certainty have been applied either to fix the proper date of the Buddhistic era, or to reduce the extravagant chronology of Asia to its proper limits, without the aid of the Siṇhalese records—the

* Pr. Max Müller's Sanskrit Literature, p. 520.

† History of Ceylon, p. 516.

Dípávansa* in particular, which identified the Dévanampiya with Asóka. When the obscure dialect of the pillar inscriptions presented philological difficulties, the Ceylon Páli Mahavansa alone served as an "infallible dictionary"† for their elucidation. When again the Cashmirean history put forth an extravagant chronology, Ceylonese chronicles alone enabled Mr. Turnour to effect an important and valuable correction, to the extent of 794 years, and thereby to adjust the chronology of the Rájataranginí.‡ When lastly, the penetrating mind of a Burnouf, from an examination into the Nepal version of the Buddhist scriptures, conceived the idea of "a fourth digest" of the Buddhists, apart from the compilations of the three Convocations in India, the Siṇhalese annals, and above all the Dípávansa,§ alone furnished the proof required for establishing the conjecture.

Although the several early historical records in the Siṇhalese language which had existed before the third

* "Mr. Turnour's Páli authorities will be of essential use in expounding our new discovery, and my only excuse for not having taken the epitome already published as my guide before, is that the identity of Piadassi was not then established."—Mr. James Prinsep, in the Bengal A. S. J. vi., p. 792, &c.

† "On turning to the infallible Tíká upon our Inscriptions, afforded by Mr. Turnour's admirable Mahawansa, we find a circumstance recorded which may help us materially to understand the obscure passage."—Prinsep; see Bengal A. S. J. vii., p. 264.

‡ See Bengal A. S. J. for September, 1836.

§ See extracts and observations on the subject, in the Introduction to Kachcháyana's Páli Grammar.

century, and from which the subsequent histories were compiled, are irretrievably lost, we nevertheless have the Dípávansa, the Daladávansa, the Bodhívansa, the Túpávansa, the Rasaváhiní, the Rájávaliya, the Rájaratnákara, Sulu-Rájaratnákara, Pújávaliya, Buddhagosa's Atthakathá, the Nikáyasangraha, and the Mahavansa, all which contain historical matter exhibiting the succession of 165 kings, during a period of 2341 years, from the time when Wijaya settled in Ceylon to the British conquest in 1798; and whose general accuracy is proved by a variety of facts and circumstances. Colonel Sykes, an indefatigable scholar, who maintains to this day the superiority of the Páli language, and its history, over the Sanskrit and the Brahman prophetical annals, says in speaking of the last named work:

"The Mahavansa, in its details, manifests the same love of the marvellous, the same credulity and superstition, the same exaggeration in description, and the same adulation of kings and princes, which is met with in the annals and religious history of heathen and Christian nations called civilized, of ancient and modern Europe. With these drawbacks, common, however, to the annals and religious history of all nations, the Chronology of the Mahavansa, from the birth of Buddha before Christ 623, does not admit of a question with respect to its general accuracy; and neither Brahmanism nor the Sanskrit language can shew any work of an unquestionable date, approaching to within many centuries of it [B.C. 623], nor a work with the shadow of a claim to its honesty of intention, and its accuracy of chronological records; and Mr. Turnour seems justified in stating that...........'from the date of the introduction of Buddhism into Ceylon, B.C. 307., that history [Mahavansa] is authenticated by the concurrence of every evidence which can contribute to verify the annals of any country.'—Introduction, p. li."*

Such are the merits of the best and most authentic historical work in the whole of Asia. It is written in Páli verse, and contains 100 chapters, of which the early portion, comprising the history of Ceylon from B.C. 543. to A.D. 301, was composed by a learned priest named Mahanáma. It was compiled from Páli and Siṇhalese annals then extant, and was composed at Anurádhapura, under the auspices of his nephew Dasan Keliya, between A D. 459 and 477. It is still doubtful whether Mahanáma was not also the author of the subsequent portion, to his own times.† Yet, when it is considered that he himself was the author of the Commentary which extends to A.D. 301, and that the subsequent portion of the work goes by the name of Sulu Wansa, it may be concluded, without much doubt, that he wrote the whole history to the date last given.

"From the period (says Turnour) at which Mahanáma's work terminated, to the reign of Parakrama

---

* Journal of the Royal Asiatic Society, vol. vi., pp. 339, &c.

† Introduction to Mahavansa, p. ii.

Bahu, in A.D. 1266, the Sulu Wansa was composed, under the patronage of the last named sovereign, by Dharma Kirti, at Dambedeniya. I have not been able to ascertain by whom the portion of the history from A.D. 1267 to the reign of Parakrama Bahu of Kurunégala was written, but from that reign to A.D. 1758, the Maha or rather Sulu, Wansa was compiled by Tibbottuváwa, by the command of Kírtissrí, partly, from the works brought to this island during his reign by the Siamese priests, (which had been procured by their predecessors during their former religious missions to Ceylon), and partly from the native histories, which had escaped the general destruction of literary records, in the reign of Rája Siṃha I."*

The entire Mahavansa, together with some other historical works, was translated and published by Mr. Upham, in 1833;† but this work is not to be trusted as a translation. Noticing its character at length the Hon. George Turnour, who subsequently (1837) published the first thirty-seven Chapters with an English translation, says;—

"This translation, which abounds in errors of the description above noticed, is stated to have been made 'under the superintendence of the late native chief of the Cinnamon department, (Rájapaxa, Maha Modliar), who was himself the best Páli and Singhalese scholar in the country.' I was

---

* Turnour's Mahavansa, p. ii.

† The Sacred and Historical Books of Ceylon, in three vols. by Edward Upham, M.R.A.S., and F.S.A., London, 1833.

personally acquainted with this individual, who was universally and deservedly respected, both in his official and private character. He possessed extensive information, and equally extensive influence, among his own caste at least, if not among his countrymen generally; and as of late years, the intercourse with the Buddhistical church in the Burmese empire had been chiefly kept up by missions from the priesthood of his (the Chalia) caste in Ceylon, the late Chief Justice could not, perhaps, have applied to any individual more competent to collect the native, as well as Burmese, Páli annals; or more capable of procuring the best qualified translators of that language into Singhalese, from among the Páli scholars resident in the maritime districts of the island, than Rájapaxa was. This was, however, the full extent to which this Chief could have efficiently assisted Sir A. Johnston, in his praiseworthy undertaking; for the Maha Modliar was not himself either a Páli, or an English scholar. That is to say, he had no better acquaintance with the Páli, than a modern European would, without studying it, have of any ancient dead language, from which his own might be derived. As to his acquaintance with the English language, though he imperfectly comprehended any ordinary question which might be put to him, he certainly could not speak, much less write, in reply, the shortest connected sentence in English.* He must, therefore (unless he has practised a most unpardonable deception on Sir A. Johnston)

* "In 1822, five years after Sir A. Johnston left Ceylon, and before I had acquired a knowledge of the colloquial Singhalese, as Magistrate of Colombo, I had to examine Rájapaxa, Maha Modliar, as a witness in my Court. On that occasion, I was obliged to employ an interpreter (the present permanent Assessor,

be at once released from all responsibility, as to the correctness both of the Páli version translated into Singhalese and of the Singhalese version into English."

In marked contrast with the above is Mr. Turnour's translation. He was the Colonial Secretary of Ceylon, and, during the time he prosecuted his study of the Singhalese language, he was the Agent of Government at Kandy. Encouraged by the publication of the Bálávatára by the Rev. B. Clough, Turnour was induced to learn the Páli, and from time to time to direct the minds of the learned in Europe to its study. The great and invaluable services which he thus rendered to the cause of Asiatic History, to Chronology, and to the study of Buddhism, is acknowledged and appreciated by every one who is now engaged in the study of the Buddhist religion, and the dialect in which its scriptures are recorded. I am indeed at a loss which to admire most—whether the disinterested zeal that animated Mr. Turnour, or the perseverance with which amidst his arduous and responsible duties, he pursued the object of his researches. "When I come to analyze the Páli books of Ceylon," says M. Burnouf,* "it will be seen what discoveries and labours we owe to the zeal of Mr. Turnour; and we shall have to admit

---

Mr. Dias, Modliar) not only to convey his Singhalese answers in English to me, but to interpret my English questions in Singhalese to him, as he was totally incapable of following me in English. With Europeans he generally conversed in the local Portuguese."

* History of Buddhism, p. iv.

that if he has given to Europe fewer original manuscripts, he has furnished us with a larger number of accurate translations." Of these valuable observations and translations, in his lengthy Introduction descriptive of the Mahawansa, I shall now proceed to make copious extracts:

"The writer opens his work with the usual invocation to Buddho, to the explanation of which he devotes no less than twenty-five pages of the Tika. Without stopping to examine these comments, I proceed to his notes on the word 'Mahawanso.'

"Mahawanso is the abbreviation of Mahantánanwanso, the genealogy of the great. It signifies both pedigree, and inheritance from generation to generation; being itself of high import, either on that account, or because it also bears the two above significations; hence 'Mahawanso.'

"What that Mahawanso contains (I proceed to explain):—Be it known, that of these (*i. e.*, of the aforesaid great) it illustrates the genealogy, as well as of the Buddhos, and of their eminently pious disciples, as of the great monarchs, commencing with Mahasammato. It is also of great import, inasmuch as it narrates the visits of Buddho (to Ceylon). Hence the work is ('Maha') great. It contains, likewise, all that was known to, or has been recorded by, the pious men of old, connected with the supreme and well defined history of those unrivalled dynasties ('wanso'). Let (my hearers) listen (to this Mahawanso).

"Be it understood, that even in the (old) Atthakathá, the words 'Dipatthutiya sadhusakkatan' are held as of deep import. They have there (in that work) exclusive reference to the visits of Buddho, and matters connected therewith.

On this subject the antient historians have thus expressed themselves:—'I will perspicuously set forth the visits of Buddha to Ceylon; the arrival of the relic and of the bo-tree; the histories of the convocations, and of the schisms of the theros; the introduction of the religion of (Buddha) into the Island; and the settlement and pedigree of the sovereign (Wijayo).' It will be evident, from the substance of the quotations here made, that the numerical extent of the dynasties (in my work) is exclusively derived from that source: (it is no invention of mine.)

"Thus the title 'Maháwanso' is adopted in imitation of the history composed by the fraternity of the Maháwiharo (at Anurádhapura.) In this work the object aimed at is, setting aside the Singhalese language in which (the former history) is composed, that I should sing in the Mágadhi. Whatever the matters may be, which were contained in the Atthakathá, without suppressing any part thereof, rejecting the dialect only, I compose my work in the supreme Mágadhi language, which is thoroughly purified from all imperfections. I will brilliantly illustrate, then, the Maháwanso, replete with information on every subject, and comprehending the amplest detail of all important events; like unto a splendid and dazzling garland, strung with every variety of flowers, rich in color, taste, and scent.

"The former historians, also, used an analogous simile. They said, 'I will celebrate the dynasties ('wanso') perpetuated from generation to generation; illustrious from the commencement, and lauded by many bards: like unto a garland strung with every variety of flowers: do ye all listen with intense interest.'

"After some further commentaries on other words of the first verse, Mahanámo thus explains his motives for undertaking the compilation of his history, before he touches on the second.

" 'Thus I, the author of the Maháwanso, by having rendered to religion the reverence due thereto, in my first verse, have procured for myself immunity from misfortune. In case it should be asked in this particular place, 'why, while there are Maháwansos composed by ancient authors in the Singhalese language, this author has written this Palapadoru-wanso?' in refutation of such an unmeaning objection, I thus explain the advantage of composing the Palapadoru-wansa, viz., that in the Maháwanso composed by the ancients, there is the defect, as well of prolixity as of brevity. There are also other inaccuracies deserving of notice. Avoiding these defects, and for the purpose of explaining the principle on which the Palapadoru-wanso I am desirous of compiling, is composed, I proceed to the second verse."

The following extracts are also made to elucidate certain particulars connected with the history of Mahanáma. Mr. Turnour says:—

"In opening the second chapter, Mahanámo supplies detailed data touching several of Gótamo's incarnations, prior to his manifestation in the person of Mahásammato, the first monarch of this creation. I shall confine myself to a translation of the portion of the commentary which treats of that particular incarnation. It will serve to assimilate his production or manifestation, by 'opapátika' or apparitional birth, with the Hindu scheme of the origination of the solar race.

" 'At the close of that existence (in the Brahma world) he was regenerated a man, at the commencement of this creation, by the process of 'opapátika.' From the circumstance of mankind being then afflicted with unendurable miseries, resulting from the uncontrolled state of the sinful passions which had been engendered, as well as from the consternation created by the murder, violence, and rapine produced by a condition of anarchy, a desire manifested itself among men to live subject to the control of a ruler. Having met and consulted together, they thus petitioned unto him (the Buddho elect), 'O great man! from henceforth it belongs to thee to provide for our protection and common weal.' The whole human race having assembled and come to this decision, the appellation was conferred on him of 'Mahásammato,' 'the great elect.'

"Valuable as the comments are on the genealogy of the Asiatic monarchs—the descendants and successors of Mahásammato,—they are still only abridged and insulated notes deduced (as already noticed) from the Piṭakaṭṭáya and the Atthakathá; to which justice would not be done in this limited sketch of the buddhistical annals. As a proof, however of Mahanámo's general rigid adherence to the data from which his history is compiled, I may here advert to one of the instances of the care with which he marks every departure, however trivial, from the authorities by which he is otherwise guided. He says, in reference to the twenty-eight kings mentioned in the 6th verse: 'In the Atthakathá composed by the Uttarawiháro priests, omitting Chétiyo, the son of Upacharako, and representing Muchalo to be the son of Upacharako, it is stated that there were only twenty-seven rájas, whose existence extended to an asankya of years.'

"The account of the first convocation on religion, after Gótamo's death, is so clearly and beautifully given in the third chapter, that no explanatory comments are requisite from me. For detailed particulars regarding the construction of the convocation hall at Rájagaha, and the proceedings held therein, the Tíká refers to the Samantapásada Atthakathá on the Díghánikáyo, and the Sumangala wilásini Atthakathá.

"The fourth and fifth chapters are the most valuable in the Maháwanso, with reference to the chronology of Indian history. It will be observed that in some respects, both in the names and in the order of succession, this line of the Mágadha kings varies from the Hindu genealogies.

"The rest of the fifth chapter, containing the account of Asóko's conversion—the history of Moggaliputtatisso, by whom the third convocation was held, as well as of that convocation, is full of interesting matter, detailed with peculiar distinctness, on which the comments of the Tíká throw no additional light.

"At this stage of his work, being at the close of the third convocation, Mahanámo abruptly interrupts his history of India, and without assigning any reason in the sixth chapter for that interruption, resumes the history of Lanká, in continuation of the visits of Buddho, given in the first chapter, commencing with the landing of Wijayo. His object in adopting this course is sufficiently manifest to his readers, when they come to the twelfth chapter. In the Tíká, however, he thus explains himself for following this course, at the opening of the sixth chapter.

"'As soon as the third convocation was closed, Maha Mahindo, who was selected for, and sent on, that mission, by his preceptor Moggaliputto, who was bent on establishing the religion of Buddho in the different countries (of Jambudípo) came to this island, which had been sanctified, and rescued from evil influences, by the three visits paid, in aforetime, by the supreme Buddho; and which had been rendered habitable from the very day on which Bhagawá attained parinibbánan.

"'Accordingly, at the expiration of two hundred and thirty-six years from that event, and in the reign of Déwánanpiyatisso, (Mahindo) arrived. Therefore (the Maháwanso) arresting the narrative of the history (of Jambudípo) here, where it was requisite that it should be shown how the inhabitants of this island were established here; with that view, and with the intent of explaining the arrival of Wijayo, it enters (at this point), in detail, into the lineage of the said Wijayo, by commencing (the sixth chapter) with the words: 'In the land of Wangu, in the capital of Wangu, &c.'"

"The Tiká adds nothing to the information contained in the Maháwanso, as to the fabulous origin of the Síhala dynasty. There are two notes on the first verse, on the words 'Wangésu' and 'puré,' which should have informed us fully as to the geographical position of the country, and the age in which the Wangu princes lived. They are however unsatisfactorily laconic, and comprised in the following meagre sentences.

"'There were certain princes named Wangu. The country in which they dwelt becoming powerful, it was called 'Wangu,' from their appellation.

"'The word 'puré' 'formerly,' signifies anterior to Bhagawá becoming Buddho.

"All that can be safely advanced in regard to the contents of the sixth chapter is that Wijayo was descended, through the male branch, from the rájas of Wangu (Bengal proper), and, through the female line, from the royal family of Kálinga (Northern Circars); that his grandmother, the issue of the alliance above mentioned, connected herself or rather eloped with, some obscure individual named Sího (which word signifies 'a lion'); that their son Síhabáhu put his own father to death, and established himself in Lála, a subdivision of Mágadha, the capital of which was Síhapura, probably the modern Synghaya on the Gunduck river; (in the vicinity of which the remains of buddhistical edifices are still to be found); and that his son Wijayo, with his seven hundred followers, landed in Lanká, outlawed in their native land, from which they came to this Island. I shall hereafter notice the probability of the date of his landing having been antedated by a considerable term, for the purpose of supporting a pretended revelation or command of Buddho, with which the seventh chapter opens.

"The fabulous tone of the narrative in which the account of Wijayo's landing in Lanka is conveyed in the seventh chapter, bears, even in its details, so close a resemblance to the landing of Ulysses at the island of Circé, that it would have been difficult to defend Mahanámo from the imputation of plagiarism, had he lived in a country in which the works of Homer could, by possibility, be accessible to him. The seizure and imprisonment of Ulysses' men and his own rencontre with Circé, are almost identical with the fate of Wijayo and his men, on their landing in Lanká, within the dominions of Kuwení.

"The narrative is too full and distinct in all requisite details, in the ensuing three chapters, to make any further remarks necessary from me.

"The twelfth chapter contains the account of the dispersion of the buddhist missionaries, at the close of the third convocation, in B.C. 307, to foreign countries, for the purpose of propagating their faith. I had intended in this place to enter into a comparison of the data contained in Professor Wilson's sketch of the Rája Taringiní, with the details furnished in this chapter of the Maháwanso, connected with the introduction of buddhism in Caṣhmir. The great length, however, of the preceding extracts from the Tíká, which has already swelled this introduction beyond the dimensions originally designed, deters me from undertaking the task in the present sketch. I shall, therefore, now only refer to the accordance between the two authorities (though of conflicting faiths) as to the facts of that conversion having taken place in the reign of Asóko; of the previous prevalence of the nága worship; and of the visitation by tempests, which each sect attributed to the impiety of the opposite party; as evidences of both authorities concurring to prove the historical event here recorded, that this mission did take place during the reign of that supreme ruler of India.

"In entering upon the thirteenth chapter, a note is given in the Tíká, which I extract in this place, as containing further particulars of the personal history of Asóko; and I would take this opportunity of correcting a mistranslation, by altering the passage 'she gave birth to the noble (twin) sons Ujjénio and Mahindo,' into 'she gave birth to the noble Ujjénian prince Mahindo.' The other children born to Asóko at Ujjéni, alluded to in a former note, were probably the offspring of different mothers.

"'Prior to this period, prince Bindusáro, the son of Chadagutto of the Móriyan dynasty, on the demise of his father, had succeeded to the monarchy, at Pátiliputta. He had two sons who were brothers. Of them (the sons) there were, also, ninety other brothers, the issue of different mothers. This monarch conferred on Asóko, who was the eldest* of all of them, the dignity of sub-king, and the government of Awanti. Subsequently, on a certain occasion, when he came

* "This is at variance with a preceding note, which made Sumano the eldest of all Bindusáro's sons."

to pay his respects to him (the monarch), addressing him, 'Sub-king, my child! repairing to thy government, reside at Ujjéni,' ordered him thither. He, who was on his way to Ujjéni, pursuant to his father's command, rested in his journey at the city of Chétiyagiri, at the house of one Déwo, a seṭṭho. Having met there the lovely and youthful daughter of the said seṭṭho, named Chétiya déwi, and becoming enamoured of her; soliciting the consent of her parents, and obtaining her from them, he lived with her. By that connection she became pregnant; and being conveyed from thence to Ujjéni, she gave birth to the prince Mahindo. At the termination of two years from that date, giving birth to her daughter Sanghamittá, she continued to dwell there. Bindusáro, the father of the sub-king, on his death bed, calling his son Asóko to his recollection, sent messengers to require his attendance. They accordingly repaired to Ujjéni, and delivered their message to Asóko. Pursuant to those instructions, he hastened to his father by rapid stages, leaving his son and daughter, in his way, at Chétiyagiri; and hurrying to his father at Pátaliputta, performed the funeral obsequies of his parent, who died immediately on his arrival. Then, putting to death the ninety-nine brothers of different mothers, and extirpating all disaffected persons, and raising the chhatta, he there solemnized his inauguration. The mother of the théro (Mahindo), sending her children to the king's court, continued to reside herself at the city of Chétiyagiri. It is from this circumstance (that the author of the Maháwanso has said), 'While prince Asóko was ruling over the Awanti country.'

"The Tíká affords no new matter, as far as regards the interesting narrative contained in the fifteenth, sixteenth, seventeenth, eighteenth, and nineteenth chapters. The twentieth chapter contains a chronological summary of the reign of Dhammásóko, at the opening of which the Tíká gives the following note, affording another proof of the minute attention paid by the author to prevent any misapprehension in regard to the chronology of his history.

"After describing the arrival of the bo-tree, and preparatory to entering upon the chapter on the subject of the théros obtaining 'parinibbánan,' the account of the death of the two monarchs, Dhammásóko and Dewánanpiyatisso, is set forth (in the Maháwanso in these words): 'In the eighteenth year of the reign of Dhammásóko, the bo-tree was placed in the Mahaméghawanna pleasure garden.'

"(In the Maháwanso it is stated), 'these years collectively amount to thirty-seven.' By that work it might appear that the total (term of his reign) amounted to forty-one years. That reckoning would be erroneous; the last year of each period being again counted as the first of the next period. By avoiding that double appropriation, the period becomes thirty-seven years. In the Atthakathá, avoiding this absurd (literally laughable) mistake, the period is correctly stated. It is there specified to be thirty-seven years."

The untranslated portion of the Mahawansa contains sixty-two chapters; (vide an Analysis of the same in Turnour's Mahawansa, p. xci.) There is not the same facility for translating this portion which Mr. Turnour had for the rendering of the first thirty-eight chapters into English; for, not only is there not a gloss or tíká to the untranslated part, but the work itself is found in almost inextricable confusion; and the only hope of securing a correct copy of the text is by careful intercomparison with old MSS. in different parts of the island, and with copies, if procurable, from Siam and Amarapura.

Having given all the information worthy of notice regarding this ancient History, we may state that Turnour has translated and published the first thirty-eight chapters, and also the fifty-ninth. It was publicly stated that he had also translated ten other chapters, but these have never been published. Mr. L. De Zoysa, Mudaliyar, has also published a translation of the lxviiith and lxixth chapters in the C. B. Royal Asiatic Society's Journal for 1856—58.

Not only as a specimen of the third part of the Mahawansa by Tibbottuváwa, but as furnishing evidence of the wanton destruction of the ancient literary records of this country, which, according to another historian, "were burnt in heaps as high as cocoa-nut trees," we here present, with a translation,

Cap. XCIII.

Atha tassachchaye tasmin samudd'ásanna raṭṭhake
Jayawaddhana koṭṭh'ádi pasiddha nagaresuhi
Tahin tahin vasantesu Suriya vansaja rájusu
Máyá dhanavho ráj'eko ási tejo janádhipo
Tass'atrajo balo ási Rájasího 'ti námako
Gantvá tahin tahin yuddhan katvána aggahí jayan
Jayaggahó mahábálo attano pitaran 'picha
Ghá tetvá saka hatthá so rajja'maggahi dummati
Sítávaka nagarasmin Rájasího 'ti vissuto
Pasanno sásane kinchi kálamhi kusalan karan
Dánan datv'ekadá rájá mahá there apuchchhi so

Pitu ghátakapápá'han kathan násemi bhítiko
Tadá therá tassadhamman desetvána visáradá
A'rádhetun asakkontá duṭṭha chittan kubuddhino
Kata pápan viná setun nasakká'ti giran sute
Daṇḍappa haṭa matteua kuddho ghora viso viya
Sivabhattike'pi puchchhitvá sakká'ti kathitan giran
Amatan viya sutvána káyan limpetva chhárikan
Sivabhattin gahetvána násentó jinasásanan
Bhikkhu Sanghancha ghátento jhápento dhammapotthake
Bhindápetvána áráme saggamaggam'pi chhádayí
Sansárakhánubhúto'va michchhádiṭṭhin aganhi so
Sumana kúṭambi uppannan sabban lábhan hi ganhitun
Niyojesi tahin pápa michchhádiṭṭhika tápase
Evan adhammiko bálo gahe tabban ajániya
Agahe tabbakan gayha mahá dukkhan agaṇhi so
Tadá rájabhayen'eva uppabbajjinsu bhikkhavo
Sansára bhíruká tesu gatá ásun tahin tahin
Sabba loka hitan buddha sásanan hi sunimmalan
Dhansetvá'kási rajjan so pubba puñña baleni'dha
A'ṇá balena yuttova sabba lankátalan hi so
Katvána attano hatthe rajjan akási pápiko
Evan rájabalen'upeta mahipo dassetva áṇá balan
Katvá so sakalan apuññanichayan márassa hatthan gato
Itthan pápa kudiṭṭhi moha vasago ádínavan jániya
Bhítá sabba pamáda bhávarahitá sádhentu atthan bahun.

Iti sujanappasáda sanvegatthâya kato Mahá-vanse Máyá Dhanavha rája dípako náma te-navutimo parichchhedo.

"Thereupon after his demise there, when several Princes of the Súrya race were resident in different localities in Jayawaddhana Kóṭṭha, and other celebrated cities adjacent to the sea, there was a mighty and supreme king named Máyádhanu. He had a valiant son named Rája Siŋha, who, having gone to different places, waged war, and achieved victory. This victorious, but very unwise and wicked person, having (next) killed his father with his own hand, ascended the throne; proclaimed himself Rája Siŋha of Sitávaka; and, for a short time, did meritorious acts in devotion to (Buddhism) religion.

One day, this timid conscience-stricken king, after feeding the Mahá theras, inquired of them: 'How shall I get over the sin of Patricide?' Thereupon, though these talented priests preached the dhamma to him, they were nevertheless unable to satisfy the wicked mind of this foolish (prince); and when he heard the reply that it was impossible to get rid of the sin which he had committed, he was provoked like a venomous (serpent) that had been struck with a stick.

Making the (same) inquiry of Saivites, but hearing their reply, that 'it was possible,' he was (filled with joy) as with ambrosia. Daubing his body with ashes, and (thus) embracing the faith of Sivá, he destroyed the religion of Buddha, murdered Bhikkhus, and Sangha, burnt the sacred works of Buddha, pulled down monastic establishments, raised a barrier to heaven, and, as if he had raised a (lasting pillar) monument to Sansára [never ceasing circle of existence], became a heretic.

He placed sinful heretical (Tápasa) Fakirs at the Sumana Mount [Adam's Peak], and directed them to take all the revenues derivable at that (establishment.) Thus this unjust and foolish personage, not knowing what was fit to be taken, and taking what was improper to take, entered into (paths) of great distress.

At this period (some of) the bhikkhus, from a dread of the king, left the priesthood; and others, from fear of Sansára, resorted to different countries.

This sinful king (however), having destroyed the unblemished religion of Buddha, which was profitable to the whole world, continued to reign by reason of his previously acquired merit, and by means of his great powers, secured the rule of the whole of Lanka into his hands.* Having thus exhibited his powers, and having also amassed a large amount of sin, he entered the hands of death.

May the (righteous), thus knowing the danger of sin, ignorance, and false religion; and, with dread, forsaking all conditions of procrastination, accomplish great felicity.

Here (ends) the ninety-third chapter of the Mahawansa, entitled 'the Dynasty called Máyádhanu,' composed equally for the delight and affliction of righteous men."

Having already noticed the Tíká to the Mahawansa, it only remains to give a specimen of the work; and we subjoin the following passage with a translation, referring to the text at p. 229.

---

* I have here omitted certain repetitions.

Thúpassa muddhani tathá 'nagghan vajira chumbaṭan-ti; tatheva mahá thúpassa muddhani satasahassagghanikan mahá maṇincha patiṭṭhápetwá tassaheṭṭhá asani upaddava viddhansa natthan ádhára valaya miva katvá anagghan vajira chumbaṭan* cha pújesí'ti† attho. That is; "Thúpassa muddhani tathá'nagghan vajira chumbaṭan" means, "having in like manner placed a large gem, of a lac in value, on the top of the great thúpa, he fixed (literally, offered) below it (*i. e.* below the gem), for the purpose of destroying the dangers of lightning, an invaluable diamond chumbaṭa, (having made it) like a supporting ring, (or annular rest.)"

DI'PAWANSA.

Though the Mahawansa is at present "the most authentic" history of Ceylon, it is by no means the only existing historical record, nor the most ancient.

---

* The word chumbaṭa is compounded of chumba 'to kiss,' and aṭa 'to go.' This is sometimes used with, and sometimes without, an affix. If with an affix, (when a euphonic change is intended) it takes navu, which is changed into aka. See Bálavatára, p. 113. Thence, the word itself is written chumbaṭaka. See also Páli Nighandu.

† A respectful term; and means 'placed,' or 'fixed as an offering' in a religious point of view. This is a very common expression. See Bengal Asiatic Society's Journal, vi. note at p. 755. In vol. vii. of the same work, at p. 259, Mr. Prinsep defines this term "propitiated by pújá."

One of the Páli Records to which Mahanamo was indebted for information, and from which he has extracted two verses without alteration, is the Dípawansa.

Mr. Turnour's conjecture, that this work* is the Mahawansa of the Uttara Vihára priests, is entitled to much weight. He says:—

"The author of the Maháwanso,† in his Tíká, declares more than once that he compiles his work from the Síhala Maháwanso and Aṭṭhakaṭhá of the Maháwiháro, and from the Síhala Aṭṭhakaṭhá of the Uttarawiháro fraternities, as well as from the Maháwanso of the Uttarawiháro priests. The last mentioned of these works alone, as far as I am able to form an opinion at present, was composed in the Páli language, at the time Mahánámo compiled his Maháwanso. I am induced to entertain this opinion from the circumstance, that Mahánámo's quotations from that work alone are in the metrical form, whereas all the translated quotations made by Páli authors from Síhala authorities are invariably, as might have been expected, rendered in prose. One of these quotations consists of the identical two verses with which the Dípawanso opens, and at the close of the Tíká a reference is made to the Dípawanso for explanation of the violation of the Maháwiháro consecration, in the reign of Mahaseno. For these reasons, and as that work bears also the title of the "Maháwanso" or "the great genealogy," my Buddhist coadjutors concur with me in thinking, that the Dípawanso now extant

* My copy is written in 328 pages, with 16 lines to the page.

† Pages xxxi., xxxii., xlii. and xliii. of the Introduction to the Maháwanso.

is the Páli Mahávanso of the Uttarawiháro fraternity. In fact the titles of Dípa and Mahá, are indiscriminately given to both these histories."

From the evidence which its contents furnishes, there can be no reasonable doubt that the Dípawansa was compiled from time to time by several official historiographers, appointed by the State, as we learn from tradition, as well as from the early Arabian travellers in Ceylon.*

I have procured several copies of this work, but they are all in great confusion. Some of the Banawáras, into which it is divided, are deficient in the necessary number of stanzas. The whole work is confused in its arrangement; the same stanza being repeated in several chapters, and sometimes several times in one and the same chapter. Some of the verses are also deficient, and perhaps owing to bad copyists, very defective in language. Such appears to have been the case, as remarked by Mr. Turnour in his essay on the Indian Inscriptions,† even in the copy which he obtained from Burma through the intervention of Nadoris De Silva, Mudaliyar.

This leads me to believe that these defects of repetition, etc., are attributable chiefly to the compilers themselves. I am the more confirmed in this belief, not only by the repetitions with which all ancient books, especially the Tepiṭaka, abound; but also by the

---

* Sir E. Tennent's History of Ceylon, i. p. 387, note.

† See Bengal Asiatic Society's Journal.

testimony contained in later writings as to their general character. Mahánáma in speaking of such works (of which the Dípawansa was doubtless one) says, "that in the Mahawansa composed by the ancients there are defects both of prolixity and brevity. There are also other inaccuracies deserving of notice." And Buddhagosa in referring to the writers he was indebted to for his Gloss, says, "I translate the Atthakathá .... into the Páli .... omitting only the frequent repetition of the same explanation."

The Dípawansa, as remarked by Turnour, from its being quoted by the Maháwansa, is unquestionably a prior work, but as its narrative extends to the reign of Mahasena in A.D. 302, its priority cannot exceed 150 years.

The most remarkable feature in this history, is the great effort which is made by its authors to complete the links of the Theraparampará chain, or the genealogy of the priesthood, and make them consistent with chronology. This is, obviously, for the purpose of shewing that the sacred teachings of Gotama had been preserved in the memory of these successive priests until they were recorded in the reign of Waṭṭagámini, as stated by the Dípawansa in the verses given below, and which are also found quoted by the author of the Maháwansa.

Piṭakaṭṭáya Pálincha tassá Aṭṭhakathancha tan
Mukhapátena ánesun pubbe bhikkhu mahámatí
Hánin disvána sattánan tadá bhikkú samágatá
Chiraṭṭhitthan dhammassa potthakesu likhápayun.

"The profoundly wise (inspired) priests had theretofore orally perpetuated the Páli Pitakattáya and its Atthakathá (commentaries). At this period, these priests foreseeing the perdition of the people (from the perversions of the true doctrines), assembled; and, in order that the religion might endure for ages, recorded the same in books."

But, from internal evidence alone, Mr. Turnour was enabled to point out to his coadjutors, that "this elaborate adjustment of the succession of preceptors" was erroneous. Mr. Turnour says:

"The author of the Dípawanso has certainly spared no pains in his endeavours to make the links of the Théraparampará chain complete, and consistent with chronology. He, however, only gives the succession of preceptors, who were the guardians of the Winéyo section of the Piṭakattayan, commencing with Upáli, whose death is placed in the sixth year of the reign of Udayo; while the incongruities I have dwelt upon in the paper No. 2, have reference to Sabhakámi, who though a cotemporary disciple of Buddho, has been represented to have presided at the second convocation, a century after Sákya's death; when he must, from the date of his upasampadá ordination, have been at last 140 years old. But even this succession of the Wínéyan line of preceptors, the chronological particulars of which are pretended to be given with so much precision in the following extracts, will not stand the test of scrutiny by a person conversant with the rules that govern the Buddhistical church. It is an inviolable law of that code, established by Buddho himself at an early period of his mission, and adhered to to this day—to which rule there are only two well-known exceptions—that no person, whether a noviciate priest called Sámanéro, or an ascetic layman, however learned or pious he may be, can be ordained an upasampadá before he has completed his twentieth year. The two exceptions alluded to are the instances of Sumano and Sopáko, who were ordained upasampadá at seven years of age.

"It will be seen that this line of preceptors, extending from the date of Buddho's death to the third convocation, a term of 236 years, is made to consist of five successions. Upáli the cotemporary of Buddho, is stated to have been 60 years old in the eighth year of the reign of Ajátasattu, which is the 16th year A. B. He is represented to have survived Buddho thirty years, and to have died in the 6th of Udayo's reign in A. B. 30. It is not, however, mentioned how many years he had been an upasampadá, and all these dates work out therefore without disclosing any discrepancy.

"Dásako is represented to be his pupil and immediate successor, and he is stated to be 45 years old in the 10th of Nagasoko's reign, which falls to A. B. 58. He was born, therefore, A. B. 13, and his preceptor Upáli died A. B. 30, Supposing his ordination had been put off to the last year of Upáli's life, he could not have been more than 17, when made an upasampadá. So far from being qualified to be the custos of the Winéyo, he wanted three years of the age to make him admissible for ordination. But we are further told, that he died at the age of 64 in the eighth of Susunágo's reign, which falls to A. B. 80: having then been an upasampadá 50 years, he must necessarily have been ordained at 14 years of age. But there is manifestly some trifling error somewhere; for, by the latter dates he must have been born not A. B. 13, but A. B. 16.

"Sónako was Dásako's successor; he was 40 in the 10th year of Kálásóko's reign, which was A. B. 100; he was born therefore in 60, and he is stated to have died at the age of 66 in the sixth of the reign of the Nandos, which falls to A. B. 124. He was therefore only 20 years old when his preceptor died: but it is specifically stated that he had been a learned upasampadá 44 years when he died; and consequently Sónako also could only have been 16 years when ordained.

"Siggawo and Chandawo or Chandawajji were the co-disciples and successors of Sónako. Siggawo was 64 years old in the second of Chandagutto's* reign A. B. 164, and he died aged 76 in the 14th of that reign A. B. 176. He was born therefore A. B. 100, and yet we are told, that it was in this very year, the 10th of the reign of Kálásóko, they were ordained upasampadá, by Sónako. There is a manifest error, therefore, in the term of five years assigned for Siggawo's upasampadáship. As his ordaining preceptor Sónako died A. B. 124, he must have been at that time only 24 years old, and at his own death an upasampadá of 76 years' standing,—a term co-equal with his natural life. In various parts of the Aṭṭhakatha, and in the fifth chapter of the Mahâwanso likewise it is stated that they were "adult priests" at the time the second convocation was held; and indeed it is specifically stated in page 30, that Siggawo was 18 years old when he was first presented to Sónako. The pretended prophecy, delivered to him and Chandawajji at the close of

* "I assign in these remarks 24 years to the reign of Chandagutto, which will bring Asoko's accession to A. B. 214, and his inauguration, four years afterwards, to A. B. 218."

that convocation, would consequently be nullified at once, if their birth be not dated anterior to A. B. 100: manifestly, therefore, these dates also are an imposition.

"Lastly, Moggaliputtatisso was their disciple; he was ordained in the second of Chandagutto A. B. 164, and he was 66 in the sixth of Dhammasóko A. B. 220; he was born, therefore, in A. B. 154, and could only have been 14 years old at the death of Siggawo, when he became the chief of the Winéyo preceptors. He is stated to have died in the 26th of Dhammasóko, A. B. 240, aged 80. This gives A. B. 160 instead of A. B. 154 for his birth, being a discrepancy of six years.

"On pointing out to my Pandits, that, even in this elaborate adjustment of the succession of preceptors, the number of lives given is found to be insufficient to fill up a term of 236 years, without bringing the several preceptors into office before they had attained the prescribed age, they at once decided, that the author of the Dípawanso has put forth an erroneous statement, and that the whole ought to be rejected as unfounded. How the discrepancies are to be rectified they do not suggest, beyond hazarding a conjecture, that each preceptor, like Sabhakámi, must have lived to a more advanced age; and that each succeeding preceptor consequently had attained a maturer standing at the period of his succession."

Mr. Turnour has published, in an analysis, some of the most interesting portions of this work, in the columns of the Bengal Asiatic Society's Journal. In reprinting the same here, I have added to it translations of other portions by myself. Where the matter was such as I thought not very interesting, I have given a summary of its contents.

Bha'nava'ra First.

Contents.—The usual adoration—introductory remarks—Gotama's attainment of Buddha-hood—his first work as Buddha—his perception of Lanká, and its affairs—his fore-knowledge of Asoka and Mahinda—his departure to Báránasí after seven weeks—the reception which he gave to "the five priests"—his visit to Uruvelá—how he overcame a Nága at Uruvelá, and was invited to spend the Hemanta (dewy) season there—his knowledge of the thoughts of Kassapa—his departure to Uttarakuru, and his perception of the Yakkhas in Lanká—his first visit to Lanká—the great wonders which he there exhibited—how he obtained permission to occupy a place, and how he terrified the Yakkhas—their removal to Giri-dípa—description of Giri-dípa—how the Yakkhas were expelled into it—Buddha's departure to Uruvelá after extending his protection to Lanká.

Bha'nava'ra Second.

Gotama's perception, whilst at Sávatti, of a contest between Nágas—description of their battle—the cause which led to Gotama's second visit to Lanká—his departure thereto—how he produced a darkness—how he reduced the Nágas to terror—his preaching to them from the sky—their conversion, and offering of a gem-set seat to Buddha—how he sat upon it, and the attentions which he received from the Nágas—the request to him by Maṇi-akkhika Nága to visit Lanká—his acceptance of the invitation, and departure from Jetavana monastery. Buddha's third visit to Lanká and Kalyáṇi—the offerings to him by Maṇi Akkhika—his dhyána meditations at Mahá Megha park—the acceptance of the said park by former Buddhas.

The following is Turnour's* translation of

BHA'NAVA'RA THIRD.

"Omitting the rájas who existed in former kappá, I will in the fullest manner narrate (the history of) the rájas of the present creation. I shall perspicuously set forth the regions in which they existed, their name and lineage, the term of their existence, and the manner in which they governed: whatever that narrative may be, attend ye thereto.

"The first individual who was inaugurated a rája, the protector of the land, was named Mahásammato; he was superlatively endowed with personal beauty; that Khattiyo exercised the functions of sovereignty.

"Rójo was his son, Wararójo, the monarch Kalyáno; Warakalyáno, Upósathó, Mandáto† the seventh in succession,

* He designates this the third Bhánaváro; see Bengal Asiatic Society's Journal, vii. p. 924. Mr. Turnour remarks, "a bhánaváro ought to contain 250 gáthá. This section is only equal to 87, and some of the verses are incomplete. I can however detect no want of continuity in the narrative."—The defect in this respect is only in the division of the sections.

† "In the Maháwanso, I have been misled by the plural Mandátá, and reckoned two kings of that name. I see by the tíká the name should be in the singular Mandáto. The twenty-eight rájas who lived for an Asankheyyán include therefore Mahásammato."

a supreme ruler of the four dípá,* endowed with great wealth; Charo, the rája Upacharo, and Chétiyo abounding in riches; Muchalo; Mahámuchalo, Muchalindo, Ságaro; Ságaredéwo, Bhárato, Bhágíratho the Khattiyo; Ruchí, Maháruchi, Patápo, Mahápatapo, Panado, Mahápanádo, the Khattiyo Sudassano, Mahásudassano, and in like manner two of the name of Néru; and Achchimá†, (were successively the sons of each preceding ruler.) The term of existence of these twenty-eight rájas was an Asankhéyyán; and the capitals in which these monarchs, whose existence extended to an Asankhéyyán, reigned, were Kusáwátí, Rájagahan and Mithílá."

(Here follows the rule by which an Asankhéyyán is to be computed.)

"The descendants of Achchimá were one hundred; and they ruled supreme in their capital called Sakulá.‡ The last of these was the Khattiyo Arindamo; his descendants, fifty-six monarchs in number, reigned supreme in their capital Ayujjhapurá.

---

* "Jambudípo, Uttarukuru, Aparagóyánan and Pubbawidého."

† "This name also has been erroneously omitted by me in the Maháwanso. Achchimá was there read Pachchima. The Tíká, however, shows that the Dípawanso is correct."

‡ "In the Tíká, it is further stated: The eldest son of Achchimá was the monarch Wattapárásáni, though his name be not preserved, quitting Mithelá in the same manner that the Okkáka family quitting Báránasi founded Kapilawatthu in a subsequent age, established himself at Kasáwati, raised the Chhata there, and there his dynasty flourished. His lineal successors in that empire were in number ninety-nine, the last of whom was Arindam, and they all ruled there under the designation of the Achchimá dynasty. I should infer from this passage that the capital called Sakula in the Dípawanso should be Kusáwati."

"The last of these was Duppasaho, a wealthy monarch: his descendants were sixty rulers, who reigned supreme in their capital Báránasi.

"The last of these was Ajitajano; his descendants, eighty-four thousand in number, ruled supreme in their capital Kapilanagaran.

"The last of these was Brahmadatto, greatly endowed with riches; his descendants were thirty-six rájas in number, who reigned supreme in their capital Hatthipura.

"The last of these was the rája Kambalawasabho; his descendants were thirty-two monarchs, who reigned supreme in their capital Ekachakkhu.

"The last of these was the illustrious Purindadéwo; his descendants were twenty-eight monarchs, who reigned supreme in their capital Wajirápura.

"The last of these was the rája Sódhano; his descendants were twenty monarchs, and they reigned supreme in their capital Madhurá.

"The last of these was the rája Dhammagutto, powerful in his armies; his descendants were eighteen monarchs, who reigned supreme in their capital Aritthapura.

"The last of these was the rája Narindasitthi*[1]; his descendants were seventeen kings, who reigned supreme in their capital Indapattapura.

"The last of these was Brahmedéwo[2] rája; his descendants were sixteen monarchs, who reigned in their capital Ekachakkhu.

---

* In the Tíká there are the following variations of appellation from the Dípawanso: 1. Brahmasíwo. 2. Brahmadatto. 3. Baladéwo. 4. Hatthidewo. 5. Samuddhadatto.

"The last of these was the monarch Baladatto[3]; his descendants were fourteen rulers, who reigned supreme in their capital Kósabinagaran.

"The last of these was celebrated under the title of Bhaddadéwo[4]; his descendants were nine kings, who reigned in their capital Kannakochchhanagaran.

"The last of these was the celebrated Naradewo; his descendants were seven monarchs, who reigned supreme in their capital Rájánanagaran.

"The last of these was the rája Mahindo; his descendants were twelve kings, who reigned supreme in their capital Champákanagaran.

"The last of these was the monarch Nágadéwo; his descendants were twenty-five rulers, who reigned supreme in their celebrated capital Mithíla.

"The last of these was Buddhadatto[5], a rája powerful by his armies; his descendants were twenty-five monarchs, who reigned supreme in their capital Rájagahan.

"The last of these was Dipankaro; his descendants were twelve rájas, who reigned supreme in their capital Takkasilá.

"The last of these was the rája Talisakaro; his descendants were twelve rulers, who reigned supreme in their capital Kusinára.

"The last of these was the rája Purindo; his descendants were nine kings, who reigned supreme in Támalîti.

"The last of these was the worthy monarch Ságaradéwo, whose son Makhádéwo* was pre-eminent for his deeds of

---

* The Tíká observes in reference to the Maháwanso, that according to the Aṭṭhakaṭhá, Makhádewo is reckoned among the eighty-five thousand successors of Sagaradéwo, whereas that number should be exclusive of him.

charity; his descendants were eighty-four thousand monarchs, who reigned supreme at Mithilá.

"The last of these was Némi, a monarch who received offerings from the Déwá and was a Chakkawatti (powerful sovereign), whose dominions were bounded by the ocean: the son of Némi was Kalákajanako*; his son was Samankuro: and his son was Asóko; and his descendants were eighty-four thousand rulers who reigned supreme in their capital Báránasi.

"The last of these was the rája Wijayo, a wealthy monarch: his son was Wijitasano who was endowed with great personal splendor. Dhammaséno, Nágaséno, Samatho, Disampati, Rainu, Kuso; Mahákuso, Nawaratho, Dasaratho, Rámo, Biláratho, Chittadassi, Atthadassi, Sujáto, Okkáko†, Okkákamukó, Nipuro, Chandimá, Chandamukho, Siriraja, Sanjayo, the monarch Wessantaro, Jalo, Sihawáhano and Sihassaro. These were enterprising monarchs, who upheld the pre-eminence of their dynasty; and his (Sihassaro's) descendants were eighty-two thousand, who (all) reigned supreme in their capital Kapilawatthu.

"The last of these was Jayaséno; his son was Séhahanu who was endowed with great personal splendor. Unto the said Séhahanu there were five sons. Those five brothers were Suddhódano, Dhotódano, Sukkódano, Ghatitodano and Amitodano. All these rájas were distinguished as Odano.‡

---

* Here also the Tíká notices in reference to the Maháwanso that the eighty-five thousand are to be reckoned exclusive of Samankuro and Asóko.

† Vide Maháwanso Introduction, p. xxxv., for the establishment of the Sakyan dynasty of Okkakamukho.

‡ This word literally signifies "boiled rice:" no reason is assigned for adopting the designation.

Siddattho, the saviour of the world, was the son of Suddhódano; and after the birth of his illustrious son Rahulo, finally relinquished (worldly grandeur) for the purpose of attaining Buddhohood.

"The whole of these monarchs, who were of great wealth and power, were in number one lakh, four nahutaní* and three hundred. Such is the mumber of monarchs of the dynasty from which the Bódhisatto (Buddho elect) is sprung.

"Perishable† things are most assuredly transitory, it being their predestiny that after being produced they should perish; they, accordingly, being produced, pass away. To arrest this (eternity of regeneration and destruction, by the attainment of nibbánan) is indeed to be blessed."

The conclusion of the Maha'ra'jawanso.

"The raja Suddhódano, the son of Séhahanu was a monarch who reigned in the city called Kapila; and the rája Bhatiyo was then the monarch who reigned at Rájagahan, a city situated in the centre of five‡ mountains. These two rulers of men, Suddhódano and Bhatiyo, the descendants (of royal dynasties) from the commencement of the kappó, were intimately attached to each other.

---

* In this sense a nahutan is 10,000, making therefore, 140,300 monarchs. According to the Tíká there were 252,539 rájas from Mahásammato to Okkako, the Ikswaku of the Hindus.

† This is a passage of the Pitakattayan as propounded by Sakya.

‡ The names of these mountains are Isigili, Wibharo, in which is situated the Sattampanni cave in which the first convocation was held; Wéputto; Pandawo and Gejjhakato, the mountain where Buddho dwelt last in the neighbourhood of Rajagahan.

"(By Bimbisaro the son of Bhatiyo) these five wishes were conceived in the eighth year of his age. 'Should my royal parent invest me with sovereignty: should a supreme of men (Buddho) be born in my dominions: should a Tathagatho select me for the first person to whom he presented himself: should he administer to me the heavenly dhammo; and should I comprehend that supreme dhammo—these will be blessings vouchsafed to me.' Such were the five wishes conceived by Bimbisaro.

"Accordingly, on the demise of his father, he was inaugurated in the fifteenth year of his age: within his dominions the supreme of the world was born: Tathagato repaired to him as the first person to whom he presented himself: propounded the heavenly dhammo: and the monarch comprehended it.

"Maháwéro was not less than thirty-five years old, and the monarch Bimbisaro was in the thirtieth year of his age. Gótamo therefore was five years senior to Bimbisaro. That monarch reigned fifty-two years, thirty-seven of which he passed contemporaneously with Buddho.

"Ajatasatto (his son) reigned thirty-two years: in the eighth year of his inauguration, the supreme Buddho attained nibbanan. From the time that the omniscient Buddho, the most revered of the world and the supreme of men attained Buddhohood, this monarch reigned twenty-four years."

BHA'NAVA'RA FOURTH.

Parinibbute cha sanbuddhe bhikkhu sangho samágato
Arahá* khíná savá suddhá sabbe [te ?] guṇa páragá
Te sabbe vichi nitvána uchchinitvá varan varan

---

* This is in the singular number. I apprehend it should be arahanto.

Pancha satánan theránan akansu sangha sammatan
Dhutavádánam'aggo so Kassapo jina sásane
Bahussutánam' A'nando vinaye Upáli paṇḍito
Dibba chakkhumhi Anuruddho Vangíso paṭibháṇako
Puṇṇo cha dhamma kathikánan chittakathí Kumára Kassapo
Vibhajjanamhi Kachcháno Koṭṭhito paṭisambhido
Aññe' p'atthi mahá therá agga dhamme patiṭṭhitá
Thehichaññehi therehi katakichchehi sádhuhi
Panchasatehi therehi dhamma vinaya sangaho
Therehi kata sangaho thera vádoti vuchchati
Upálin vinayan puchchhitvá dhamman A'nanda yavhayan
Akansu dhamma sangahan vinayan chápi bhikkhavo
Mahákassapa thero cha Anuruddho mahá gaṇí
Upáli thero satimá A'nando cha bahussuto
Aññe bahú abhiññátá sávaká satthu vaṇṇitá
Pattapaṭi sambhidá chhaḷa bhiññá mahiddhiká
Samádhijjhána manuchiṇṇá saddhamme páramingatá
Sabbe pancha satá therá navangan jina sásanan
Uggahetvána dháresun buddha seṭṭhassa santike
Bhagavato sammukhá sutá patiggahítá cha sammukhá
Dhammancha vinayan chápi kevalan buddha desitan
Dhammadhará vinaya dhará sabbepi ágatá'gamá
Asanhírá asankuppá satthukappá sadá garu
Aggasantike gahetvá agga dhamman tathágatá
Agganikkhittaká therá aggan akansu sangahan
Sabbopi so thera vádo agga vádo ti vuchchati
Sattapaṇṇi guhe* ramme therá pancha satá gaṇí

---

* Guhá is a feminine noun. In the locative it should be guháyan, as Buddhagosa has correctly rendered it in the Atthakathá—"sattapanne guháyan." It is here treated as a masculine or neuter noun, for which I find no authority.

Nisinná paṭigajjinsu navangan satthu sásanan
Suttan Geyyan Veyyákaranan Gathudánitivuttakan
Játak 'Abbhuta Vedallan navanga satthu sásanan
Pavibhattá iman therá saddhamman avinásanan
Vagga paññásakan náma sanyuttancha nipátakan
A'gama piṭakan náma akansu sutta sammatan
Yáva tiṭṭhati saddhammo sangahonavinassati
Távatá sásanaddhánan chiran tiṭṭhati satthuno
Katancha dhamma Vinaya Sangahan sasaná rahan
Asankampi achalan daḷhan appaṭi vattiyan
Yo kochi samaṇo vápi bráhmano cha bahussuto
Parappa váda kusalo válavedhi samágato
Nasakká paṭi vattetun sineruva suppatiṭṭhito
Devo máro cha brahmá vá ye kechi paṭhavi nissitá
Napassanti anuppattan kinchi dubbhásitan padan
Evan sabbaṅga sampannan dhamma Vinaya sangahan
Suvibhattan supaṭichchhannan satthu sabbaññutáya cha
Mahá Kassapa pámokkhá therá pancha sátá cha te
Katá dhamman cha vinayan sangahan avinásanan
Sammá sambuddha sadisan dhammakáyan sabhávato
Ñatvá janassa sandehan akansu dhamma sangahan*
Anuññá vádo sáratto saddhammá anurakkhato
Ṭhitiyá sásanaddhánan thera vádo sahetuko
Yávatá ariyá atthi sásane buddha sávaká
Sabbe pi samanuññanti paṭhaman dhamma sangahan
Múla nidánan paṭhaman ádi pubbangaman dhurá
Pancha sata katá aggá ajániyá aná kulan... ti
Mahá Kassapa sangahan niṭṭhitan.

---

* There are many doubtful expressions in this extract; but I have not thought proper to revise the text.

'When Buddha had attained nibbáṇa, the assembled priesthood, who were all pure Arahantas of eminent virtues and whose clinging to existence was extinct, having consulted together, and selected pre-eminent théras, held a Council of five hundred.

Kasappa, who was the chief, amongst the Dhutavádas* in the Buddhist faith; A'nanda, amongst those who had much heard (the original discourses); Upáli, amongst those who were versed in the Vinaya; Anuruddha, amongst those gifted with divine perception; Vangísa, amongst those who were of prompt speech; Puṇṇa, amongst the preachers; Kumárakassapa, amongst those who could (adorn) expatiate on a subject; Kachchána, amongst those who were able to consider a matter in all its bearings; Koṭṭhita, amongst those versed in the Paṭisambhida;† and others of pre-eminent virtues; as well as various other pious, sanctified theras, (in all) five hundred, made a collection‡ of the doctrines of the Dhamma and Vinaya. The compilation so made by them is called Thera Váda,§ 'the discourses of the Theras.'

* Observers of thirteen religious ordinances. See Telesdhutánga, in Clough's Siṇhalese Dictionary, p. 242.

† Four eminent qualifications, peculiar to the highest order of Arahantas; a knowledge of ethics; of dhamma or religious doctrines; of the philological comments and expositions thereon; and a supernatural discrimination.

‡ Sangaha, 'collection,' 'compilation.'

§ This is an important and remarkable admission, and it is consistent with the facts which every section of the Piṭakattáya discloses.

The Bhikkhús made the collection of the Dhamma* and the Vinaya, having first consulted (him who was called) A'nanda on the former, and Upáli on the latter.

The Theras, Mahákassapa; Anuruddha of immense retinue; Upáli of retentive memory; A'nanda of profound learning,† and many other celebrated disciples‡ —in all 500 principal theras, endowed with the six perceptions,§ and mighty powers; who had been complimented by Buddha (himself); who were versed in the Paṭisambhidá; who practised Samádhi‖ and Jhána;¶ who were perfect masters of the doctrines, and the sustainers of them; and who had, moreover, learnt the nine-branched** religion in the very presence of the supreme Buddha; heard and received the entire body of Buddha's Sermons (comprising) the Vinaya and Dhamma (in the presence of) from Buddha himself.

---

* Dhamma, here comprehends the doctrines of the Sutta and Abhidhamma piṭakas, as opposed to the Vinaya, which is on Discipline.

† Bahussutá, 'much heard.'

‡ Sávaka, 'hearer,' thence 'a disciple.'

§ Chhaḷabhiññá—1, The power to assume any shape. 2, Supernatural hearing of any sound, however low. 3, The power of knowing the thoughts of others. 4, The knowledge of previous states of existence. 5, The power of vision at any distance; and 6, The subjugation of all desires.

‖ 'Deep and devout meditation.'

¶ Jhána, 'meditation and reflection, so as to bring their object fully and undisturbedly before the mind.'

** Lit. 'nine-bodied'—vide the text.

All these pre-eminent, ever venerable theras of undeviating orthodoxy, and unchangeable (principles), like Buddha himself, who were the sustainers of the Dhamma and Vinaya, who were well versed in the doctrines, and who learnt the supreme dhamma in the presence of their chief, made the first Compilation. All the discourses of the Theras are (thence) called the chief discourses.

The Council of five hundred Theras sat in the delightful cave Sattapaṇṇi, and chaunted the nine-bodied discourses of Buddha, which, with a view to their perpetuation,* they apportioned into Sutta, Geyya, Veyyákaraṇa, Gáthá, Udána, Itivuttaka, Játaka, Abbhuta, (Dhamma), and Vedalla. They also constituted (the foregoing) into Vagga, Paññásaka, Saṇyutta, Nipátaka, A'gama, Piṭaka, and Sutta.

As long as the Dhamma shall stand, so long shall this Compilation last;—and by its means the religion (itself) of Buddha shall endure for a long time.

The Compilation thus made of the Dhamma and Vinaya was in conformity to the doctrines—firm, durable, immovable, and unchangeable. Like the steadfast Sineru, it could not be shaken by any association, either of Samaṇas or Bráhmaṇas, however much they might be endowed with hair-splitting ingenuity, (acuteness), and (however) well learned, and greatly distinguished for dialectic disputation. Neither Gods, Máras, Brahamas, nor any inhabitants

* Avinásayan, 'That they may not perish.'

of the earth will (ever) perceive in it a single improper expression. Thus, this perfect Compilation of the Dhamma and Vinaya is well defined; and is conformable to the dictates (omniscience) of Buddha himself.

The five hundred theras, headed by Mahákassapa, made the compilation of Dhamma and Vinaya, with a view to its preservation; and regarding the doubts of the people, they made this compilation of the entire body of Dhamma (in purity) like Buddha himself.

To him who maintains its doctrines, this compilation is a mandate, and is full of instruction. It is destined to endure long.

All the venerable members of the faith, the disciples of Buddha, participated in the first compilation of the Dhamma.

The first (in point of time,) the prior (in respect of others,) the leading, the principal, and the chief original nidána (cause) is to be known without confusion."*

The end of the Convocation of Kassapa.

"This chapter then proceeds with a chronological narrative of the history of India, specifying also the contemporaneous dates of the reigns of the monarchs of Ceylon, and of the death of those inspired therá, who are considered to have constituted the connecting links of the chain called the Theraparampará, or generation of Preceptors.

---

* Here is a play upon words, an alliteration of the word agga which we have rendered 'pre-eminent,' 'supreme' 'chief,' 'first.'

"The following are the most important passages of this section:

"The sixteenth year after the nibbánan of the saviour of the world was the twenty-fourth of Ajátasattu, and the sixteenth of Wijaya (the rájá of Laṅká.) The learned Upáli was then sixty years old. Dásako entered into the upasampadâ order in the fraternity of Upáli. Whatever may be the extent of the doctrines of the most revered Buddho which had been promulgated by that vanquisher as the nine integral portions of his dispensation, the whole thereof Upáli taught. The said Upáli thus taught the same, having learnt in the most perfect manner the whole of the nine portions of his doctrine, which have been auricularly perpetuated, from Buddho himself. Buddho has declared of Upáli in the midst of the congregated priesthood, 'Upáli, being the first in the knowledge of winaya, is the chief in my religion.' He who had thus been selected and approved in the midst of the assembled priesthood, and who had a numerous fraternity, taught the three Piṭakas to a fraternity of a thousand bhikkhús, of whom Dásako was the chief disciple: he taught them (especially) to Dásako, and to five hundred Théras, who had overcome the dominion of sin, were of immaculate purity and morals, and versed in the wáda (history of the schisms). The thero Upáli, who had a great fraternity, continued to teach the winayo for full thirty years after the nibbánan of the supreme Buddho. The said Upáli taught the whole of the eighty-four thousand component parts of the doctrines of the divine teacher to the learned Dásako.

"Dásako, having learned the whole of the Piṭaka in the fraternity of Upáli, and held the office of Upajjháya (conferrer of the sacerdotal ordination of upasampadá) propounded the same. The chief of the great fraternity (Upáli) having deposited (ṭhapetwána) the whole winayo in the charge of the learned Dásako, died. The monarch Udayo reigned sixteen years. It was in the sixth year of his reign that the thero Upáli demised.

"A certain trader named Sóṇako, who had come from the Kási country, and was proud of his high descent, entered the sacerdotal order in the religion of the divine teacher (Buddho) at the Wéluwana* wihára in the mountain-girt city Rájagahan. Dásako, the chief of the confraternity, sojourned in the mountain-girt city, the capital of the Magadha nation, thirty-seven years, and initiated Sóṇako into the sacerdotal order. The learned Dásako was forty-five years old, in the tenth year of the reign of the rájá Nágadasa, and twentieth of the reign of the rájá Panḍu (of Lańká).

"The thero Sóṇako became an upasampadá in the fraternity of the thera Dásako, and the thero Dásako taught Sóṇako the nine component parts of the faith; and having learned the same from the preceptor who ordained him, he also taught the same. The thero Dásako having invested Sóṇako thera, who was the senior pupil in his fraternity, with the office of chief over the winayo, died in the sixty-fourth year of his age.

"At the expiration of ten years and half a month of the reign of the rája Kálásoka, the thero named Sóṇako was forty years old, and he had been a thero learned in the doctrines for fourteen years; and at the period of the expiration of ten years and six months, the thero Sóṇako, who was the chief of a great fraternity, conferred the upasampadá ordination on Siggawo and Chanḍawo.

---

* This word signifies 'the bamboo grove.'

"At that period a century had expired from the time that Bhagawá had attained nibbánan, and certain (bhikkhús) of Wesálí, native of Wajjís, set forth these ten (new) tenets of discipline."

This Bhánavára concludes with a brief account of the schism of the ten innovations* which led to the second Convocation, held by the orthodox priests of the time.

BHÁNAVÁRA FIFTH.

The first Convocation referred to—the hierarchs connected with it—how it was held—the ten innovations again referred to—the confusion made by Vajjiyans in the Dhamma and Vinaya—is thus related:

Uddhamman ubbinayañcha apagataŋ satthu sásane;
Atthaŋ dhammaŋ cha bhinditvá vilomaŋ dípayiŋsu te
Tesaŋ ŋiggahaŋatthúya bahú buddhassa sávaká;
Dvá dasa satasahassáni jina puttá samágatá.
Etasmiŋ sannipátasmiŋ pámokkhá aṭṭha bhikkhavo;
Satthukappá maháŋágá durásadá mahágaṇí
Sabbakámí cha Sáḷho cha Revato Khujja-sobhito;
Vásabhagámi Sumano Sána vásícha Sambhuto;
Yaso Kákaṇḍa putto cha jinadiṭṭhá ime isí;
Pápánaŋ niggahattháya Vesáliyaŋ samágatá;
Vásabhagámí cha Sumano Anuruddhassá'nuvattaká;
Avasesá A'nandassa diṭṭhapubbá tathágataŋ.
Susunágassa putto Asoko'si mahípati;
Páṭaliputta nagaramhi rajjaŋ káresi khattiyo
Tañcha pakkhaŋ labhitvána aṭṭha therá mahiddhiká;
Dasavatthúnaŋ ninditvá pápe nimmaddayiŋsu te.

---

* For an account of this, see Introduction to Kachcháyana's Páli Grammar, p. 53.

Niddhametvá pápa bhikkû madditvá váda pápakaŋ ;
Saka-váda sodhanatthaya aṭṭha therá mahiddhiká
Arahantánaŋ sattasatan uchchiṇitvána bhikkhavo ;
Varaŋ varaŋ gahetvána akaŋsu·dhammasaṅgahaŋ.
Kúṭágára sáláyaŋ Vesáliyaŋ puruttame ;
Aṭṭha máschi niṭṭhúsí dutíyo saṅgaho ayaŋ.
Nikkaḍḍhitá pápa bhikkhú therehi Vajji puttaká ;
Aññan pakkhaŋ labhitvána adhammavádí bahú janá ;*
Dasa sahassá samágantvá akaŋsu dhammasaṅgahaŋ
Tasmáyaŋ dhammasaṅgítí mahá saṅgíti vuchchatí
Mahá saṅgítiká bhikkhú vilomaŋ akaŋsu sásanaŋ ;
Bhinditvá múla saṅgahaŋ aññaŋ akaŋsu saṅgahaŋ.
Aññattha saṅgahítan suttaŋ aññattha akariŋsu te—
Atthan dhammañcha bhindiŋsú nikáyesu cha pañchasu
Pariyúyadesitan vápí atho nippariyáyadesitaŋ ;
Nítatthañcheva neyyatthaŋ ajánitvána bhikkhavo
Aññan sandháya bhaṇitaŋ aññattha ṭhapayiŋsu te ;
Vyañjanachháyáya te bhikkú bahuŋ atthaŋ vinásayuŋ.
Chhaḍḍetvá eka desañcha suttaŋ vinaya gambhíraŋ ;
Patirúpaŋ sutta vinayaŋ tantiŋ cha akariŋsu te
Parivúraŋ atthuddháraŋ abhidhammaŋ chhappakaraṇaŋ ;
Paṭisambhidañcha niddesaŋ eka desañcha Játakaŋ
Etta kaŋ vissajitvána aññaŋ va akariŋsu te
Námaliṅgaparikkháraŋ ákappakaraṇáni cha ;
Pakatibhávaŋ vijahitvá tañcha aññaŋ akaŋsu te
Pubbaṅgamá bhinnavádá mahá saṅgíti káraká ;
Tesañcha anukárena bhinna vádá bahú ahú.
Tato aparakálamhí tasmiŋ bhedo ajáyatha ;
Gokuliká Ekabbohárí dvidhá bhijjittha bhikkhavo

* Buddhaghosa has quoted portions of this section in his Pañchappakaraṇaṭṭhakathá.

Gokulikánaŋ dveva bhedá apara kálamhi jáyatha ;
Bahussutiká cha paññattí dvidhá bhijjittha bhikkhavo.
Chetiyácha punavádí mahásaṅgíti bhedaká ;
Pañcha vádá ime sabbe Mahásaṅgíti múlaká.
Atthan dhammañcha bhindiŋsu eka desañcha saṅgahaŋ ;
Ganthaŋ cha ekadesaŋhí chhaḍḍetv'aññaŋ akaŋsu te
Námaliṅgaŋ parikkháraŋ ákappakaraṇáni cha ;
Pakatibhávaŋ vijahitvá tañcha aññan akaŋsu te.
Visuddha-theravádambí puna bhedo ajáyatha ;
Mahiŋsásaká Vajjiputtá dvidhá bhijjittha bhikkhavo
Vajjiputtaka-vádamhí chatudhá bhedo ajáyatha ;
Dhammuttariká Bhadrayání Chhannágariká cha Sammití.
Mahiŋsásakánan dve bhedá apara kálamhi jáyatha ;
Sabbatthi vádá Dhammaguttá dvidhá bhijjittha bhikkhavo
Sabbatthivádá Kassapiká Kassapikena'pi Saṅkantiká ;
Saṅkantito Suttavádí anupubbena bhijjatha.
Ime eká-dasa vádá pabhinná thera-vádato,
Atthan dhammañcha bhindiŋsu ekadesañcha saṅgahaŋ ;
Ganthañcha ekadesamhi chhaḍḍetvána akaŋsu te
Námaliṅgaŋ parikkháraŋ ákappakaraṇáni cha ;
Pakatibhávaŋ vijahitvá tañcha aññaŋ akaŋsu te *
Sattarasa bhinnavádá eko vádo abhinnako ;
Sabbe v'aṭṭhádasa hontí bhinnavádena te saha.
Nigrodho'va mahárukkho thero vádána muttamo,
Anúnánadhikañche'va kevalaŋ Jina sásanaŋ ;†

* It is remarkable that the repetition of an act is conveyed by a repetition of the same stanza, a circumstance which proves the truth of the tradition, that the Dipáwansa was compiled by royal chroniclers, to whom it was assigned as a task.

† In reprinting this sheet we have inadvertently adopted ŋ for the niggahíta.

Kaṇṭaká viya rukkhamhi nibbattá váda sesaká
Paṭhame vassa sate natthi dutiye vassa satantare;
Bhinnásattarasa vádá uppanná Jina sásane
A'chariya vádan niṭṭhitan.

They (the sinful priests) made an absurd mixture by departing from the sense and phraseology of the dhamma and vinaya, the doctrines of Buddha.

With a view (therefore), to degrade them, many priests, disciples of Buddha, (in all) twelve hundred thousand, assembled together. In this congregation there were eight pre-eminent principal bhikkhus, who had a large retinue, who were (unapproachable, *i. e.*) without their equals, and not inferior to (Buddha himself; viz.) Sabbakámí Sáḷha, Revata, Khujjasobhita, Vásabhagámí, Sumana, Sambhúta of Sána, and Yasa, son of Kákanḍa, all who had seen Buddha. They assembled at Vesáli with a view to reproach the sinful priests.

Vásabhagámí and Sumana were the disciples of Anuruddha, and the rest of A'nanda. They had all seen Buddha.

[At this time] Asoka, the son of Susunága, a Khattiya prince, reigned in Páṭaliputta.

The (abovenamed) eight pre-eminent theras, having gained (this prince) to their side, censured the ten indulgences, and (oppressed) inflicted pains and penalties on the sinful innovators. Having (thus) overcome the sinful bhikkhus, and suppressed their heresies; these illustrious eight priests, with the object of purifying their own discourses, assembled seven

U

hundred arahantas—pre-eminent bhikkhus; and held a Council of dhamma.

This second Sangíti was brought to a close in eight months, at the Kúṭágára Hall, in the renowned city of Vesáli.

Many individuals (viz.) ten thousand sinful Vajjian* bhikkhus, who had been expelled by the theras, assembled together; and, having formed another party, held a council of dhamma. This is thence called Mahá Sangíti.

The bhikkhus who held the Mahá Sangíti reduced the religion into confusion,† set aside‡ the first compilation,§ and made another.‖ They placed in different places the Suttans which occurred in different other places, and distorted the sense, and the words¶ of the five

---

* Vajji—the inhabitants of Vesáli, a territory on the north of Petna in which the Lichchhavi Princes were settled. It is however not stated where the Council was held. Doubtless it was at a distance from the principal seat of Government and Buddhism, which at this period was at Vesáli.

† Vilomaṇakansu, 'made to bristle,' 'ruffled,' 'crossed,' 'reversed,' 'confused.'

‡ Bhinditvá—'having broken,' 'split,' 'set aside.'

§ Sangahan. From the context I would render this word 'compilation' and not 'rehearsal.' The acts here related, taken in connection with the original import of the word, can only refer to a written and not a mental collection.

‖ Akarinsu 'maḍe,' 'done,' 'effected.' The same word is used in the following sentence, wherein I have rendered it 'placed.'

¶ Dhamma here means phraseology of the Scriptures, as opposed to their attha, 'sense' or 'import.'

nikáya. They did so, ignorant of (the difference between) the general discourses, and those (delivered) on particular occasions, and also (between) their natural and implied significations. They expressed* in a sense different from that which was declared, and set aside various significations under the unwarranted authority (shadow of) words.† They omitted a portion of the Sutta, and Vinaya of deep import, and substituted‡ (their own) version§ of them and the text.‖ They left out the Parívárau annotations,¶ the six books** of the Abhidhamma, the Paṭisambhidá, the Niddesa, and a portion of the Játakas†† without replacing

* Ṭhapayinsu—'They made to stand.'

† Vyanjana, 'letters,' and in some of the Buddhist writings, 'words' or 'sentences.'

‡ Patirúpa—placed another figure or 'counterpart.'

§ From a comparison of the Ceylon and Nepal versions of the sacred writings I find the latter has three sections, the Vaipulya, the Nidan, and the Upadesa; all which are additions to the original discourses. Compare the following list taken from Hodgson's Illustrations, with the list from Buddhagosa's atthakathá, given in Introduction to Kachcháyana's Páli Grammar, p. 61. Hodgson says; "The Bauddha scriptures are of twelve kinds, known by the following twelve names, 1 Sútra; 2 Geyya; 3 Vyákarana; 4 Gáthá; 5 Udan; 6 Nidan; 7 Ityukta; 8 Játaka; 9 Vaipulya; 10 Adbhúta dharma; 11 Avadán; and 12 Upadesa."

‖ Tantin. The text; see my remarks hereon in the Introduction to Kachch. Páli Grammar, p. v.

¶ Atthuddháran, 'explanatory discourses.'

** Pakarana, 'compilation,' 'something made methodically,' 'an original composition.'

†† The version of the Játakas in Ceylon is, I believe, deficient.

any thing in their stead. They moreover, disregarded* the nature of nouns, their gender, and (other) accidents,† as well as the (various) requirements of style,‡ and corrupted the same by different forms.

The originators of the Mahá Sangíti were the first seceders. Many followed their example. Since then, there was a breach in that association, and the Priests were divided into two sections—the Gokulika and Ekabbohárika. Subsequently the Gokulikas branched off into two others, viz., Bahussutika and Paññatti. Subsequently still, there arose a schism (called) the Chetiya. Then there were altogether five schisms which had sprung up from the Mahá Sangíti—the same, which was the first, (being a sixth)

These heretics (also) distorted the sense and the phraseology (of the scriptures); omitted a portion of the (original) compilation, and of the gáthás, and substituted others (in lieu of them). They (further) disregarded the nature of nouns, their gender, and other

---

* A'kappakarana—also 'decorations, embellishments, niceties of style or composition, or figures of speech.'

† The peculiarities here noticed, when compared with those of the Gáthá dialect of the Nepal Scriptures (see Essay thereon by Babu Rajendralal Mitra in the Bl. A. S. J. for 1854, p. 604, et seq.), there can be no doubt of the identity between this fourth code of the Buddhists and the Nepal version. The differences of style therein illustrated by Mr. Mitra exactly correspond with the defects of composition here described.

‡ Parikkháran—'attributes,' 'decorations,' 'accidents.'

accidents, as well as the various requisites of style, and corrupted the same by different substitutions.*

In the doctrines of the orthodox priests there was again a breach (which resulted in the establishment) of two sects called the Mahinsaka and Vajjiputtaka. From the latter arose four sects, called Dhammuttarika, Bhadrayáni, Chhannágárika, and Sammiti. Afterwards, two (more) schisms, the Sabbatthiváda and Dhammagutta arose out of the Mahinsaka; and from the Sabbattiká gradually sprung up the Kassapika, and from the latter the Sankantika, and from it the Suttavadí schism. These eleven emanated from the orthodox party.

They (likewise) made a compilation by distorting the sense, and the phraseology of the sacred discourses; and by omitting a portion of the text and of the gáthás. They too disregarded the forms of nouns, their gender, and other accidents, as well as the various requirements of style, and corrupted the same by different substitutions.

The schisms of the seceders were (thus) seventeen, the váda† of those who had not seceded, was one; and with it there were altogether eighteen sects.

---

* "In the Gáthá, says Mr. Mitra, we find the old forms of the Sanskrit Grammar gradually losing their impressive power, and prepositions and periphrastic expressions supplying their places, and time-hallowed verbs and conjugations juxtaposed to vulgar slangs and uncouth provincialisms."

† The word váda, which we have differently translated at different places to convey 'heresy,' 'schism,' &c., means simply as in this place, 'discourse,' 'discussion,' 'demonstrated conclusion,' 'doctrine,' 'principle.'

Like the great Nigrodha (among) trees, the orthodox discourses alone are supreme among doctrines; and they are moreover the pure (very) word of Buddha, without retrenchment or addition. The doctrines which have arisen from it are like the thorns of a tree.

There were no (heresies) in the first century (anno Buddhæ) but in the second, seventeen sprung up in the religion of Buddha.

END OF THE A'CHARIYA VA'DA.

This section then proceeds to narrate the division amongst the preceptors. The life of Moggaliputta Tissa thera is thus translated by Turnour.

"In the second year of the reign of Chandagutto, when Siggawo was sixty-four years old, which was the fifty-eighth year of the reign of Paṇḍukabhayo, the raja (of Lanka) Moggaliputto was ordained an upasampada in the fraternity of Siggawo; and the said Moggaliputtatisso, having acquired the knowledge of the winéyo in the fraternity of Chandawajji, was released from the sins inseparable from liability to future regeneration. Both Siggawa and Chandawajji taught the whole of the Pitako, which embraces both (the wineyo, discipline, and dhammo, doctrine), to the pre-eminently endowed Muggaliputto. Siggawo of profound wisdom died at the age of seventy-six, having constituted the pre-eminently endowed Moggaliputto the chief of the wineyo Chandagutto reigned twenty-four years. In the fourteenth year of his reign Siggawo died.

"In the sixth year of the reign of Dhammasoko, Moggaliputto was sixty-six years old. Mahindo was then ordained an upasampada in his fraternity, and acquired a knowledge of the Pitako.

"Upali attained his seventy-fourth, Dasako his sixty-fourth, the thero Sónako his sixty-sixth, Siggawo his seventy-sixth, and Moggaliputto his eightieth year. The following are the periods that all of these theros were upasampada, of whom at all times the learned Upali was recognized as the first chief, viz., Dasako was an upasampada fifty, Sónoko, forty-four, Siggawo five,* and Moggaliputto, sixty-eight years.

"Udayo reigned sixteen years, and in the sixth year of Udayo's reign, Upali died.

"Susanago, the opulent monarch, reigned ten years, in the eighth year of Susanago's reign Dasako died.

"At† the demise of Susanago he had ten brothers, who collectively reigned twenty-two years, in great celebrity. In the sixth year of their reign Sónako died.

"Chandagutto reigned twenty-four years, and in the fourteenth year of his reign Siggawo died.

"The celebrated Dhammasóko the son of Bindasaro reigned thirty-seven years. In the twenty-sixth year of his reign, Moggaliputto died, having caused religion to be glorified, and having completed the full measure of human existence.

"The learned Upali, the chief of a great fraternity died at the age of seventy-four, having appointed his learned disciple Dasako to the office of chief wineyo.

"Dasako, died at the age of sixty-four, having appointed his senior learned disciple Sonako to the office of chief of the wineyo.

---

* "This is evidently a mistake.

† "The reign of Kálásóko is omitted, who was the father of the Nandos who are here designated the brothers of Susanago.

"Sónako, who was endowed with the six abinna, died at the age of sixty-six, having appointed his arahat son (disciple) Siggawo to the office of chief of wineyo.

"Siggawo who was endowed with the six abinna died at the age of seventy-six, having appointed his son (disciple) Moggaliputto to the office of chief of wineyo.

"Moggaliputtatisso died at the age of eighty, having appointed his disciple Mahindo to the office of chief of wineyo.

THE CONCLUSION OF THE FIFTH BHA'NAWA'RO.

BHA'NAVA'RA SIXTH.

"Piyadassano* was inaugurated in the two hundred and eighteenth year after the death of the supreme Buddho. At the installation of Piyadassano preternatural manifestations took place.

"(For these manifestations I must refer to the Mahawanso.)

"That royal youth, who was the grand-son of Chandagutto and the son of Bindusáro was at that time the (karmalino) ruler of Ujjeni.

"In the course of an official circuit he visited Wessanagaran; where lived a damsel, the daughter of a Sitthi, who became celebrated under the name of Dewi. By his connection with her, an illustrious son was born. (The said son) Mahindo and (his daughter) Sangamitta formed the resolution to enter the order of priesthood. Both these individuals having been thus ordained, overcame subjection

---

* "Having erroneously written this name "Piyadasino" in a former paper, (Beng. A. S. Journal) vol. vi. p. 1056, you have been led to suppose it was the genitive case of Piyadasi."

to regeneration. Asóko was then reigning in the illustrious Pataliputto. In the third year of his inauguration he became a convert to the religion of the supreme Buddho. (If it be asked) what the duration of the term is, from the date of the parinibbánan of the Supreme Buddho to the date of the birth of Mahindo, who was descended from the Moriyan dynasty, (the answer is) two hundred and five years. In that year Mahindo the son of Asóko was born. In Mahindo's tenth year, his father put his own brothers to death; and he past four years in reducing Jambudipo to order. Having put to death his hundred brothers, and reduced the dynasty to one (family), they (the people) inaugurated him in the fourteenth year of Mahindo's age. Asoko, who was endowed with great personal superiority and good fortune, and was destined to rule the world, was inaugurated under miraculous manifestations. They installed Piyadassano on his completing his twentieth year."*

This bhánavára concludes with Nigrodha's visit to the Palace—his preaching to Asoka—the admission of the latter to Buddhist religion—his interview with sixty thousand priests—a city festival—alms-giving—the offering of garments—inquiry by Asoka into the division of the dhamma—its enumeration—eighty-four thousand monumental erections by Asoka.†

* "This is evidently a clerical error, his son Mahindo being then fourteen years old. It was subsequently mentioned that Asóko-dhammo was forty-five years old at his inauguration.

† There is a great deal of confusion and repetition in this section. I have retained the spelling of Mr. Turnour; and have not thought proper to interpose any observations on his translation.

BHA'NAVA'RA SEVENTH

"Begins with the account of Mahindo and Sangamittá being admitted into the order of the priesthood, (the former was at once ordained upasampadá, being of the age of twenty; but the latter remained a samanéri for two years, being only eighteen,) in the sixth year of Asóko's inauguration. These particulars will be found in the Maháwanso.

"Asókadhammo was fifty-four years old at the time of his inauguration, and at the time of Asókadhammo being inaugurated, Moggaliputtatisso was sixty-six. Mahindo entered into the order of priesthood in the fraternity of Moggaliputtatisso. Mahádéwo performed the ceremony of admission, and Mojjhanto, the ceremony of the upasampadá ordination. These were the three preceptors who qualified Mahindo for the priesthood. The said preceptor Moggaliputtatisso taught Mahindo, who illuminated (Lanká) dípo, the whole of the Pitako, both as regards its import and its doctrine. In the tenth year of Mahindo's (ordination) having acquired a perfect knowledge of the whole creed, he became the head of a fraternity, and (pachariyo) a sub-preceptor (under Moggali). The said Mahindo, having thus acquired a knowledge of the perfectly profound and well arranged (Piṭakattayan), containing the two doctrinal portions (the wineyo and the abhidhammo) and the suttako (the parables) as well as the history of the schisms of the preceptors, became a perpetuator of the same. Moggaliputtatisso thus perfected Mahindo the son of Asóko, in the knowledge of the three wejja and the four paṭisambhidá, and (thereby) Moggaliputtatisso permanently established in his disciple Mahindo, the whole of the Piṭakattayán which had been thus handed down to him.

"Nigródho was admitted into the priesthood in the third year of Asóko's reign, his brother (Tisso) in the fourth, and in the sixth his son Mahindo. Tisso and Sumittako, the two theros who were descended from the Kunti, and were endowed with supernatural powers, died in the eighth year of the reign of Asóko. From these two princes having entered the order of priesthood, and from (the manner in which) these two theros died, multitudes of the khattiya and brahman castes proclaimed themselves to be devotees in this creed, and great benefits and honors resulted to the religion of the vanquisher; and the heretics, who had been influential schismatics, lost all their ascendancy. The pándarangá, the jaṭila, niganthá, chétaká and other sects for seven years continued, however, to perform the upósatha in separate fraternities. The sanctified, pious, and virtuous ministers (of Buddho) would not attend those upósatha meetings. At this conjuncture, it was the two hundred and thirty-sixth year (of the Buddhistical era.)

BHA'NAVA'RA EIGHTH.

After relating the working of wonders, and the inquiries made of the priesthood regarding religion, this section proceeds to give a brief account of the third convocation of which the following is a translation:

'The heretics, who, seeing the gains (of the Buddhists), and the very great attentions (paid to them), fraudulently associated (with them), were sixty thousand. (Owing to their intrusions the observance of) the Pátimokkha*

* The meeting of the priesthood once in 15 days; or, on the full-moon day and on the new-moon day,—when they usually recite and explain the rules of discipline.

was discontinued in the Asokáráma monastery; and a minister who ceased to hold the Pátimokkha killed some of the priests.*

With a view (therefore) to eject the heretics, many Buddhist priests, about sixty thousand in number, assembled. In this assembly Moggaliputta thera was the chief. He was equal to Buddha himself—pre-eminent, and peerless; and, having been requested by the king (to declare who would incur) the sin of having killed the priests, he dispelled the Sovereign's doubts by working a miracle.

When the king had learnt the religion from (this) thera, he extirpated the imposters by removing their (sacerdotal) garments. (These were) the inimical heretics, who had entered the priesthood, and who, by means of their own doctrines, set aside the word of Buddha, which was as pure as gold. All those doctrines were false,† and opposed to the discourses of the theras. To render (therefore) the orthodox doctrines pure, and to eject the heretics, Moggaliputta delivered the Katháyatthupakaraṇa‡ on the Abhidhamma. For the suppression of heresies, there was not a better (instrument of) reproof than this.

---

* For a detailed account of this proceeding, see the Maháwansa.

† Lit.—'Broken, imperfect.'

‡ A 'book-on-the-substance-of-the-discourses.' This is the name given to the additional pakaraṇa or 'book' of the Abhidhamma. It was composed by amplifying the pre-existing mátiká, and it is devoted to the consideration of five hundred points of difference between the Buddhists and the heretics, and five hundred errors of the orthodox party.

This done,* with a view to the stability of religion, and the purification of its doctrines, this hierarch assembled a thousand arahantá; and, having selected a pre-eminent and highly erudite thera, held a Council of dhamma.

This third convocation was brought to a termination in nine months, at the Asokaráma monastery, founded by the pious king of that name.

This section concludes with the dispersion of missionaries for the promulgation of Buddhism into different parts of Asia, viz., Gandhára, Mahinsa, Aparantaka, Maháraṭṭha, Yonaka, Himawanta, Suvaṇṇabhúmi, and Lankádípa.

Bha'nava'ra Ninth

Commences with the history of Lanká, thus:—

"This island Lanká acquired the name of Síhala from Siho†. Listen to this narrative of mine, being the account of the origin of this island and this dynasty. The daughter of a king of Wango, having formed a connection with a certain Sího, who found his livelihood in a wilderness, gave birth to two children. These two children named Síhabáhu

---

* Lit —'the thera having delivered the Katháwatthu-pakaraṇa on the Abhidhamma.'

† "Pachchantan," I have translated, "foreign" in the Mahawanso, as the word is compounded of "pati" and "antan." It would be better rendered as "situated on the confines."

Wanawási is here omitted, probably by an error of transcription.

This passage is important. Mátácha Susimánáma, pitácha Síhasawhayo. If "Sího" was intended for a "lion," "sawhayo," which signifies "named" or "called," would not be used.

and Sewalí were of prepossessing appearance. The mother was named Susimá, and the father was called Sího, and at the termination of sixteen years, secretly quitting that wilderness, he (Síhabáhu) founded a city, to which capital he gave the name of Síhapura. In that Lála kingdom, the son of Síbo becoming a powerful monarch, reigned supreme in his capital Síhapura."

This Bhánavára proceeds to relate the history of Wijaya, his arrival in Lanká, the names of which are embodied in the following verse.

Ojadípo Vara-dípo Manḍa-dípo cha tadá ahú
Lanká-dípo cha paṇṇatti Taubapaṇṇíti ñáyati.

And its magnitude is described to be 'thirty six yojanas in length, eighteen in width, and a hundred in circumference'

Battinsa yojanan díghan aṭṭhúrasahi vitthatan
Yojanánan satan ávaṭṭan ságarena parikkhitan*

Gotama's request to Indra concerning Lanká [regarding which we quote the following gathás].

Parinibbána samaye sambhuddho dipa duttamo
Síhabáhussayan putto Wijayo náma Khattiyo
Lankádípamanuppatto jahitvá Jambu-dípakan
Byákási Buddhaseṭṭho so rájá hessati khattiyo
Tato ámantayí satthá Sakkan devánamissaran
Lankádípassa ussukkan samápajjatha† Kosiya
Sambuddhassa vacho sutvá deva rájá Sujanpati
Uppalavaṇṇassa áchikkhi dípassárakkha káranan

---

* 'Surrounded by the ocean.' It is quite clear that at this period at least this island was not a part of India.

† This should be in the singular number.

Sakkassa vachanan sutvá deva putto mahiddhiko
Lankádípassa árakkhan ṭhapesi Vásu-devako.

'At the period of the parinibbána of Buddha, who was superior to bipeds, the Khattiya named Wijaya, son of Síhabáhu, left Jambudípa, and arrived in the island of Lanká. The supreme Buddha, having declared that Wijaya would be king, summoned Sakka, the chief of the devas (and said to him)—'Kosiya, exert thyself in regard to the island of Lanká. Sujápati, the king of the devas, on hearing the word of Buddha, intrusted to Uppalavaṇṇa the protection of the island of Lanká; and he Vásudeva, the great mighty deva, on hearing the word of Sakka, extended his protection to Lanká.'

As regards the origin of the name Tambapaṇṇa for this island, the Dípawansa has the following:

Ukkhittá váta vegena disá múḷhá mahá janá
Lanká dípa'mupá gamma orohitvá thale ṭhitá
Patiṭṭhitá dharani tale dubbalá'ti jighachchhitá
Pipásitá kilantácha padasá gamanena cha
Ubhohi páṇi jannúhi viaggan katvá puthúviyan
Majjhe vuṭṭháya ṭhatvána nahipassanti sobhanan
Surattan pansu bhúmi bhága hattha pádanhi makkhitan
Náma deyyan tadá ási Tambapaṇṇí 'ti dípitan.

'By the fury of the tempest the large assemblage of people lost their way, and reached Lanká-dípa; (where) having disembarked, and landed, they [lit. those who thus stood on land] were weak and hungry. When they became thirsty and faint by walking on foot, they rested on the ground, with both their palms and knees: and, when they rose and stood up, they saw in the interval [the space occupied by them] nothing beautiful. The dust, however, which stuck to the palms of their hands and feet, was very ruddy. Thence the celebrated name Tambapaṇṇi.'

Analysis continued—The first city is also called Tambapaṇṇi—Wijaya's reign in Lanká [interpolation regarding Buddha's visit to Lanká] Wijaya's embassy to his brother Sumitta—King Paṇduvása and his sons—his reign.

Bha'nava'ra Tenth.

King Abhaya—Paṇḍukabhaya— Prince Pakuṇḍaka —Paṇḍukabhaya again —Mutasíva— interregnum — Mutsaíva's children.*

Bha'nava'ra Eleventh and Twelfth.

Inauguration of Devánanpiyatissa—his good fortune —his alliance with Asoka—the offerings of the latter to the former—Mahinda's visit to Lanká—preliminaries connected with his departure—Indra's interview with Mahinda—particulars connected with his journey —his arrival in Lanká—Devánanpiyatissa's excursion on a deer-hunt—his invitation and visit to Mahinda—Mahinda preaches to the king—entrance into the city —ordination of Sumana—Mahinda's missionary labours at Anurádhapura—his stay at Mahá Meghavana—description of this Park—its dedication—acceptance—preternatural indications—the earth quakes eight times.

---

* This as well as several other Bháṇavâras are found short of the required number of stanzas.

BHA'NAVA'RA THIRTEENTH.

Mahinda's visit to the palace--second visit--his preaching in the Nandana Park--the ecclesiastical limits of Lanká—the city included, and why?—limits fixed—Mahinda's visit to the palace—he preaches in the Nandana—accepts the Mahá Vihára—preaches at the palace—the departure of the priests to Mount Missaka, where the king rejoins them—Mahinda's interview with the king—his preparation for Vassa—his proposal to define the ecclesiastical limits about the mountain—limits defined—ordination of Prince Ariṭṭha—the monastery on the mountain.

BHA'NAVA'RA FOURTEENTH.

As the portion which follows the above is sufficiently interesting we give a translation of it below, omitting repetitions.

'We,' (said Mahinda), who have arrived from Jambudípa in the first month of the Gimhána* season, and on the full-moon Sabbath (day,) have resided in the celebrated mountain. We purpose returning to Jambudípa in the fifth month of our residence in the mountain, and in Tissáráma. O Monarch, permit (us to do) so.

[The king answered and said]; 'All the people have taken refuge. (They) have pleased you with eatables and drinkables, with raiment and habitations. Wherefore (then) is your dissatisfaction?'

* The hot season.

'Monarch,' (replied Mahinda), 'it is very long since Buddha, the chief of the bipeds, was (worshipped by) prostration, by rising from one's seat, by salutation, and by reverent attention.'

'Lord,' (returned Devánanpiyatissa), 'what you have (said) is indeed understood by me. I shall erect a splendid Thúpa. I shall build it for Buddha. Look out for a suitable locality.'

[Whereupon Mahinda thus spoke]: 'Sumana, come hither. Go to the city of Páṭaliputta, and say thus to king Dhammásoka; Mahá rája, thy ally has embraced Buddhism. He will build a thúpa for Buddha. Bestow upon him (some) valuable relics.'

The eloquent, and meek (Sumana) of great erudition,—the sustainer of learning, who had achieved iddhi, and who was on the mount, instantly took his bowl and robe, and went to king Dhammásoka, and delivered the message (thus): 'Mahá rája, hear thou the word of the spiritual preceptor. Mahá rája, thy ally has embraced Buddhism. Bestow on him some valuable relics, and he will erect a Thúpa for Buddha.'

The king hearing the (above) speech was highly pleased and became very anxious. He (immediately) filled (for him) a vessel of relics, (and said) 'O! virtuous, depart quickly.'

Whereupon the eloquent and meek (Sumana) taking the relics, ascended the sky, and went to Kosiya.* And, when he had approached Kosiya's presence, the

* Indra.

pious (ascetic) spoke thus: 'Mahá rája, hear thou the words of the spiritual teacher. The king-beloved of the gods has embraced Buddhism. Give him valuable relics, and he will construct a great Thúpa.'

Hearing his words, and being pleased, Kosiya bestowed the right collar-bone (of the sage, and said) 'O virtuous, depart quickly.'

Sumana, the Sámanera, having thus gone to Kosiya, and received the right collar-bone, returned to the celebrated mountain.

* * * * * * Thereupon the king of immense forces, with his brother, preceded by the bhikkhús and sanghas, repaired to meet the relic of the illustrious Buddha. On the day which completed the fourth month (of the seasons), in the full moon night of Komudí,* the Mahá Víra, who had come (thither) took his place on the frontal globes of the elephant.

There (in honor of) Buddha's arrival at Pachchanta, the elephant roared, the earth quaked, like a stroked basin, and chanks and musical instruments were played. Immense was the noise of drums; and the king, attended by his retinue, made offerings unto the great being.

The royal elephant, which had its face towards the west, went away from amongst (other) elephants, and entered the city through the eastern gate; when both men and women made offerings (unto the relic) with all kinds of scents and flowers.

---

* Kattika, 'Oct.—Nov.'

The elephant, when proceeding through the southern gate, (halted) in the ancient capital, the region consecrated by Kakusandha, Konágamana, and Kassapa

* * * * * * * *

Buddhas; where the king enshrined the relics of Sakyaputta; and at this event the gods rejoiced, and the earth quaked miraculously and frightfully.

The Sámanera, called Sumana, with his brother (or cousin,) having consulted the Ministers of State, and the inhabitants of the country, constructed bricks for the thúpa.'

Analysis continued: Kakusandha Buddha's visit to Lanká—his missionary operations—Konágamana Buddha's visit to Lanká—success of his operations—Gotama's mental perception of Lanká—the cause of Sangamitta's visit to Lanká—preliminaries connected with her visit—permission granted to her by Asoka.

Bha'nava'ra Fifteenth.

Sangamitta's departure with the Bodhi branch—Asoka staying behind—how evil spirits surrounded the Bodhi—offerings thereto by gods and Nágás—Lanká's king's offering to the same—ordination of Anulá.

Bha'nava'ra Sixteenth.

The size of Lanká (repetitions) names of Lanká—and of Anurádhapura—the relics of former Buddhas deposited in Lanká—the names of mountains in aforetimes—Konágamana's relics deposited in Lanká—the name given at that period to the spot on which the

Bodhi now stands—Kakusandha Buddha's visit to, and stay in, Lanká—his aspirations whilst in Lanká—the prayers of the people of Lanká—Kakusandha's visit to Mahátittha Park—his acceptance of the Park—the planting of his memorial tree in Lanká—the offerings to the same by devas—(repetitions) the planting of Gotama's Bodhi in Mahá Meghavana—the computation of time from the death of Gotama to the reign of Devánanpiyatissa—the exchange of presents between that sovereign and Dammásoka—the second inauguration of Devánanpiyatissa—the erection of a chetiya by him—reign of Uttiya—the cremation of Mahinda—the designation given to the place.

BHA'NAVA'RA SEVENTEENTH.

Lanká abounded with good and great—therí-parampará or the succession of preceptresses,—which is thus translated by Turnour.

"She who was renowned under the appellation of Pajápati, and was of the Gotamo family, endowed with six abiññá and with supernatural gifts, the younger sister, born of the same mother, of Mahámáyá (the mother of Buddo): and who, with the same affection as Máyá herself nourished Bhagawá at her breast, was established in the highest office (among priestesses.)

"The following are the priestesses who (in succession) acquired a perfect knowledge of the wineyo, viz.: Khémá Uppalawanná, two of each name, and Paṭáachári, Dhammadinná, Sóbhitá, Isidásiká, Wisákhá, Asóká, Sapalá, Sanghadási, gifted with wisdom, Nandá and Dhammapálá, celebrated for her knowledge of Winéyo.

"The therí Sanghamittá, Uttará, who was gifted with wisdom, Hémapása, Dassalá, Aggamittá, Dasiká, Pheggupabbattá, Mattá, Salalá, Dhammadásiya—these juvenile priestesses came hither from Jambudipo, and propounded the Winayapiṭako in the capital designated Anurádhapura—they propounded not only the five divisions of the Wineyo, but also the seven Pakaranáni.

"The females who were ordained upasampadá by them in this island were Sóma, devoted to dhammo, Goridípí, Dhammadasiyí, Dhammapálá versed in the wineyo, Mahila conversant in the dhutawádá, Sóbhana, Dhammata, Passanagamissá, also versed in the wineyo, and Sátakáli profound in the theri controversy, and Uttará.

"Under the instructions of Abhayo* celebrated for his illustrious descent, the aforesaid priestesses as well as Sumana† renowned for the doctrinal knowledge among her sisterhood, a maintainer of the Dhutangá, a vanquisher of the passions, of great purity of mind, devoted to dhammo and wineyo, and Uttará endowed with wisdom, together with their thirty thousand priestesses, were the first priestesses who propounded at Anurádhapura, the wineyo, the five Nikáye (of the Suttapiṭako) and the Suttapakarané of the Abhidhammo.

"Mahála equally illustrious for her knowledge of the dhammo and for her piety, was the daughter of the monarch Kákawanno. Girikáli, profoundly versed by rote, was the daughter of his Pooróhito (the almoner of Kákawannó); Káladási and Sabbapápiká were the daughters of Gutto. These priestesses, who always maintained the orthodox texts,

---

* "Abhayo, the brother of Déwánanpiyatisso."

† "Vide Index of the Maháwanso for this name."

and of perfect purity of mind, were versed in the dhammo and wineyo, and having returned from the Róhana division maintained by the illustrious ruler of men Abhayo*, propounded the Winéyo, at Anurádhapura."

[Analysis continued] the reign of King Síva—reign of Súratissa and Elára.

Bha'nava'ra Eighteenth.

Reign of Duṭṭhagámaní—the building of a large Palace—the arrival of priests from Asia—the erection of preaching halls—death of Duṭṭhagámaní.

Bha'nava'ra Nineteenth

Treats of the religious acts of Saddhátissa—that he placed a glass pinnacle on the Thúpa†—the reigns of Thúlathana and Lajjitissa--the reigns of Khalláṭa and Kammahárattaka—the reigns of Waṭṭagámaní and a Damiḷa king—Waṭṭagámaní (continued). Reduction of Buddha's discourses to writing;‡—the reign of Maháchúlí Mahá Tissa—reign of Chora Nága —[Chúla] Tissa—Anulá—Síva Waṭuka—Kaṭṭhahára —Tilaya Damiḷa—Kuṭikaṇṇa-Tissa—the acts of the last named.

* "Vide Index for Gamini Abhayo, the name of Duṭṭhagámaní before he recovered the kingdom."

† For the original see my Attanagaluvansa, p. xxvi.

‡ See extract, ante p. 121.

Bha'nava'ra Twentieth.

Abhaya the son of Kuṭikaṇṇa—the desire of the king to see the interior of the thúpa—the desire realized by the help of Indra—the light offering by the king—the offerings to the chetiya—the flower offerings by the king—donations—the erection of a building for the observance of the Sabbath—King Nága—A'maṭṭagámaní—Tissa—Chúlábhaya—Sívalí—Ilanága and Síva—Yasa—Lála Tissa, and Subha.

Bha'nava'ra Twenty-first

Contains an account of King Vasabha—his acts—construction of subterranean aqueducts for irrigation—King Tissa—Gajabáhu—Gámaní and Mahalla Nága—A'yutissa—the opening of the Ramaní Tank—Bhátikatissa—the acts of Tissa—King Vankanásika—the history of Vankanásika, Tissa, Gajabáhu, &c.—Khujjanága—Kunjanága, Sirinága—King Abhaya—his acts—King Sirinága—Wijaya—Sanghatissa—Sanghabodhi—Abhaya—Meghavaṇṇa—the acts of the two last—Jeṭṭha Tissa, his acts—King Mahásena, his acts.

The conclusion of Di'pawansa.

Anuruddha S'ataka.

This is one of the few Sanskrit works now extant in Ceylon. It contains an account of Gotama Buddha. The three first verses are devoted to the usual adoration;

the next seven to a brief history of Gotama's twenty-four predecessors, from whom he had received the sanction of becoming Buddha; and the next nine to an explanation of the ten Páramitás.* The 21st and 22nd stanzas relate his birth in the heaven named Tusita, and his final nativity at Kapilavastu in this world, and the attainment of Buddhahood; the 23rd gives the allegory of his contest with Mára; the 24th alludes to his first sermon; 25 to 61 delineate his personal accomplishments from head to foot; 62 to 71 narrate his virtues, [including Vidyá and charaṇa†]; and 72 to 90 describe his miraculous powers. Five following stanzas embody the narratives of several of his incarnations. The 96th contains a rebuke to those who do not embrace Buddhism. The next three express the writer's own devotion to Buddhism, followed by three others, embodying some observations of the author with reference to his work. The whole book concludes with a stanza containing the aspirations of the writer; but, since there is no translation of it into Siṇhalese, it is supposed that the same was introduced by the Translator.

The language of the original is elegant, though there are a few grammatical inaccuracies which have been noticed by my pandit. He points out in the Preface, which he has given to the work in publishing

* See Attanagaluwansa, note (4) at p. 64.

† For an explanation, see Introduction to Kachcháyana's Páli Grammar, p. xxxiv.

it with the Siṇhalese paraphrase,* that "bhindante s'abare" in the 13th stanza should be "bhindati s'abare;" and that the insertion of r in "saranirivarupetá" is not sanctioned by Sanskrit Grammar.

The work is composed in several metres. Thirty-two stanzas are in the S'árdúlavikkríḍita metre; five in the Mandákrántá; eighteen in the Máliní; ten in the Sragdhará; thirty-two in the Vasantatilaká; one in the Vans'astha; and two (including the Translator's) in the Upajáti.

We have again to record the omission of the date of the work, though we are told that the name of the author was Anuruddha, a Buddhist priest, after whom the work is named.

It is, however, stated in the Saddhamma Sańgaha that this S'ataka, as well as Abhidhammattha Sańgaha, was composed by one and the same Anuruddha. Now, there is a Sanna to the last work by a very learned Priest named Sáriputta,† in the reign of Parákkramabáhu of Poḷonnaruwa 1153—1186 A.D. The text must therefore be placed before the last date, and we cannot ascertain exactly how much earlier. Yet, since according to the Maháwansa, the very Uttaramúla fraternity, to which the writer under review belonged, came to existence about the period when the seat of

---

* See this Edition 1866, octo. pp. 41.

† He was also the author of Sáratthadípaní, a Tíká to the Vinaya, Anguttara Tíká, a Commentary on the Grammar of Chandragomi, Páli Muttaka Vinaya Vinichchhaya, etc.

government was finally removed from Anurádhapura (1023 A.D.) to Poḷonnaruwa, we may place the work before us between 1023—1186 A.D.

It only remains to give a specimen of this work, and we quote stanzas 1 and 96.

1.

Lakshmí sanvadanan himáns'u vadanan
dharmámritasyandanan
Maudrálápakalan guṇai'ravi kalan
pápadvipé pákalan,
Satvánán nayanoddhavan matidhavan
maitrílatá mádhavam
Kalyáṇápaghanan rajóhatighanan
bhaktyá name s'ríghanan.

96.

Yah s'rotrá bharaṇan karoti na muneh
saddharma váṇí maṇin
Yasyá'sít saphalan na lochanayugan
saundarya sandars'anaih
No'pas'lokayaté yadíyarasaná
chitran charitrá mritan
Na s'rotran nacha lochanan na rasaná
tasyá'nginah sádhavah.

'I devoutly bow unto Buddha, the source of the ambrosia-of-dharma, the consort of wisdom; who exhibits beauty, has a moon-like visage, and a good deep-intoned speech; who is full of goodness, and possesses a handsome body; and who is like fever to the elephant-of-sin, a feast to the eyes of mankind, the (season of) spring to the creeper-of-mercy, and the very rain to the dust-of-sin.'*

'O wise! He has no ear who does not make an ear-ornament of the gem-of-Buddhá's (Saddharma) doctrines. He has no sight, whose pair of eyes does not become fruitful by the look of the sage's beauty. He has no tongue, who does not praise the nectar-of-his-marvellous conduct.'

As we have already noticed, there is a

SIṆHALESE SANNA

to this S'ataka. It is used, together with the Text, as a school-book for the instruction of the young in the Buddhist monasteries.† The Translator has neither given his name nor the date of his gloss. It is sufficient to give, as a specimen, the translation of line first in

Verse First.

Laks'mí, s'rikántávage ákarshanayaṭa ; sanvadanan, maṇi-mantrádiyak vẹnivú ; himáns'u, chandrayá há samána ; vadanan, mukha ẹti ; dharma, saddharma nẹmati ; amrita syandanan, amávẹhennávú, etc., etc.

BAUDDHA S'ATAKA

is the common name by which the Bhaktis'ataka is generally known amongst us. It is in Sanskrit verse, and was composed by a Bráhmaṇ of Calcutta converted

---

* Rajo means both 'dust' and 'sin;' and it is used in the latter sense.

† See Sidatsangará, p. 224.

to Buddhism in Ceylon. He was named Mukunda, alias Chandra Bhárati. He presented a copy of his work to the king, Parákkrama Bahu VI. of Cotta, who rewarded him with the honorary title of Bauddhágama Chakravarti.

This work contains 112 s'lokas, of which five have been added by a subsequent writer. The entire book is devoted to the 'Praise of Buddha,' and is written in several metres. There are eleven s'lokas in the S'árdúla-vikríḍita, twelve in the Sragdhará; nine in the S'ikhariṇí; four in the Máliní; fifty-nine in the Pushpitágrá; four in the Vasantatiláká; one in the Dritavilambita; two in the Bhujangaprayáta; two in the Prithví; two in the Ratoddhatá; and one in the Pathyávaktra.

It was printed and published, with its Paraphrase, in 1868 by Frederick Coorey. We select as a specimen the 3rd and 107th s'lokas.

Brahmá'vidyábhibhúto duradhigama mahá
máyayá'lingito savu
Vishṇú rágáti rekún nija vapushi dhritá
Párvatí s'aṅkareṇa
Vítá vidyo vimáyo jagati sa bhagaván
vítarágo munindrah
Kas sevyo buddhi madbhir vadata vadata me
bhrátaras teshu muktyai.

107.

Bhásvad bhánukulámbujanma mihire
rájádhirájes'vare
S'ri Lankádhipatau Parákramabhuje
nítyá mahíns'ásati

Sad Gauḍah kavibháratih kshitisurah
s'ri Ramachandras sudís'
S'rotrúná' makarot sa bhakti-s'atakau
dharmártha mokshappradam.

'Brahmá is overcome by ignorance; the well-known Vishṇu is full of very mysterious deceptions; owing to an excess of lust Parvatí is borne in his own body by Sivá; (but) this Bhagavá, the chief of Munís in the world, is one who is destitute of ignorance, devoid of deceptions, and free from lust. My brethren! say, say, which of these should be adored by the wise to obtain Nirvána.'

'During the equitable reign of Parákramabáhu, king of Lanká, supreme to all emperors, dazzling (in splendour) like a sun on the lotus-of-his-súrya race,—Srí Ráma Chandra, a wise Bráhmaṇ, born in Gauḍa, a very Sarasvatí to poets, composed this Bhakti-s'ataka, which is productive to its hearers, merit, wealth, and Nirvána.'

THE SIṆHALESE SANNA,

or the paraphrase to the above, was by Sumangala, a priest and a pupil of Toṭagamuve Srí Ráhula, who was also preceptor to Chandra. We select the following elegant and beautiful Introduction by the Siṇhalese Translator:—

S'rí maj Jambudvípayehi sakala vidyá nidhánavú Gauḍa des'ayen s'rí lanká-dvípayaṭa pemini tarka vyákaraṇa kávya náṭakádí samasta s'ástrayehi nipuṇa Kátyáyana gotra sambhúta s'rí Ráma Chandra bhárati nam Bráhmaṇa paṇḍito'ttama keṇek, s'rí Sańghabodhi

S'rí Wijayabáhu parivéṇádhipati tripiṭakavágís'vará'chárya s'rí Ráhula sthavirapádayan vahansé keren, tripiṭaka dharmaya asá igeṇa ratnatthaya s'araṇa paráyaṇawa s'ásanábhi prasanna chitta ẹtiva parama vis'uddha s'rardhátís'aya bhaktiyen Bhakti-s'ataka namvú buddhastotraprakaraṇayak karannáhú—'Jñánan yasya samasta vastu vishayan'—yanádín s'lókayan rachanákalo.

'S'rí Rámachandrabhárati, an illustrious Bráhman, born of the family of Kátyáyana, learned in all the rich sciences of Logic, Grammar, Poetry, Music, &c., having arrived in the beautiful Island of Lanká, from the treasury (seat) of all sciences, Gauḍa in the prosperous Jambudvípa, and having inquired and learnt the Tripiṭaka doctrines from the reverend and venerable S'rí Ráhulasthavira—supreme master of the Tripiṭaka doctrines, and Principal of the Temple S'rí Saṅghabodhi S'rí Wijayabáhu—and being (also) greatly pleased in mind (delighted) with the religion (or the doctrines)—hath, with supreme, sincere, and greatly devout faith, paraphrased, "Yñánan yasya samasta vastu vishayan," and other stanzas of the book composed by himself, in praise of Buddha, and called Bhaktis'ataka—a hundred of faith.'*

VRITTA MA'LA'KHYA'

was also written by Chandra Bhárati. It is a work taught to advanced students in the Buddhist monasteries

---

* The printed Edition contains 42 octavo pages.

of Ceylon. The writer devotes the entire work, consisting of 52 stanzas, to the elucidation of Sanskrit metres by examples. Four stanzas embody an invocation to Buddha, and a few introductory remarks have reference to Ceylon, and the reigning Prince Parákkrama. The 5th to the 18th stanza contain particulars regarding the minister Wikrama Sinha-deva of Umagamuva, the father of a celebrated priest named Rammungoda. The 18th to the 23rd give particulars regarding A'bharaṇavatí, the consort of Wikrama Sinha-deva. From thence to the 51st stanza the writer gives the life of Rammungoda, the incumbent of the Galapáta Temple at Bentoṭa. The 52nd alludes to a brother of Rammungoda, who was named Mańgaḷa, and held the office of Sańga-rája.

The metres in this work may be thus tabularized:—

Stanza	1.	...	is in the Pathy'áryá.
	2.	...	A'rya-gíti.
	3.	...	Vaitálíya.
	4.	...	Dakshiṇántiká.
	5...29.		Pathyá vaktra.
	30.	...	Pramáṇiká.
	31.	...	Bhujańga s'is'u bhritá.
	32.	...	Megha-vitána.
	33.	...	Indra-vajrá.
	34.	...	Upendra vajrá.
	35.	...	Upajáti.
	36.	...	Indravans'á.
	37.	...	Manjarikávalí.
	38.	...	Vasantatilaká.
	39.	...	Máliní.

40. ... Váṇiní.
41. ... Prithví.
42. ... Hara-nartaka.
43. ... S'árdúla vikríḍita.
44. .. Mattebha vikríḍita.
45. ... Sragdhará.
46. ... Prabhadraka.
47. ... As'valalita.
48. ... Tanví.
49. ... Kraunchapadá.
50. ... Bhujaṅga-Vijrimbhita.
51. ... Chaṇḍavrishti-prapáta.
52. ... Arna.

The following we select for a specimen:—

2.

Kavayas santi jagatyám
bahavah kavayastu náma te taih kim me
Ye guṇa-dos'a vidhijñá
viralás te sádhavastu sarasáh práyah.

'There are many poets in the world—they are (indeed) called poets! what care I of them? Those who know to discriminate between merits and defects (of poetry) are (alone) the real (poets) who know the niceties of poetry: and they are very rare.'

This work with its Siṇhalese translation (whose author is unknown) has been printed and published by Pandit Baṭuvantudáve, and contains 27 octavo pages.

VRITTA-RATNÁKARA-PAÑCHIKÁ

is another work by the same writer, undertaken and completed at the request of a friend named Subrahmaṇya. It is a commentary on the well known prosodial work called Vritta Ratnákara by Kedárabhaṭṭa, and was written in the year of Buddha 1999, or 1456 A.D. The writer seems to have been ignorant of the Gloss by Divákara. We subjoin the following comment on the 4th and 5th stanzas of the Vritta Ratnákara.*

Iha vritta-ratnákarákkhye s'ástre, tat chhandah kathyate prakás'yate, tat iti kim? Yat laukikam lokeviditam, tat chhandah dvidhá proktam, kena? mátrá varṇa vibhedena, nimeshonmeshábhyám anyatareṇa tulitah kálo mátrá, tasmin kále yo varṇa uchcháriyate sa ekamátrah, tathá choktam.

'Eka mátro bhaveddrasvo dvimátro dírgha uchyate
Trimáttrastu pluto jñeyo vyaunjanan tvardha mátrakam.'

Attra varṇá akárádayah teshám varnánám, mátrábhedena varṇa bhedena cha dviprakáram kathitam it'yarthah, kaih proktam? A'cháryaih, taih kim bhútaih? Piṅgaládibhih, Piṅgalo náma munis'chhandasám ádi kartá ádi s'abdo'tra prakáravachanah, Piṅgalaevádir yeshám S'aitavanága Vardhamána prabritínám—te Piṅgaládayah, iti bahubrihih taih. 2. Pramíyate anene'ti pramáṇam asyachchhandasah etasya chhandas's'ástrasya pramáṇa'mapi parisphuṭam pravyaktam yathá syád vijñeyam,'kriyá-vis'eshaṇánám karmatva'me-

---

* Piṅgaládibhi'rácháryair yaduktan laukikan dvidhá
Mátrá varṇa vibhedena chhandas tadiha kathyate.
Shaḍadhyáya nibaddhasya chhandaso'sya parisphuṭam
Pramáṇam'api vijñeyan shaṭtrins'a dadhikan s'atan.

katvavam napunsakatvañche'ti vacahnát parisphuṭa-s'abdassya karmatvádi siddham, asya kim vis'ishṭasya? Shaḍadhyáya-nibaddhasya addhyáyo granthánám sandhih shaṭ cha te addhyáyásche'ti, shaḍadyáyáh, taih nibaddhasya nis'chitasya kídris'am pramáṇam? S'atam, kim bhútam? Shaṭtrins'a dadhikam, saṭ cha trinsachcha, shaṭtrins'at: athavá, shaṭbhi'radhiká trins'at, shaṭ trins'at, s'ákapárthiváditván maddhyapada lopí samásah tayá shaṭtrins'atá adhikan atiriktam. Etena granthagauravabhírúṇám bálánám pravritti'ratra granthakritá dars'itá.

Ru'pa-Siddhi

is a Páli Grammar on the model of Kachcháyana. It is more lengthy and abstruse than Bálavatára. Its proper designation is Pada-Rúpa-siddhi, 'Etymology of parts of speech.' That it is an ancient work may be gathered from the fact, that it was composed at a time when Buddhism flourished in the (Dakshiná) Dekhan. But the writer is not, as stated by Mr. Turnour, 'the oldest compiler from Kachcháyana;' although he acknowledges that he has 'consulted' Kachcháyana-Vaṇṇanádi in his opening adoration. This we give below, with a translation:—

Kachcháyananchá'chariyan namitvá
nissáya Kachcháyana Vaṇṇaná'din
Bálappabodhattha'mujuṅ karissan
vyattan sukhaṇḍan Pada-rúpa-siddhin.

'Having also bowed to A'chariya Kachcháyana, and having also consulted the Kachcháyana Vaṇṇaná, &c., I shall perspicuously compose Pada-Rúpa-siddhi, distinctly divided into Khaṇḍas, for the instruction of the young.'

At the end of the Rúpa-siddhi the writer gives his name in the following stanza,

Vikkhyátánanda theravhaya vara gurunan
Tambapaṇṇiddhajánan
Sisso Dípankarákkhyo Damiḷavasu matí
dípaladdhappakáso
Báládichchádi vásadvitaya'madhivasán
sásanan jotayí yo
So'yam Buddhappiyavho yati ima'mujukan
Rúpasiddhin akásí.

'This perfect Rúpa-siddhi was composed by the Priest, who received the appellation of Buddhappiya, (and) was named Dípankara,—a disciple of A'nanda, who was an eminent preceptor, like unto a standard (hoisted up) in Tambapaṇṇi (Ceylon), was renowned like a lamp in the Damiḷa country (Chola), was the resident superior (there) of two (monastic) establishments—the Báládichcha, etc.,* and caused the religion of Buddha to shine forth.'

The tradition in the country is, that this Buddhappiya was a native of Ceylon, and that his preceptor, though the head of certain establishments on the continent,

* The other fraternity was, according to the commentator, the Chúḍámáṇikkya.

was nevertheless a teacher renowned in Ceylon. That Buddhist priests from Chola (Tanjore) have visited this island, and have rendered much service to the cause of the established religion in it, we learn from the Maháwansa. For instance, it is expressly stated in that history, that "king Parákrama appointed, as (his) royal preceptor, a very humane Mahá-thera of the country of Chola, accomplished in different languages, logic, and religion; that, having continually heard and studied under him all the Játakas, and having (moreover) committed to memory their significations, (he) thence gradually translated all the five hundred and fifty Játakas from the Páli into the Sinhalese language; and that having thoroughly revised them, after reading the same to (an assembly of) venerable priests, who were masters of the Tepiṭaka, he caused them to be written and published throughout Lanká."* We need not therefore hesitate to credit the tradition above referred to, and give to the writer under review a locus in this island.

Though we have the name, we have nevertheless no means at present of ascertaining the age of the writer.

The Rúpa-siddhi is devoted to seven books, following the order of the subjects treated in Kachcháyana, and including the Uṇádí into the seventh Chapter.

---

* For the Páli text, see Journal of the C. B. Royal Asiatic Society for 1867—70, p. 26.

The sections, however, differ from those given by Kachcháyana. Of them we give the following analysis:—

The work is divided into seven chapters

I.—Sandhi.—Combination.

- i. Saññá—Signs 'Orthoepy.'
- ii. Sara-Sandhi—Combinations of vowels.
- iii. Pakati—Normal state of words where combination is not desirable.
- iv. Vyanjana-Sandhi—Combination of consonants.
- v. Niggahíta—Combination of anusvára.

II.—Na'ma—Declension of Nouns.

- i. Masculine gender.
- ii. Feminine gender (and its formation).
- iii. Neuter gender.
- iv. Pro-nominals (and numerals).
- v. Personal pronouns, devoid of gender.
- vi. Indeclinables (Topachchâyâ'di).
- vii. Inseparable prepositions and particles.

III.—Ka'raka—Syntax.

IV.—Sama'sa.

- i. Avyayí-bháva.
- ii. Kamma-dháraya.
- iii. Digu.
- iv. Tappurisa.
- v. Bahubbíhi.
- vi. Dvanda.

} Compounds. See Wilson's S. Gr. p. 353, *et. seq.*

V.—Tadhita—Nominal Derivatives.

VI.—A'kkhya'ta—Verbs.

VII.—Kitaka, and Uṇádi—Verbal Derivatives and Uṇṇádi.

From the above analysis it would seem that the following account of the work, given by the author himself, is slightly different. He says:—

Tedhá sandhin chatuddhá pada'mapi chatudhá panchadhá-námikañcha

Byásá chhakkárakan chhassamasana'mapi chhabbhedato taddhitañcha

A'khyátam aṭṭhadhá chhabbidha'mapi kitakam pachchayánan pabhedá

Dípenṭí Rúpa-siddhí chira'midha janatábuddhivuddhin karotu.*

MOGGALLÁNA VYÁKARAṆA.

This Páli Grammar belongs to a school different from that of Kachcháyana. The Grammar derives its name from its author, who was named Moggallána, a priest who flourished in the reign of Parákramabáhu I., 1153—1186 A. D., and lived in the Thúpáráma monastery at Anurádhapura.† He was doubtless a distinguished scholar, for he is mentioned in high complimentary terms, not only by Medhankara, the author of the Vinayattha Samuchchaya, but by others, among whom we notice the learned author of the Pañchikápadípa. There are several points of difference between this writer, and those belonging to the schools of Kachcháyana, and the author of the Saddaníti. A

---

* The copy in my possession contains 164 pages of one-and-half feet long, with 8 lines to the page.

† The grammarian is different from the author of the Abhidhánappadípiká, who lived at Jétavana in Polonnaruva.

few examples may suffice:—He disputes the correctness of the Sutta, Akkharápádayo eka chattáḷísan; Kach. lib. 1. sec. 1. § 2., and contends that the Páli alphabet contains forty-three letters including the short *e* (epsilon) and *o* (omicron). With reference to Kachcháyana, lib. 2., and the Sutta—Tayon'eva cha sabbanámehi—'The three [substitutes, áya, á, and e for sa (dat. sing.) smá (abl. sing.), and smin (loc. sing.), which are optionally used after nouns, are never used after Pronouns;' Moggallána denies this, and states that those substitutions do take place, and that he has the authority of Nirutti, and of the language of Buddha, which he quotes as follows:—1. asmá loká *paramhá* cha ubhayá dhansatena ro; 2. *tyá*'han mante paratthaddho; (?) 3. *yáye*'va kho pana'ttháya ágachcheyyátho tamev'atthan sádhukan manasikareyyátho.

Again, where Kachcháyana, in accordance with Sanskrit Grammar, lays down—Yassavá dátukámo rochate dhárayate tam sampadánan—that which expresses a wish to give, that which pleases, or holds, takes a Dative case—Moggallána takes exception to the Rule and states, that though words of giving, govern a Dative; and though the forms of the two cases are identical, yet words expressing 'pleasure' and 'holding' govern a Genitive, *e. g.*, má áyasmantánan'pi sanghabhedo ruchchittha; rañño satan dháreti; rañño chhattan dháreti.

This work contains six Chapters. The first explains his terminology, and treats briefly on Sandhi 'Combination,' the second on Siyádi 'Declension'; the third on Samása

'Compounds,' the fourth on Nádi,' Nominal derivatives,' the fifth on Khádi, 'Derivative verbs, and Verbal derivatives,' and the sixth on Tyádi or verbs.*

As a specimen we present the following :—

INTRODUCTION.

Siddha 'middha gunam sádhu, namassitvá Tathágatam
Saddhamma Sańgham bhásissan Mágadhan Sadda lakkhanam.

CONCLUSION.

Yassa raññο pabhávena bhávitattasamákulam
Aná 'kulan duladdhíhi pápa bhikkhúhi sabbaso.
Lańkáya munirájassa sásanam sádhu saṇṭhitam
Puṇṇachandasamáyogá váridhí'va vivaddhate.
Parakkamabhuje tasmin saddhábuddhiguṇodite
Manuvansaddhajákáre Lańkádípan pasásati.
Moggallánena therena dhímatá suchivuttiná
Rachitan yam suviññeyya 'masandiddha 'manákulam.
Asesavisayavyápi jinavyappathanissayam
Sadda sattha 'manáyása sádhíyam buddhi vaddhanam.
Tassa vutti samásena vipulatthappakásiní
Rachitá puna ten'eva sásanujjota kariná.

1. 'After appropriately bowing unto Buddha, who has achieved [his own] status, and [also after bowing unto] dhamma and sańgha, I shall declare the Grammar† of the Mágadhí.

2. 'When the monarch Parakkama, like a banner to the solar-race, and distinguished for the virtues of

---

* The entire work contains six bhánavâras, and is written on 103 palm-leaf pages of 20 inches in length, with 8 lines to a page.

† Sadda lakkhana "Forms of Words;" but these words are used to denote—Verbal science, Grammar, or Philology.

faith and wisdom, was ruling in the Lanká-dípa; and (when) by his prestige the church of the king of Munis, which is well established in Lanká, and which is entirely composed of those who have achieved dhyána, etc.,* and is wholly destitute of heretical sinful bhikkhus, has shone forth like the ocean by the contact of the rays of the full-moon; [this] Sadda-Sattha [work on verbal science], which is understood with facility, acquired without labour, and calculated to promote wisdom; and which is free from (ambiguity) doubt, is plain and [pervades] is applicable to all the [grammatical] studies, sanctioned by the usage of Buddha's language, has been composed by the wise, and well-conducted Moggallána thera. Again, its Vutti, explanatory of the broad sense [of the Suttáni], has been briefly composed by himself, who is a distinguished member of the church.'

VUTTODAYA

is, so far as we have yet ascertained, the only Páli work now extant, on Páli Prosody. It is partly in verse, and partly in prose; and the first and last chapters are entirely in verse. It is evidently composed on the basis of previous Sanskrit works on the same subject. Its terminology, too, is entirely that of Sanskrit writers. Entire passages are taken from Piṅgala, to whom the Vuttodaya also refers by name.

---

* Or, rather uttari manussa dhamma 'super-human power;' see Vinaya Piṭaka, lib. 4. sec. i.

The adaptation of the Sanskrit rules into the Páli may be exhibited, thus; *e. g.*

San:—Vritta Ratnákara.

Na na ma ya yayuteyam Máliní bhogilokaih.

Páli—Vuttodaya.

Na na ma ya yayutáyam Máliní bhogisíhí.

The writer himself explains the plan of the work in the introductory part of his first chapter, which we subjoin.

Nam'atthu janasantánatamasantána bhedino
Dhammujjalantaruchino munindodátarochino
Pingaláchariyádíhi chhandanyam'uditam purá
Suddhamágadhikánan tan na sádheti yathichchhitam.
Tato Mágadhabhásáya mattávaṇṇavibhedanan
Lakkhalakkhaṇa samyuttan pasannatthapadakkamam
Idam Vuttodayan náma lokiyachchhandanissitam
A'rabhissa'mahan dáni tesam sukhavibuddhiyá.

'Be obeisance to the moon-like chief of Munis, who dazzles in the luminous rays of the Dhamma, and who destroys the dense darkness in the mind of man.

'The works on Prosody, composed afore by Pingala A'chariya and others, are not such as to afford satisfaction to those who study the pure Mágadhí. Therefore, for their easy comprehension, do I now commence, in the Mágadhí language, this which is named Vuttodaya, applicable to popular poetical metres, distinguished into the different (metres of) Mattá and Vaṇṇa, composed in language, pleasing, and (abounding) in sense, and embodying [at once]* both rule and example.

* Vide supra, Rule on the metre Máliní.

The entire work is divided into six chapters. The first treats of the eight prosodial feet, and of technical terms; the second is on Mattá metre, or poetry measured by the number of syllabic instants, without reference to prosodial feet; the third on Sama-vutta, or poetry, of which every line is alike; the fourth and fifth on Addha-samavutta, or poetry, where every half-gáthá is alike, and on Visama vutta, or poetry where the four pádá of a gáthá are not equal; and the sixth on the chap-pachchayá, 'six kinds of knowledge,' having reference to patthára, (1) symbolical 'spreading of the rythm;' Naṭṭha (2) 'the finding out of a forgotten metre;' uddiṭṭha (3) 'ascertaining the number of the tune of a given piece of poetry;' lagakriyá (4) 'the finding out of laghu and garu syllabic instants;' sankháṇa (5) 'enumeration of the number of tunes in a class;' and addha-yoga, (6) 'the measurement of the space necessary for spreading the symbols of rythm.'

The writer concludes the work with his own name, Sangharákkhita Thera; but the date is not given.*

JÁNAKI'HARAṆA

is a very ancient, and very interesting Sanskrit poem. A Siṇhalese sanna, or literal translation of it alone has yet been discovered. It is however possible that

---

* Mr. Childers has given a more lengthy description of this work in his Khuddaka Páṭha, p. 22. et seq.

the original work may still be found in some nook of an old monastic library.

Like all Siṇhalese sannas this translation quotes the words of the original in their integrity, and it is therefore not impossible to restore the words into their original poetical form; though, we confess, the MS. in our possession requires much correction, after comparison with other copies, which we hope may yet be found. But its restoration into metre is undoubtedly a very arduous work. Considering, however, that this poem, according to the opinion of the learned in Ceylon, is "not inferior to the works of Kálidása," the Indian Shakspeare, and that it may be ranked amongst the "Mahá Kavu" or "great poems," it may be well worth the trouble of some oriental scholar in Europe to undertake the work of restoration.

The original work was, as stated in the Sanna, composed by Kumáradása, or Kumára Dhátu sena, one of the celebrated Siṇhalese kings, who reigned between 513—522 A.D. It is not only expressly stated in the Sanna that he was the author, but there are other authorities who ascribe its authorship to him. The Pẹrakumbá Sirita thus notices both author and work:—

'King Kumáradás, who on the very same day celebrated a three-fold feast in honor of the inauguration of the Queen-Consort, the installation into office of a number of priests, and the founding of 18 temples and 18 tanks; and who in masterly and elegant strains composed Jánakíharana and other [mahá kavu] great poems, offered his life for the poet Kálidása.'*

The Mahávansa thus notices the acts of this celebrated Prince:—

Tass'achchaye Kumárádí Dhátuseno'ti vissuto
Ahú tassa suto rájá deva-rúpo mahá-balo
Káritepituná'kási viháre nava kammakam
Káretvá dhamma Sangítin parisodhesi sásanam
Santappesi mahá sanghan pachchayehi chatuhi'pi
Katvá puññáni'nekáni navame háyane'tigá.

'After his (Moggalana's) demise, his son, who was known as Kumára Dhátusena, (both) mighty and godlike, became king. He repaired the temple which had been built by his father, held a convocation of [Dhamma] the Bauddha Scriptures, and purified the religion. He pleased the priesthood with the four pachchayá; and, having done many meritorious actions, passed away in the ninth year.'

I am indebted to my pandit for the ten following s'lokas which he has restored to the original rythm. To them I add my own translation, as well as a specimen of the literal translation, or the sanna, of the first verse of the reclaimed s'lokas.

---

* For particulars regarding this tradition the reader is referred to the Sidatsangará, p. cliii. et seq., where too, the original of the above from Pęrakumbá Sirita is given. The Kálidása here mentioned was not the poet of that name known as the "Indian Shakspeare."

Chap. IX.

Iti mese, *sukhena* suvayen, *pravritasya* pẹvẹttávú, *sutasya* putrayáhaṭa, *keshuchit más'esu gateshu* [satsu] kípa másayak giya kalhi, *sa-bhúpatih* é Das'aratha tema, *itarat sutánántrayam* anik putrayan tundená, *vanitá-parigrahaih* añganávange pánigrahayen samarpya yodá, *puram* purayaṭa, *pratasthe* giye.

1. Iti pravrittasya sutasya keshuchit
Gateshu máseshu sukhena bhúpatih
Trayam sutánám'itarat samarpya sah
Puram pratasthe vanitáparigrahaih.

2. Nitambabháreṇa cha s'okasampadá
Bhuvahsutá mantharavikramá pituh
Tatána pádáv'udabindubhir dris'or—
Upetya patyá'bhimukhí pravrittaye.

3. Gurustato'sau guṇapaksha vartiním
Matim samálambya guṇaih puraskritán
Apatyakán sádhu giram garíyasím
Jagau satíná'muchitavratás'rayán.

4. Paran prakarshó vapushah samunnatir
Guṇasya tátó nripatirvayo navam
Iti sma má mánini mána'mágamáh
Patiprasádonnatayo hi yoshitah.

5. Striyo na pumsá'mudayasya sádhanan
Taeva taddhámavibhútihetavah
Taḍidviyuktó'pi ghanah prajrimbhate
Viná na megham vilasanti vidyutah.

6. Giro'krithá má purushártadípanír
Gatá'pi bharttre parikopa'máyatam
Kulastriyo bhartrijanasya bhartsane
Vadanti maunam paramam prasádhanam.

7. Pativritá vasya'mavasya'mañganá
Karoti s'ílena guṇasprihampatim
Vinashṭacháritraguṇá guṇaishiṇah
Parábhavam bhartturupaiti dustaram

8. Alan tvayi vyáhritivistareṇa me
S'rutim prayátañ charitan tvadásrayam
Na dírayed yaj jarasai'va jarjaram
Sahasradhe'dan hridayañ kurushva tat.

9. Ayan tvade'kapravaṇo manoratho
Vrithá'dya daivádapináma no bhavet
Iti pravaktur vachanáni manyuná
Nigrihya kaṇṭhe jarato nirásire

10. Udagrabhásah s'ikhayá s'ikhámaṇeh
Srajá cha dhammilla kiríṭa dashṭayá
Pramrijya pádau Janakasya jampatí
Kshayád'ayátám'athalambhitás'ishau.

1. When thus, the son (Ráma), had happily passed several months, that monarch [Dasaratha] started for the city, having concluded marriages for his remaining three sons.

2. The princess, with her husband, entering upon her journey, and slowly moving, owing to the languor* of her limbs, and the sorrow (of separation), covered her sire's feet with the tears of her eyes.

---

* Lit. 'weight.'

3. Then this parent, depending on his notions of social wisdom, gracefully addressed his virtuous daughter in language powerful, and indicative of courses of chastity, (thus):—

4. Honorable woman! do not be arrogant (thinking) of the high accomplishments of thy person, thy transcendent virtues, and that thy father is king, and that thou art youthful in age; for, women's happiness consists in the very love of their husbands.

5. Women are not the source of the accomplishment of their husbands' prosperity, but the very husbands are the cause of their wives' dignified and happy status: for, a rain-cloud, even in the absence of lightning, is distinctly visible; but shafts of lightning never shine without a rain-cloud.

6. Though thou mayest be greatly wroth with thy husband, do not use language unbecoming thy sex*; for, ladies say, that when husbands reprove (their wives) silence is the highest means of pacification.

7. A woman devoted to her husband, by her chastity, verily charms† a good husband: a woman (on the other hand) who has abandoned a virtuous life, incurs the irredeemable displeasure of a virtue-loving husband.

8. It is unnecessary that I should enlarge on the topic of my discourse concerning thee. Do thou pursue that conduct, which, when it reaches this old

* Lit. 'masculine language.'

† Vasyan karoti—charms, conciliates.

and infirm heart (of mine) shall not rend it in a thousand ways.

9. Well would it (indeed) be, if this one urgent desire of (my) heart concerning thee, do not hence, fortunately, prove to be in vain. The words thus spoken by the old man, died away, choked in the throat by sorrow.

10. Thereafter, the wedded couple, having kissed (swept) the feet of Janaka with the top of the highly lustrous gem-studded chaplet [of the one], and with the garland-encircling coronal head-knot [of the other], went away, blessed, from home.

In the book* which we have discovered, there are only fifteen chapters; and the last chapter is called the twenty-fifth. Poems which were anciently designated "mahá kavu," seldom fell short of twenty or twenty-five chapters. There is moreover a want of continuity in the narrative. Each chapter, except the last which is very short, contains on an average eighty s'lokas. The first chapter treats of the history of Dasaratha; the second, of the visit of Indra, and other gods, to Vishnu in the Nága-loka, after they were defeated by Rávaṇá, and Vishnu's promise to be born in the human world; the third is on Ritu Varṇaná; the fourth, on the worship of Agni, and the birth of Ráma in the womb of Kausalyá, the Queen of Dasaratha—his education—his departure with Lakshmana on the application

---

* The copy in our possession contains 101 palm-leaves, of 18 inches in length, with 8 lines to the page.

of Vas'ishṭha to fight with Rákshasas, etc.; the fifth gives a description of, and particulars connected with, the jungle-residence of Vas'ishṭha; the sixth treats of the departure of Ráma, etc., to Mithilá, where a marriage was concluded for him; the arrival there of Dasaratha etc.; the seventh, on Ráma's marriage with Sítá, the daughter of king Janaka; the eighth treats of their honey-moon; the ninth, the departure of Dasaratha and the new-married couple to Ayodhya—the battles fought during their journey, etc.; the tenth relates the circumstances attending Ráma's expulsion by the infirm Dasaratha, owing to the application for the throne by Kaikei for her own son, the invitation by Baratha to Ráma, and the abduction of Sítá by Rávaṇá; the eleventh contains the fight between Garuḍa and Rávaṇá to prevent Sítá being carried away, the death of Garuḍa, the flight of Rávaṇá with Sítá to Lanká, and the acts of Ráma in connection with the battle of Sugríva and Váli; the twelfth gives a description of Sarat Varṇná or Autumn, and Sugríva's visit to Ráma; the thirteenth records Ráma's lament for the loss of Sítá, gives a description of Varshá, or the rainy season, Sugríva's attempt at consoling Ráma, etc.; the fourteenth mentions the construction of Adam's bridge; and the fifteenth (which is called the twenty-fifth, and which is evidently deficient in matter) gives a glowing picture of (the blessings of) Peace, as opposed to (the ravages of) War; which is introduced as a message sent by Ráma to Rávaṇá.

THE KÁVIYASÉKARA

is one of several valuable Siŋhalese poetical works by a priest generally known as Toṭagamuvé Srí Ráhula. He is said to have been the grand-pupil of Uttra múla. Beyond this nothing is known of either his parentage, or early history, though a tradition represents him as a natural, or an adopted son of Parákkrama Báhu VI. of Cotta, in whose reign he flourished, and that he commenced to write poetry from his early youth. There is no doubt 'he was born a poet'; and in the language of poetry it may be said of him, as of Pindar, that, 'when he lay in his cradle'

'The bees swarmed about his mouth.'

He was unquestionably

'The bard that first *adorn'd* our native tongue.'

There are few authors whose works are regarded by us with greater veneration than those of the Principal of the ancient College of Wijébáhu. It is of him that the poet of Mulgirigala has sung,

"In Wijayabáhu, oh bird! the priest supreme behold,
Whose master-mind the Piṭakas like golden chains enfold;
Whose lyre six languages adorns; who still in each doth shine
As shone in perfect beauty Kanda Kumára divine,—
His presence enter'd, say, thou dost a treasured letter bear,
Whose words the weal of Indra-like Prince Sapumal declare."

W. S.

In correctness of versification, in the splendour of his diction, and in the originality of his thoughts, few Siŋhalese poets have excelled him. He stands foremost amongst all our poets, as one who revived the dying literature of the land, and who gave a new tone to Siŋhalese poetry, which was fast declining in the early part of the fifteenth century. His writings present correct models for imitation. When the Grammar of the Siŋhalese is silent on any point, they frequently furnish us with the rule. When philologers differ as to the force or meaning of a Siŋhalese word, a reference to his works often enables them to settle their difficulties. Where versification is pronounced to be at fault, to the final arbitration of his poetry do the disputants generally refer their differences. Where again, students are in search of an elegant trope, metaphor, or simile, the inexhaustible treasures of the Káviyasékara, the Paravi-Sandésa, and the Sẹlalihini Sandésa supply the desired examples. There is indeed such an irresistible fascination in his language, and such a magic influence does his poetry exercise on the soul, that his readers cannot fail to be conscious of what Horace says,—

> .... 'Meum qui pectus inaniter angit,
> Irritat, mulcet, falsis terroribus implet
> Ut magus.'

Srí Ráhula of Toṭagamuva had a very retentive memory, and could repeat a considerable number of verses after hearing or reading them but once. He became master of every kind of learning which he chose to profess. As Johnson said of Goldsmith, he never touched a subject which he did not adorn. He possessed a correct acquaintance with several oriental languages besides the Siṇhalese—a fact which establishes the truth of what Sir W. Jones says, in his works, vol. ii. p. 317—that "a sublime poet may become a master of any kind of learning which he chooses to profess, since a fine imagination, a lively wit, an easy and copious style, cannot possibly obstruct the acquisition of any science whatever, but must necessarily assist him in his studies and shorten his labours." Gifted with these faculties Toṭagamuva did not fail to establish in his own times that literary renown for which his memory has been since distinguished. The foreign languages, of which he was a proficient, are enumerated in the paraphrase to his Sẹlalihini Sandésa. They were six in number; viz. Sanskrit, Mágadhí (or Páli), Apabbransa, Paisáchí, Saurasena, and Tamil. He was ṭhence called, " Shaḍ-bháshápárameshwara."*

Toṭagamuva was a great favourite of Parákkrama Báhu; and, it is believed, that, as he was fostered in the king's household previous to his taking holy orders, so he continued after that event to benefit by the patronage of his royal master. Nor was he ungrateful to his benefactor. Of his devotion to Parákkrama and the royal family, his writings contain many tokens. The king inspired some of his best and most melodious strains. He gave to him the most invaluable token of his regard, the use of his pen; and dedicated besides his Káviyasékara (a poetical version, in 885 stanzas, of

* "Chief [linguist], acquainted with six languages."

one of the incarnations of Buddha, called the Sénaka Játaka) to the Princess-Royal, Ulakudá Déwí, at whose request it was composed. This work—"a garland of flowers on the crown of poetry,"—has been scarcely surpassed by any other in respect of originality, depth of thought, elegance, and correctness of expression. Like Milton's Paradise Lost, "it stands on a height by itself." And of its author it might well be said, what a critic says of Milton—"He cannot want the praise of copiousness and vivacity. He was master of his language in its full extent, and has used the melodious words with such diligence, that from his book alone the art of poetry might be learned." No Siṇhalese scholar reads it, much less hears its name pronounced, without mingled feelings of esteem and veneration. Its style is elaborate and energetic; and its versification correct, smooth, and elegant. We must however state it as our opinion, that in some parts it is inferior in imagery to the Kavu-Silumina.

A deficiency of the Páli and Sanskrit classics may be supplied by a close study of Káviyasékara; and, if one thoroughly understands that work, he may be considered as being possessed of a pretty good acquaintance with the Siṇhalese language. This forms the last of the last series of books in a course of reading prescribed by several pandits to scholars advanced in the study of the Siṇhalese.

It is an admitted fact, that poets of all countries and at all times have been vastly vain of their learning. Even such great characters as Sir Walter Scott and

Milton, are by no means free from unnecessary ostentation of learning. Addison says of the latter, that "he seems ambitious of discovering, by his excursions on free-will and predestination, and his many glances upon History, Astronomy, Geography, and the like, as well as by the terms and phrases he sometimes makes use of, that he was acquainted with the whole circle of arts and sciences." Indian poets, in reference to their knowledge of the Sanskrit, to which is ascribed a divine origin, have called themselves "gods on earth;" and similarly Toṭagamuva compared himself to Brahaspati;* and, with the arrogance of an Ovid when he said—

'Jamque opus exegi; quod me Jovis ira, me ignis
Nec poterit ferem, nec edax rectustas;'—

and with the self-complacency of a host of Indian and Siṃhalese writers, he speaks of himself in the following strain:—

"Attain'd to fullest knowledge of every science known,
In every holy duty to pure perfection grown,
Like to a Brahaspati am I upon this earth,
The gem borne in the chaplets that crown the wide world's worth."

W. S.

---

* Brahaspati—the teacher of the Hindu gods—is often designated by a term supposed to be its equivalent, Jupiter. But this we believe is incorrect, since the one has nothing in common with the other. The Grecian Zeus or the Roman Jupiter is more like Brahama in one sense, and like Indra in another. He is the Sire of gods and men; also the 'Thunderer.'

The Káviyasékara is a work which cost the poet years of great labour, although judging from its easy and unlaboured style we are almost led to disbelieve the writer's own account of it, viz., that it was commenced A.B. 1958 or A.D. 1415, and was concluded in the 34th year of the reign of Prákkrama Bahu VI., who ascended the throne A.B. 1953 or A.D. 1410. We select the following as a specimen of the writer's language.

1. Piya Bamunu so(n)davá
Neti nena kandulu ra(n)davá
Duva langaṭa kẹ(n)davá
Mesé avaváda kí so(n)davá.

2. Nokiyá siya himiṭa
Nẹtivada uturusalupaṭa
Gaman ikmankoṭa
Noyan nuba vasana gen piṭataṭa.

---

1. "The Brahman her good father
Then said, restrain'd his tears,
Now learn from me, lov'd daughter,
What most a wife endears.

2. Without your husband's knowledge
Leave not his house, your home;
Nor vagrant gadding, venture
Unshawl'd abroad to roam.

---

* *Lit.*—1. 'The Bráhman (her) good father, having restrained the tears that flowed from his eyes, called his daughter near, and advised her as follows:—2. Go not out of your residence, either without informing your husband, or without covering yourself

3. Mahaluvada Sama-nana
Ẹra noyeka sesu pirimina
Samaga siṭa eka tẹna
Katá nokarava nurá tepulina.

4. Pekaniya nodakvá
Salu e(n)da bolaṭa dakvú
Nopava tana sakvá
Siná nomasen dasan dakvá.

5. Himi nẹ́ haṭada guru
Pavatuva lesin mehekaru
Sẹtirin avẹḍakaru
Karava yehelin lesin piyakaru.

---

3. Though aged be your consort,
In privacy alone,
With other males, no converse
Hold of an amorous tone.

4. In dress, waist, ancle, ever
And bosom fair, conceal;
And when inclined to laughter
Do not your teeth reveal.

5. Serve readily your husband,
His parents, kith and kin;
The women-folk, when spiteful,
As friends most cherish'd, win.

---

with a shawl, or in haste (i.e. quickly walking.)—3. Although your consort is old, stand not in one place, and hold converse of love with other males, who are many.—4. Dress your garment abovẹ the navel, so as to reach the ancle bone, and without exposing the fair bosom: and expose not your teeth in laughing (or laugh not so as to expose your teeth.)—5. Be like a servant to your husband, his relations, and parents; and befriend inimical bad

6. Ẹta mehekaru daná·
Pavatu duka sẹpa samaná
Sẹpata ẹta vi(n)diná
Garuva madakut noveva nomaná.

7. Abisaru liya tẹpala
Sera vesi dẹsi nala(m)ba kala
Malkaru ridí kala
Saba(n)da nokarava sitaṭa topakula.

8. Iṅguru duru ẹ́yutu
Malgomuhá vẹvú vatu
Gava mí tamá natu
Dasun pilivisa balava ẹti tatu.

---

6. Your servants treat with kindness
Alike in weal or woe ;
In happiness unduly
No proud elation shew.

7. Yet race, and rank and station,
Regard with honor meet ;
Disreputable females,
In friendly terms ne'er greet.

8. Your gardens, herds, and cattle,
Your herbs, fruits, flow'rs, inspect ;
Inquiries make, and careful
All negligence correct.

---

women, as your intimate female associates.—6. If you have servants treat them equally in prosperity and adversity; and if you enjoy happiness be not at all elated.—7. If you love your honor (race), be not friendly with loose, dissolute women, or with knavish, whorish, slavish, nauchi, flower, or dhoby girls.--8. See (for thy self,) after inquiry from thy servants, the actual condition of your clean cattle, buffaloes, the planted gardens, containing

9. Iru gilena davasé
Gahaná depódavasé
Sa(n)da sikuru davasé
Gomin piribaḍa ganuvȧ nivesé.

10. Niti gé dora ẹmada
Kẹli kasala dẹka noma i(n)da
Udẹ́sana savasada
Pahan dalvava vimana novarada.

11. Navaham mẹdindina
Pẹminena mẹdí pohodina
Edavas udẹ́sana
Gedevi puda bat-pahan suva(n)dina.

---

9. On each fresh asterism,
Eclipse, new moon and full,
On Mondays, Fridays, house-floors
With cleansing cow-dung cool.

10. No dirt about your dwelling
Nor filth endure to see ;
Each morning and each evening
Let lights there burning be.

11. Each full-moon day in Navan*
And Mẹdindina,† wake
At dawn, gifts, incense, off'rings,
Thy household-gods to make.

---

flower bushes, ginger, cumin, etc.—9. On the day when the sun enters a new asterism, on the day on which an eclipse takes place, on the full moon and new-moon days, on Monday and on Friday, daub (the floor of) thy residence with cow-dung.—10. Seeing dirt and filth, suffer not the same to be; but constantly clean your house; yea, morning and evening do thou without fail burn a light.—11. Early on the mornings of the full-moon day in

* Month answering from January 13th to February 11th.
† February 11th to March 12th.

12. Himi gamanak gosin
Geṭa ú kalaṭa satosin
Noçṇa vá dásin
Nṇbama payasódavan vesesin.

13. Dorakaḍa rẹkasiṭum
Uyan vatuvala ẹvidum
Mehevaraṭa mẹlikam
Nokara mé kí siyalu notaram

14. Nokaratat viyadam
Karatat itá viyadam
Kiyamin ẹti padam
Rahasa danvan himiṭa karapem.

---

12. When travel-worn thy husband
Comes home with wearied feet ;
Thy maidens stay—to wash them
Be thine the office meet.

13. Be not at doors a watcher
Nor pleasure grounds frequent ;
Nor set unto the household
Example indolent.

14. Extravagant or niggard
If such thy husband prove,
With gentle speech in private
Seek kindly him to move.

Navam and Mẹdindina, make oblations of food, light and scents to the household gods.—12. When thy husband has returned home after a journey, order not thy maidens, but do thou thyself wash his feet.—13. Be not guilty of watching at the door, of walking in pleasure grounds; and be not lazy to (household) work. 14. Whether thy husband spends too much, or does not spend at all, speak to him kindly and privately, informing him (of the fact), and

15. Geyi ẹti noyekabaḍu
Dakimin niti nokara aḍu
Daruvan haṭada vẹḍu
Noden nokiyá yali nodẹnapuḍu

16. Tamá himi situ lesa
Duṭuvot venata senehasa
Nuvan ka(n)dulen misa
Yalit nokiyan basin pilivisa.

17. Himihaṭa ita kẹmati
Dena batmálu ẹ́ niti
Pisa kavamin kẹmati
Dakin duk sẹpa mavaka sé iti.

---

15. Thy goods preserve, nor 'minish
Without thy husband's ken;
Not measureless to children
Give, e'en though they be men.

16. If from thee to another
Thy husband's love should stray,
In bitter haste reproach not,
Tears best the heart then sway.

17. The food he most delights in,
Which chief prefers, provide;
For him as mother caring,
Though good, though ill betide.

---

stating the actual state [of funds].—15. Preserve, without diminution, the various things in the house; and give not even to grown-up children without informing (of it to thy husband), and without measure.—16. If thou seest thy husband form an attachment to another, speak not [to him on the subject], except after inquiry, and except in tears.—17. Feed thy dear husband with the rice and curry which he ever likes; and thus be to him a mother

18. Himi vetaṭa yana kala
Abarana suva(n)da manakala
Paṭapiliyen udula
Yạnna sẹrasí lesin Siri kala.

19. Pẹminenakala yahana
So(n)da mudu sihin saluvena
Giv kan abaraṇina
Malin suva(n)diu sẹdeva risivana.

20. Hevapasukoṭa ẹmaṭa
Aluyama palamunẹgisiṭa
Himi pubudina kalaṭa
La(ń)gama siṭinéya rẹkavalkoṭa.

---

18. When thou to him approachest
  Bedeck thyself with care,
Clad in thy silks, and perfumed
  Like Lakshmí, goddess fair.

19. So when his bed thou seekest
  Soft be thy garb and fine;
Thy neck and ears be jewell'd,
  Sweet flowers thy locks entwine.

20. To rest, to sleep, the latest,
  Be first at dawn to rise,
That when thy husband wakens
  Thy 'tendance he may prize.

---

in both adversity and prosperity.—18. When thou approachest thy husband, go delightfully dressed and perfumed; and decked in silks, like Lakshmí.—19. When thou goest to bed, be delightfully attired in fine soft garments, with ear and neck ornaments, and decked in flowers and perfumes.—20. Go to rest after all (others); be first to rise at dawn; and at the time thy husband

21. Matut dęna vanavęḍa
Dęnagaṇa noví aḍudaḍa
Nokoṭa senehasa kaḍa
Yamak nokaran himin atmeḍa.

22. Himi uvada uraná
Nokiyá tepul daruná
Vaḍava sita karuná
Velit nosiṭava detęnasaraná.

23. Piya Bamunu sakasá
Ová bas dí melesá
Si(m)ba duvage sirasá
Yanṭa kí himisamaga nolasá.

---

21. The present and the future
Regarding, let thy love
Be studious thy husband
To please all else above.

22. If anger'd, him provoke not,
Nor for fresh marriage sigh,
But ever with affection
Strive love to intensify.—

23. The Brahman his sage counsels
Thus giv'n, with yearning heart
His daughter kiss'd, and bade her
Thence with her lord depart."

W. S.

---

awakes be thou on attendance upon him.—21. Having regard to the present and future happiness, be not confused (in your acts); and, not wanting in thy love to thy husband, do nothing that is distasteful to him.—22. Even if thy husband be angry, do not use harsh expressions, but rather promote feelings of affection; and think not of a second marriage.—23. The Bráhman, her father, having thus advised, and having kissed his daughter's head, desired her to depart with her husband.'

THE SẸLALIHIṆI SANDÉSA,

'The Sẹla*-Messenger,' is another of Toṭagamuva's celebrated works. Well indeed may it be compared to the Megha Dúta of Kalidása. The writer's thoughts, brilliant and original, sparkle as we go along his elegant and flowing rhymes. His language is free and fascinating; his illustrations are original and lively; and his versification unexceptionable.

Toṭagamuva undertook this work with grateful affection for the king and his country. He felt interested in the welfare of the young family of Parákkrama Báhu, and sympathised with the Princess Ulakuḍá, who pined for want of a son and heir. It is a Message to Vibíshana, the presiding deity of the Kẹlani temple, invoking the blessing of a grandson to the king, or rather a son to the princess.

The poem consists of 107 stanzas. The first four (called sẹ̀heli) are introductory, and are addressed to

* "The Sarica (Gracula Religiosa) is a small bird better known by the name of Mina. It is represented as a female; while the Parrot is described as a male bird; and as these two have in all Hindu tales the faculty of human speech, they are constantly introduced, the one inveighing against the faults of the male sex, and the other exposing the defects of the female."—Megha Dúta, pp. 92-93.

the Messenger. We give them below as a specimen.*

1. Sẹrada sulakaḷa kuru-miyuru tepulen ra(n)daná
Raja kula rahasẹ mẹtiniya-siyanchi Sẹlalihiṇi sa(n)da.

2. Pulmal kesaru men ranwaṇi tela saraṇa yuga
Sapu mal kẹnew tuḍa mada ratini manahara.
Nilupul delew samawaṇi piya piya patara
Malin kaḷa rúvew ebẹwin nubin ena wara.

Nilúda lada Sida(m)buwo digu waraḷẹ nilu
Nilúdawaṭa bi(n)gu peḷa ada ta(m)bara nilu.

---

1. "Hail Sarica, high gifted! endow'd like sages wise
Whose bosoms hold state secrets, with whom crown'd heads [advise!
Thy words, in tones that ravish, sweet music's notes excel:
Amongst thy kin beloved, long, long, oh may'st thou dwell!

2. Fair bird! whose limbs, gold-colour'd, in lustrous tint compare
With pollen full-blown flowers in beauteous corols bear;
Whose glittering beak is ruddy as champak blossoms red;
Whose wings, dark blue and glossy, like upul petals spread;—
When like a flow'r-clad fairy thou dartedst through the sky,
Did not, to meet thee, swiftly, the youthful Siddhas fly,

---

* *Lit.*—1. O Sarica! in wisdom equal to that of ministers of Princes—and of speech sweet, and composed of excellent notes, mayest thou in the company of thy species live long!—2. When thou, whose (two) feet are of golden hue, like unto the pollen of a full-blown blossom, whose partially red and glistening beak is like unto a cluster of champaka flowers, and whose black and delightfully wide-spread wings are like unto the leaves of the blue lotus;—(when thou) takest thy airy flight like a flowery figure, have not youthful goddesses worn thee on their long jet-black hair? Have not swarms of bees, which make the lotuses their habitation, approached, and encircled thee? Have not the god-

Wanadew liyó nokaḷoda sawaṇa ambaraṇa
Ena maga dukek nowída saba(n)dini kalana
Senchasa bẹndunu ṭena noharina karọ diwuṇa
Wena ṣẹpa kumaṭa topa dakiná ema pamaṇa.

3. Lapa noma wan sa(n)da men somi guṇa gibiṇí
Opa wẹḍi gata helmẹli siwmẹli pẹmiṇí
Sẹpa siri dena wẹni rasa basẹti situminí
Topa dẹkumen apa pinkala bawa dẹnuṇí.

Place thee their flowing tresses, their jetty locks among,
While bees from lotus dwellings around in circles hung?—
Say, has no forest goddess of thee an ear-drop made,—
No hindrances or mishaps thee on thy way delay'd?—
Ah, happy one! whose friendship, tried by whatever tests,
Where once 'tis placed is rooted, there grows, there ever rests,
Let those who list, enjoyments in other pleasures own,
For us, blest with thy presence, no greater joy is known.

3. And since in thee dwell virtues as with the moon dwells light,
And delicate and spotless as water-lily white
Appears thy graceful body, while thy sweet-sounding voice
Is like the chintámani, that makes the heart rejoice,
That brings its blest possessor each long'd-for boon of wealth
Or whatsoe'er he wishes of happiness or health:—
A consciousness thou bring'st us, in former births our life
Was one of merits fruitful, with righteous deeds was rife.

---

desses of the forest made thee their ear-ornaments? Has no (other) ill befallen thee in thy journey? Happy friend, who possessest inviolate and with increasing vigour, any attachment which thou mayest form! What is bliss save that which is known in thy presence!—3. When we behold thee, who art equal to a spotless moon, full of (goodness) brilliancy, of an exceedingly smooth body like a delicate white lotus, of sweet speech; and like unto a situmini gem, which produces (bestows) wished-for health

4. Mituru tumó duk sẹpa dẹkehima pẹwatí
Bitu situyam rú men piṭu nopáwití
Yutu matu wẹḍa matepala ewẹni guṇa ẹti
Situ natukarẹ asa yahaluwa waḍana rutí.

---

4. Like pictures on walls painted so fix'd true friends remain;
To turn their backs they cannot, nor can their friendship wane;
Alike amid reverses or fortune's fav'ring smiles,
Hearts still to hearts united, nor look nor thought beguiles;—
Such to the core thee knowing, unto my words, oh friend!
Much future good involving, with heedful care attend."

W. S.

Stanzas 5 to 51 are occupied with graphic descriptions of Kóṭṭa, its busy streets, palaces and temples; the intervening scenery between it and Kẹlani; the route to be followed in journeying from one city to the other; the villages and their inhabitants; the religious rites and customs of the people; and the banks of the Kẹlani-gaṇga. From 52 to 76, Kẹlani, its temples, dágobas, and other sacred sites (of many of which, as in Kóṭṭa, only traditional traces now remain), its dancing girls, and singing women, are the subjects of the poet's theme. The next sixteen stanzas contain

---

and prosperity—we feel that we committed meritorious acts (*i.e.*) in a previous existence.—4. Excellent friends, like a picture on a wall (which does not or cannot turn away), are immutable both in prosperity and adversity. Friend of the like character, having rivetted thy attention, give ear unto my words, both pleasing and prognostic of future happiness.

a glowing description of the God Vibíshana. 93 to 104 contain the message and prayer, in the course of which admirable sketches are given of the minister Nallurutanayá, the king Parákkrama, and Ulakuda-devi, the Princess-Royal. 105 and 106 give shrewd advice as to the best methods of furthering the suit, and 107 ends the poem with the author's benediction on the bird. Two additional stanzas give information concerning the writer, and the date at which he wrote.*

---

* In some copies there are 108 stanzas;—one, descriptive of Kóṭṭa, being inserted as the 10th. This however is considered an interpolation by some authorities.

The text of the Sẹla-lihini Sandésa, with an ancient sanne, was first published by Tudâve pandit in 1859. The same work, with an English metrical translation, literally rendered, and with notes and a glossary for the use of students, was published, in 1865, by W. C. Macready, Esq., of the Ceylon Civil Service. It forms a useful volume of 100 8vo. pages, from which we extract the following specimen:—

CI. "4...On *her his daughter*, beauteous and renowned
Princess Ulukudé, 1...who learned is
In poetry and eloquence, 2 ..who shews
Great zeal and love for Buddha's Páli law,
Neglecting not the pure observances
Of the eight Sílas on moon's quarter days,
C. 4.. Like one with reason and with wisdom born
The ten good works to practice, *and* who keeps
The obligations of her marriage vow
And morals pure, 2...raining a rain of wealth
Kindly upon her maids and men, 1...*best* pleased
To share her joys among her women friends,
XCIX. 4...Fair as the new moon which th' inhabitants
Of earth, loving, adore 3...in wisdom like
Divine Saraswati apparent made,

As a further specimen we quote stanzas 99 to 102.*

99. Sirisa(n)da wan saw siri diyunuwẹ ra(n)dana
Situ mina wan yadi yadinaṭa danin dena
Sarasawi wan nuwanin pahalawẹ penena
Nawa sa(n)da wan lew wẹsi adarin wa(n)dina.

[sweet,
99. "To her—his youthful daughter—like peerless Lakshmí
Or new moon cloudless rising, which men adoring greet;
Who learn'd as Saraswatí, and graced with beauty's charms,
Is famed alike for wisdom, for bounty, and for alms,—
Whose suppliants see daily, she more and more to them
Is, in generous donations, the wish-conferring gem:—

From almsgiving to suppliant mendicants
The wishing gem resembling, like Síri
In whom reside, in whom increase all charms;—
4...On her, as fitting is, a jewel fair
A son bestow, 3...with glory, wisdom wealth,
And length of years, cheering the hearts *of men:*
Give this, great God, eye of the triple worlds,
Whose sacred feet are wetted 1.. with the drops
Of perfumed honey from the flower wreaths
Upon the crowns of bending deities."

* *Lit.*—102. O great God (Vibhíshana)—the eye of the three worlds, and whose beauteous feet are laved in the sweet nectar that proceeds from the flowery chaplets of the Dáityas! [101] On Princess Ulakuḍá, happy and renowned,—99. who lives, like Siri, in the enjoyment of great prosperity,—like the Situmini, by reason of her gifts to supplicating mendicants,—like Sarasvatí, who is famed for her wisdom,—and like the new moon which is affectionately adored by people; 100. who possesses a very mind cherished with (as much) affection towards her friends, as to herself; who is like a rainy-cloud, which graciously showers (wealth) upon her maids and servants; who observes inviolate a

100. Yehelin keré saki sẹpa samaga sit mé
Kulunen dẹsi dasun weta wasina watmé
Rakimin patini dam yahapat sirit mé
Sihinẹn nipan wan dasa pin pẹwẹtmé.

101. Mihiri tepala tan wẹsi kiwikam purudú
Itiri bẹti pemẹti pela dahamehi Muni(n)dú
Nohẹri póya aṭa sil rẹkuma pirisidú
Sasiri Ulakuḍaya déwíhaṭa pasidú.

[bonds
100. To her—the high-born princess—who, natheless, friendship's
Delights in; with her ladies shares joys, to theirs responds;—
Whose men and maids are by her, with kindly liberal hand
Enrich'd, as by the rain-clouds is fertilized the land;
Who from her inborn wisdom and intellectual ken
Appreciates, adheres to, Religion's precepts ten;
Who with pure heart unswerving the Patini-Dam obeys,
A model is of virtue, a wife above all praise:—

101. Who gracious in her language, with soft and 'suasive voice
Selects, and fluent utters, words eloquent and choice;
Who skill'd in arts poetic, evinces earnest zeal
For all that sacred writings, our Sage's laws reveal;
Who each recurring póya neglects no holy rite,
Nor fails the eight-fold Síla with fervor to recite:—

---

course of pure chastity; and who is born, endowed with wisdom and sound memory, for the observance of the ten meritorious deeds;—101. who is accustomed to speech, sweet and apropos; who is skilled in the art of poetry—evincing great and affectionate zeal for Buddha's doctrinal texts; and who never fails the observance of the sabbath, and the eight pure religious obligations;—[on this happy and renowned princess] 102 bestow [I pray thee],

102. Dit rupu silu maldam suwa(n)da mí wẹsa
Tet siripáyut suri(n)duni tiló ẹsa
Sit pinawana ẹti ásiri nuwana yasa
Put ruwanak so(u)da duna mẹṇawi nisi lesa.

---

102. Eye of the world—worlds triple—whose beauteous feet are wet
With nectar-drops sweet-scented from floral chaplets set
On crowns of bow'd Dáityas,—oh Vibíshana! give,
With glory, wisdom, power, and destined long to live—
To Ulakuḍá-Dewí—belov'd, renown'd, most fair,
Oh give, as best thou seest, to her a son, an heir!—
Th' inestimable blessing in season due bestow;
To king, princess, and people, thy favor great thus shew."

W. S.

PARAVI SANDÉSA,

'The Pigeon-Messenger' is also a poem by the same writer. It is a work of great merit, and is generally of a piece with the last in style, although in many parts inferior to it in imagery. It was a Message to Krishna, invoking blessings upon the army, the king's brother of the name of Parákkrama of Máyádunu, who had the government of Jaffna, and upon Chandrawatí, a near relation of king Parákkrama Báhu VI.

The poet's attachment to the family of his sovereign seems to have been very great. Even in this poem there are tender allusions to the royal family. That Chandrawatí might soon enter the bonds of matrimony,

---

as it seemeth best, an invaluable son, acceptable, replete with wisdom, wealth, years and renown.

and that, allied to a noble prince, she might become the mother of a virtuous son, are amongst the warmest aspirations of the writer, and the topics of his song. No date is given to this work; but from the slight difference of style to which allusion has been made, we are led to suppose that it was written shortly after the last.

Similar in plan to the Seḷa-lihiṇi Sandésa, this poem commences with an address to the Paravi, his messenger. The opening stanzas (séheḷi,) we here quote:—

Sẹrada parevi(n)du sa(ṇ)da pa(n)duwan surat saraṇin
Pahala kirimuhudin saha pabala pẹlasak wan
Mituru turu sarahana mamituru nawa wasatayuru
Nu(m)binena sa(n)da nada mada mada pawanẹlelí
Hebipul Kumudu hẹ(n)gẹ nogatuda atingilí.
Suraga(n)gi nalanelu(m)bu dẹlisandahasa novetapata.*

"Long be thy life extended, sweet Paravi, dear friend!
Who with thy plumes cream-tinted and feet of reddest hue
Art like a chank with corals, Milk-ocean's product fair,
Or sun with stars bright shining in azure autumn sky.—
When hither gently wafted, on breeze delightful borne,
Did not the nymphs who saw thee thy form believe to be
A full bloom'd snow-white lily from Swarga blown to earth?
Did not the rája-hansas thee deem, when gathering round,
A lotus-bud fresh fallen from heaven's own river clear?—

---

* *Lit.*— Mayest thou, O noble Paravi! live long; My friend! who by reason of thy yellow-white hue, and deeply red feet, art like unto a chank with coral plants produced from the milky-ocean, and unto the clear autumnal sky bespangled with the sun and the stars! When thou wast slowly moving in the sky, and in

Sudubudu nivesinena topa dẹka lew esa(n)da
Sudubudu rẹs piḍekẹyi nokalóda puda

Sa(n)dekin Nadunuyaninena maleka surana(m)bé
Sa(n)dekin lobin waṭalá nodamúda i(m)bé
Nidukin avudasakisa(n)da ataramaga nu(m)bé
Itikin apaṭa sẹpanam dẹkma mayi nu(m)bé

Did not the world, deluded, thee for Buddha's ray mistake,
His ray of purest white, and hasten offerings to make?—

Did not goddesses embrace thee, caress with fond delight,
And imagine thee a flower from Nandana's gardens bright?—
Hast thou scatheless hither come, hath unhinder'd been thy flight?
Then trebly welcome friend to us thy bliss-producing sight."

W. S.

The route of the intended journey is then sketched out; Koṭṭa, the chief city; the reigning sovereign, the temples and dewálas are described; and particular notice is taken of Pẹpiliyána-vihára, founded by the king in honor of his mother—to which fact a stone inscription on the spot still bears witness. Attiḍiya and Moratu Eliya [plain] are then noticed, and the scenery from thence to Pánaduré and on to Kalutara,

---

a delightfully gentle breeze, were not (goddesses) deceived in thee for a beautifully full-blown white lily dropt from (heaven)? Did not rája-hansas approach thee under a belief that thou wast a lotus-bud fallen off from the celestial river? Did they (the world) not make offerings to thee under an impression that thou wast a white ray emitted from Buddha's pure court? Did not goddesses kiss thee with delight under the mistaken idea that thou wast a flower from Nandana, the heavenly park? Hast thou arrived scatheless in thy aërial journey? Noble friend, to us thy sight is bliss!

occupy the poet up to stanza 66. Towns, villages, temples, streams, tanks and ponds, and scenery of sky, land, and sea, with all objects worthy of note from Kalutara to Bentoṭa, on to Galle and Mátara, and thence to Dondra head, are themes for stanzas 67 to 147; and the reader will observe that the route which was known 400 years ago, is, with very slight deviation, the principal line of communication now existing between Koṭṭa and Dondra. The latter is then described (similarly to Kẹlani in the Seḷa-lihini Sandésa) in 33 stanzas. The 181st stanza commences a description of the god Krishna, which ends with the 195th. The Message, to the god, with prayers on behalf of the king, his brother the sub-king at Máyádunu, and the royal army, bring the poem to the concluding stanza, the 212th, in which the author gives his name. The whole is full of most interesting topographic and historic notices. As a further sample of the author's style we here give stanzas 71 to 73.

71. Ran tẹṭi ayuru tu(n)gu pun piyayuru udula
Man aṭi karana a(n)ganó ra(n)ga dena ipila
Un sẹṭi balásiṭi salelun nopẹ́ ẹla
Bentoṭinetara sẹtapewa Kálikówila.*

"Bentoṭa cross, and nigh the stream where Kali's temple stands
For sleep repair, observing well the gay and sprightly bands
That fascinated nightly there the dancing girls behold,
Whose heaving bosoms to their gaze seem rounded cups of gold.

---

* *Lit.*—71. Cross Bentoṭa, and sleep thou at Káli-kovila, where sprightly youths, unmoved witness, the lovely hopping nautch girls,

72. Eta dadarada eguwana wana wásayaṭa
A(n)duru rupun wan sa(n)da wana wásayaṭa
Gosin tosin Bentoṭa Wanawásayaṭa
Wadu mituri(n)du rẹ dina wana wásayaṭa.

73. Evu Riwi himi wil kata kirana ran pata
Evu kiyawana bi(n)gu revu watini siyapata
Sivu digineta esa(n)dehi nala suwa(n)da yuta
Yavu mamituru wẹ(n)da muni(n)dun bẹtin sita.

When next the Moon possession shall have taken of the sky,
And to solitude hath Darkness his foe compell'd to fly,
To Bentoṭa with gladness then, oh friend! direct thy way,
And at Wanawása quietly repose till break of day.

When to the Plain her lord the Sun his message sends of light,
And with the hum of bees its lines her lotus-lips recite,
To Buddha great then worship give with true and faithful heart,
And on the fragrant balmy breeze that fills all space depart."

W. S.

---

whose full heaving bosoms resemble golden cups. 72. When the Moon shall have taken possession of the sky, and the Enemy of Darkness has retired into solitude; noble friend! gladly enter thou the Wanawása [temple] of Bentoṭa for (thy) rest at night. 73. [But] when the Consort of the Plain shall, with her lotus-mouth, and the hum of bees, have read the Epistle of Light, forwarded by her lord, the Sun,—then in the soft fragrant breeze which fills all sides, do thou depart, after worshipping Buddha with a faithful heart.

The Sidat-Sangará

is the only standard Grammar of the Siṇhalese. There are several editions of this work, and one, with an English translation, published in 1853. The text has been also published by Pandit Tudáve, with a gloss, and vocabulary.

Sidat-Sangará means 'a compilation of First Principles.' This Grammar is designed 'for beginners,' and is stated to have been compiled 'on the standard of previous works on Grammar.' We thus learn that many Siṇhalese Grammars were extant in this Island from a very early period; a fact which, without this direct testimony, is rendered highly probable from the evidence which is furnished by the literature of the land.

The work under notice contains twelve chapters. The first treats on Signs, or Orthœpy, and Orthography; the second on Permutation; the third on Gender; the fourth on Declension; the fifth on Compound words; the sixth on Concord; the seventh on Verbs; the eighth on Derivatives; the ninth on Voices; the tenth on Syntax; the eleventh on good and evil Characters, etc.; and the twelfth on Rhetoric.

Since there is a translation of this work with a lengthy Introduction, an extended notice of it here is unnecessary; a few descriptive observations may not however be deemed unacceptable.

The correspondence between the terminology of the writer before us, and that of Buddhagosa, has been already briefly noticed.—See *ante*, p. 68.

The language used, and the grammatical forms treated of, prove, beyond all manner of doubt, that the Siŋhalese is a North-Indian dialect. For full particulars on the subject the reader is referred to two articles published in the Journal of the Ceylon Branch of the Royal Asiatic Society for 1866 and 1867.

The following extract from the concluding part of the work, which we present as a specimen, contains allusion to the writer, and his patron:

> Mẹ́ pela pamana si(m)bi kivi man danan pasasata
> Garahata yalidu kam kim pa(n)duvóma mehi pamanó.
> Duhuna dana haṭa mut mekudu Sidatin viyatini
> Piriyatnaṭa nẹta datak mehi kaḷa matẹta tusvá.
> Dakana Laka siyal bujamahavuruṇi rakná
> Dedev radalagam vimanaga patirájadevsẹradené
> Adaren yadata ohu vibatẹ tiraṇa siya basẹ
> Palakaranuvas mekelem kulunen Sidatsangará.
>
> Mehi padanuvaga dẹna viyaraṇa vidi bajamina
> Nitetinimana pasi(n)da vida danada pini pilena
> Yasaraladigela(m)bena vitara pata sayuru mena
> Naganu melaka niti diya dada narasahamina.

'What signifies the praise or censure of pretended Pandits, who only acquired the first elements (of Grammar)? Learned Pandits alone are competent critics. O Pandits, although this little Sidata, except to the beginner, has nothing original in it (to recommend itself) to the erudite; rejoice ye at my labours. May Patirája, like unto a flag on the summit of the mansion-like village Radula, and who, by the arm of his extensive ramparts, governs the whole of the

Southern Lanka, be long prosperous! I have composed the Sidat-Sangará at his kind request, and with a view to disseminate (the knowledge of) the rudiments of cases, etc., in the Siŋhalese language. The wise man who has learned its rules (both) primary and secondary, and made Grammar his study, will, having with facility removed the pretensions of the learned, who are elated with pride, constantly hoist up the flag of success in (this island of) Lanka, like the boundless ocean with the renown of his waves, wide-spread in all directions.'

We are unable to identify the village Radula; and there is no reliable evidence to indicate the situation of the Patirájapirivena, of which the author was the superior incumbent; See Sidat-Sangará, p. 43. But, since the temple was named after its founder, and he is said to have been the Governor of Southern Lanka, it may not be difficult to place it somewhere in the Southern Province of Ceylon. But we have yet to learn the name of the author, and to identify the founder of the monastery.

A tradition states that the writer is identical with the author of the Bálavatára; but this is contradicted by another tradition which identifies the Grammarian with the author of the Sidat-Sangará. That tradition is founded on the facts stated in the following passage in the Rasaváhiní.

Yoká síhala bhásáya síhala sadda Lakkhanan tena Vedeha therena katháya Rasaváhiní.—'This book called the) Rasaváhiní was composed by the same

Reverend Vedeha who had composed the Siṇhalese Grammar in the Siṇhalese language.' Before however we attempt to identify the minister Patirája, we shall, from internal evidence, which the Sidat-Sangará furnishes, endeavour to ascertain the chronological position which it occupies with reference to the known literature of the land.

The writer, it would appear, quotes from several authors, and among others from the Asakdá, a poem which is no longer extant, and of which little or nothing is known beyond that it was a poem of great merit; and from the Kavu Silumina, whose author was King Pandita Parákrama Báhu III—1266 A. D.

As pointed out by the translator at page cxvi., a stanza in the Káviasékara quotes a few words which are given as examples in the Sidat-Sangará. Now, it is true that there is a belief among some Siṇhalese scholars, that the grammarian, who professes to write his work upon 'the precepts of unerring custom, or after the established usage of eminent writers, has borrowed most of his illustrations such as 'nat for anat, from the Káviasékara;' yet, we believe, apart from the modernism of the style and poetry of the last-mentioned work—a fact which sufficiently refutes the above opinion—there is almost conclusive evidence to support the more generally prevailing belief, that the Káviasékara was subsequent to the date of this Grammar. We say there is nearly conclusive evidence, because the poet, as will be seen on reference to the stanza quoted in the Sidat-Sangará at p. clxxx., places the Verb in the "seventh section or chapter of the Grammar," a division which agrees accurately with that given in the Sidat-Sangará.

Assuming then that the above refers to the Grammar under notice, we find no difficulty to assign to it a date between the age of Parákrama in 1266 and 1410 A. D., when the Káviasékara was written.

We have yet another fact, by which the interval between these two dates, which gives a period of 144 years, may be reduced, and that is, if possible, by the identification of Patirája.

We read of several celebrated ministers of that name in our historical books. In the Introduction to the Sidat-Sangará (see p. clxxxii), we were inclined to identify him with the Wírasiṇha Patirája mentioned in the Introduction to the Siṇhalese version of the Pansiyapanas Játaka. But recent researches enable us to identify him with the Patirája deva, whom Parákrama III—1266 A. D. despatched to South Ceylon to repair dilapidated religious edifices,* and generally for the promotion of religion, and to whom we have already alluded at p. 23.

* See Mahávansa.

APPENDIX.

APPENDIX.

Professor Max Müller to Mr. Herbert.

Parks End, Oxford,
March 21st, 1870.

SIR,

I HAVE read with great interest the papers forwarded to Lord Granville by Sir Hercules Robinson, stating the measures which have lately been taken by the Ceylon Government for making a collection of MSS.—Páli, Siṇhalese and Sanskrit—that are still to be found in Ceylon, and publishing without delay a Catalogue of the same.

In taking measures for the preservation of the ancient Literature of India and Ceylon, the Government is performing a duty which, in the present state of the country, could be efficiently performed by no one else.

Whatever, according to the varying judgment of European Scholars, the intrinsic value of the ancient Literature of India may be, the fact remains that, through all the vicissitudes of their past history, the inhabitants of that country have from century to century handed down their literary treasures with the greatest care, and have thus preserved to us a literature which in antiquity exceeds that of Italy and Greece, nay, possibly of evey other country in the world. From the days of Sir William Jones, the interest excited by the ancient Literature of India among European scholars has been steadily increasing, and it seems certainly a strange fact, that while English education is rapidly spreading all over India, Professorships should be founded in every University of

Europe for teaching the ancient language and Literature of the Brahmans.

It would by no means be fair to charge the English Government with indifference as to the ancient Literature of its Indian subjects.

Both the East India Company and the Indian Ministry have repeatedly afforded their patronage to Editions of texts and translations from Sanskrit Literature, and the collection of Sanskrit MSS. which has gradually been brought together in the East India House, and is now preserved at the India Office, is without comparison the largest and most valuable in Europe.

At the same time it cannot be doubted, that more energetic measures are required, in order to prevent the loss of a Literature which exists chiefly in MSS., and which, with the progress of English education and the spread of English ideas in India, is losing in the eyes of many of the natives that importance which it formerly possessed. In former days, most native princes considered it their duty to keep up a Library and to maintain a staff of Librarians, whose office it was to copy each MS. as soon as it began to shew signs of decay. Sanskrit MSS. are mostly written on paper made of vegetable substances, and unless preserved with great care, they seldom last in the sultry climate of India beyond three or four centuries. When the native princes were mediatised and pensioned by the English Government, one of the first retrenchments in their establishments consisted in the abolition of their libraries, and the dismissal of their librarians. Some of the Rajahs offered their libraries as presents to the East India Company, but report says that a rule was passed excluding libraries from the class of presents acceptable to the Company.

The result is, that in different parts of India collections of ancient MSS. have crumbled to dust, and that literary works which had been preserved for centuries have been lost for ever.

During and after the late mutiny, so many accounts of the wanton destruction of Libraries came to my knowledge, that I ventured to make a representation to Lord Elgin before he left England as Governor-General, urging him to sanction some plan for the preservation of the ancient literature of India. Lord Elgin promised to keep the matter in mind, and I doubt not that if his life had been spared we should have had an Elgin collection of Oriental MSS., which need not have feared comparison with the Elgin collection of Marbles at the British Museum. My letter to Lord Elgin would probably be found in his official correspondence.

I was much pleased therefore to find, when reading the letter from Pandit Radha Kisu to His Excellency the Viceroy, dated 10th May, 1868, that what I had so long advocated had at last taken a practical shape, and I trust that nothing will now interfere with the carrying out of the judicious measures sanctioned by the Indian Government for the collection and preservation of Sanskrit MSS.

With regard to Ceylon, it seems to me that it would there be even easier to carry out the plan adopted by the Indian Government than in India itself.

The literature of Ceylon is much more limited. It is the literature of an Island, and what is important in it is almost entirely restricted to the sacred literature of Buddhism. I doubt whether in Ceylon there are MSS. more ancient than those of India, for although the materials on which they are written, palm or bamboo leaves, are far more durable than paper, political and religious convulsions seem to have caused the destruction of the ancient libraries of the temples and monasteries; still there is no reason why a careful search should not be made for ancient MSS., or fragments of ancient MSS., and in case they should be found it would seem expedient to preserve carefully-made copies in Ceylon, but to transfer the originals to England, where they would be in safer keeping than anywhere else. It is important to observe, that even paper MSS. which begin to shew signs of decay in India, are perfectly safe as soon as they are brought to the colder climate of England. I possess myself MSS. which had suffered much from damp and insects while in India, but which now seem to resist all further ravages.

The principal object of the collectors should be to bring together a complete set of the canonical books of the Buddhists, with their commentaries, whether in Páli or Siṇhalese.* The titles and contents of most of these books are known to every student of Buddhism, and the munificent present of a complete copy of the Buddhist Canon from the

* It will be satisfactory to know that a carefully revised copy of the Tepiṭaka is being transcribed for the Ceylon Oriental Library; that "the munificent present" of the Burmese Government is already in its shelves, and that ere long a third copy of the Texts, from Siam, in Kámboja character, the gift of which has also been promised, will be added to the collection. There is no real difference between these three national Records, since they are all copies of the work originally brought over to Ceylon by Mahinda. But, we apprehend, great difference will be found to exist between the Siṇhalese version of the Tepiṭaka and its Commentaries, and the version of the Northern Buddhists; and we have no doubt that the Government of this Island will, at no distant date, add to its Library a copy of the Nepal version of the Buddhist Scriptures, including their Commentaries,—works which will certainly enable scholars to detect, by intercomparison, the frauds and impostures which have in process of time crept into both.

king of Burmah, would enable any Páli Scholar to make out an accurate list of the books contained in it. It would thus be easy, after the most accessible MSS. have been brought together, to draw up a list of deficiencies, and to send it to the principal monasteries and libraries in Ceylon. It would not require any large outlay to have the whole of the now existing Páli literature of Ceylon carefully transcribed, and the copies preserved in a safe place. It would be still better, wherever it is possible, that the original MSS. should be bought and preserved; and I may state, that on several occasions I have found possessors of ancient and slightly damaged MSS. in India ready to exchange them for a modern copy.

The publication of a Catalogue of the MSS. thus collected would be of great use to scholars in Europe, and it is much to be desired that the making of such a Catalogue should be entrusted to one or several really competent Páli scholars. It might be well at first to print a specimen only, and to send that specimen for approval to some Páli scholars in Europe. In printing extracts, it would be most desirable to adopt the Roman alphabet, and strictly to adhere to some definite system in transcribing Páli letters by Roman letters. Great care should also be taken that the extracts are given correctly, and, if possible, with a literal translation.

I return the original enclosures.

I have, &c.,
(Signed) MAX MÜLLER.

R. G. W. HERBERT, Esq.

The Scheme of Orthography

adopted in this work, to express, in Roman characters, the Páli, Sanskrit, and Siŋhalese words and extracts, demands a brief explanation. It will be observed that that scheme is in the main identical with the one sanctioned by the Government Minute of the 28th August, 1866, and is as follows :—

Sanskrit, Páli, and Siŋhalese.

Vowels.

අ ආ ඉ ඊ උ ඌ ඍ ඎ ඏ ඐ

a á i í u ú ṛ ṝ ḷṛ ḷṝ

Diphthongs.

ඒ ඓ ඕ ඖ

e ai o au

Semi-Consonants.

ං ṃ ; ඃ ḥ

Consonants.

Gutterals ...	ක k	ඛ kh	ග g	ඝ gh	ඞ ń
Palatals ...	ච ch	ඡ chh	ජ j	ඣ jh	ඤ ñ
Linguals ...	ට ṭ	ඨ ṭh	ඩ ḍ	ඪ ḍh	ණ ṇ
Dentals ...	ත t	ථ th	ද d	ධ dh	න n
Labials ...	ප p	ඵ ph	බ b	භ bh	ම m
Semi-vowels	ය y	ර r	ල l	ළ ḷ	ව v
Sibilants ...	ස s	ශ s'	ෂ sh	හ h	

The Siŋhalese

Vowels.

ඇ ẹ; ඈ ẹ́; ඒ é; ඕ ó;

Consonants.

ඟ (ṇ)g ඦ (ñ)j ඬ (ṇ)ḍ ඳ (n)d ; ඹ (m)b.

Remarks.

For the vowels ඍ and ඎ, the Government Minute gives ṛi, ṝi ; and there is neither provision for ඏ ḷṛ, and ඐ ḷṝ, nor the necessary type for the signs adopted and given above. For the anusvára again, the same Minute gives ṇ ; but since the use of n, with an open dot below, may lead many, as it has led me, to confound it with the lingual ṇ; I have adopted an ṃ with a dot below. That symbol, however, is not to be found in the Printing Establishment, and the consequence is, that I have been compelled to use the simple dental n or the labial m in its stead, leaving it to the reader to discern the correct character from the sense of the word. Owing to the same cause I have not been able to express the semi-consonant ඃ ḥ properly.

In proceeding to the Consonants I may remark that ච ch, is unnecessarily expressed in two letters; and the inconvenience is doubly great when we have to express it with its aspirate, thus chchh. As the scheme adopted by Fausböll is in this respect, as in others, very simple, it is my intention in the second volume to use c and ch in all cases, where in this volume I have used ch, and chh. There is only one other remark necessary under this head, and that is, that I have not been able to confine the last semi vowel in the list to a simple *v*, but have adopted the promiscuous use of *v* and *w*.

Under the head of the Siṇhalese Vowels the reader will observe that in the Siṇhalese extracts I had to use ç, ḉ, characters which are not found in the Sanskrit and Páli alphabets; and also é, and ó, which in the Siṇhalese are found with marked accent.

The Sanskrit anubandhas ṇg, ñj, ṇḍ, nd and mb possess different sounds in the Siṇhalese (see Sidatsangará, p. lxi.) and are, metrically, one syllabic instant. No signs have been appropriated authoritatively for these sounds ; nor are there any types to represent them. I have therefore (though somewhat unwillingly) resorted to the plan indicated in the above table for expressing them.

In presenting the first volume of this work to the Public, I may be permitted to state that the materials for the second volume are ready, and in the press. It will contain a complete Analysis of the VINAYA-PIṬAKA, with preliminary observations on several important subjects. I have, with the assistance of two of the most talented Pandits in this island, Batuvantudáve, and Sumańgala, High Priest, literally rendered into English all that may fairly be ascribed to Gotama Buddha. I have also given, to an appreciable extent, all the Precepts, Legends, Explanations, and Sútras, extracting only those parts of the Text, which, in my opinion, might lead to important investigations. The literal translations are invariably preceded by the Texts, which have been collated with several authentic copies, Siŋhalese, Burmese, and Siamese. A copious Table of Contents will serve all the purposes of a Descriptive Catalogue, whilst no pains will be spared to make the separate Index, intended for the second volume, as full as is desirable.

If the Analysis of this Piṭaka should fall short of the prescribed limits, which are the same as those assigned to the present volume, I purpose to commence with an analysis of the SU'TRA-PIṬAKA, but I do not believe I shall be able to present as many extracts from it as I have done from the Vinaya.

RULES OF THE GOVERNMENT ORIENTAL LIBRARY.*

I. That the Sanskrit, Páli, and Siŋhalese Library established by the Government of Ceylon, be called "The Government Oriental Library."

II. That the same be under the immediate control and supervision of the Colonial Secretary for the time being.

III. That all affairs connected with the said Library be conducted and managed by a paid Librarian, and one or more servants appointed by the Governor.

IV. That the Librarian be required to give security to the satisfaction of the Colonial Secretary for the due preservation of the books and records, and generally for the observance of the rules of the institution, and the due performance of all the duties required of him.

V. That the Library be kept open every day from 11 o'clock in the forenoon till 4 o'clock in the afternoon, except on Sundays and other Government holidays, and except after 2 o'clock on Saturdays.

VI. That on no account whatsoever shall any person be allowed to remove any book belonging to the Library beyond the precincts of the Library.

---

* "His Excellency the Governor has been pleased to direct, that the following Rules framed by the Government Oriental Library Committee, and approved by His Excellency, be published for general information.

"By His Excellency's Command,

"Colonial Secretary's Office, Colombo, 26th September, 1870.

HENRY T. IRVING, Colonial Secretary."

—[*Ceylon Government Gazette. No.* 3,787. *October* 1, 1870.]

VII. That the books belonging to the Library shall be kept clear of dust, shall always during office hours be exposed to the air, and shall at intervals of two months be exposed to the sun ; the Librarian shall moreover do all things necessary for the due preservation of books and olas.

VIII. That the Librarian shall himself keep the keys of the Library shelves, and shall not permit any person access to the books of the Library except in his presence, or except in the manner provided for by Rule IX.

IX. That the Librarian shall be responsible for any book that may be taken out of the shelf for purposes of copying, comparison, or inspection, and that the same shall on no account be removed beyond the limits of the Library premises.

X. That the Librarian shall from time to time, as may be expedient, cause a printed Catalogue of the Library, both in English and Siŋhalese, to be issued to the public, and for a price to be fixed by the Colonial Secretary.

XI. That the Librarian shall be at liberty to issue extracts on ola or paper of any of the books, or parts of the books, of the Library, on the written application of a party, and on payment of such a reasonable fee as the Colonial Secretary may from time to time sanction.

XII. That the Librarian shall keep

(1) A classified Catalogue of the books of the Library, the numbers in which shall correspond with the numbers borne by the books. All additions to the Library shall from time to time be inserted in the said catalogue ;

(2) A register, in a form to be approved of by the Colonial Secretary, of references made and of extracts or copies issued by him ;

(3) A memorandum of all the fees so received as aforesaid, an account whereof the Librarian shall, moreover, from time to time render to the Colonial Secretary, shewing the receipts on the one hand, and disbursements on the other ; and

(4) Such further catalogues, lists, or other memoranda, as the Colonial Secretary may from time to time prescribe.

XIII. That all extracts shall be made within the Library premises either by copyists employed by the Librarian, or by the person or persons requiring such extracts. No one shall be employed as copyist without the previous sanction of the Colonial Secretary.

XIV. That any one desirous of inspecting or comparing a book of the Library with his own, shall be at liberty to do so in the presence of the Librarian within the Library premises, and free of any charge whatever.

XV. That any one desirous of obtaining an extract from a book belonging to the Library, may employ his own copyist to make it at his sole cost and expense, or he may obtain the extract on a written application to the Librarian, and on his tendering the regulated fee for that purpose.

XVI. That no one should be allowed to smoke, or chew betel, or spit within the Library premises.

CORRECTIONS.

PAGE.		LINE.	
xi	...	29	*for* Pitaka *read* Piṭaka.
2	...	13	*for* kunjará *read* kuñjará.
„	...	19	*for* Ganam'pi páni *read* gaṇam'pi páṇí.
„	...	20	*for* guno *read* guṇo.
„	...	21	*for* lingesu *read* liṅgesu.
„	...	22	*for* káranan *read* káraṇan.
3	...	4	*for* Abhidhána'padípikan *read* Abhidhánappadípikan.
4	...	22	*for* ánara *read* anara.
7	...	10	*for* Bhikkhus and Sanghas *read* Council of bhikkhús.
11	...	7	*for* Pali *read* Páli; *also elsewhere.*
„	...	24	*for* Lambakanna *read* Lambakaṇṇa.
31	...	16	*for* affected *read* afflicted.
33	...	23	*for* lekhanakárayi *read* lekhamakárayi.
35	...	7	*for* Jyotigñána...Purána *read* Jyotirjñána...Puráṇa
„	...	11	*for* visiṇ *read* visin.
„	...	13	*for* rachanákarana *read* rachanákaraṇa.
„	...	18	*for* panjara *read* pañjara.
„	...	20	*for* saṇchíkrita Vaṇchí *read* Sañchíkrita Vañchí.
„	...	22	*for* lanká *read* laṅká.
36	...	7	*for* patam *read* patan.
37	...	4	*for* Sátru *read* S'atru.
40	...	6	*for* abhivandi yaggan *read* abhivandiya'ggan.
„	...	7	*for* gana'mutta mancha *read* gaṇa'mutta mañcha.
„	...	13	*for* suneyya *read* suṇeyya.
41	...	17	*for* byanjaná *read* byañjaná.
„	...	20	*for* Each (set of) five, etc, *read* Lit. '(There are) classes, from five to five, to the end of *m*.'

PAGE.	LINE.	
41	... 23	*for* Suttan *read* Sutta.
42	... 2	*for* composition *read* usage ; *also at* p. 60.
43	9 & 10	*for* sanyoge *read* saṇyoge.
47	... 4	*for* udako bako *read* udakabako.
„	... 5	*for* in a pot *read* on a pot.
„	... 20	*for* Vannaná *read* Vaṇṇaná.
„	... 21	*for* udáharana *read* udáharaṇa.
„	... 22	*for* pakaranan *read* pakaraṇan.
49	... 20	*for* vannita *read* vaṇṇita.
„	... 22	*for* parampará *read* párampará.
„	... „	*for* vinichchaya nichchayan *read* vinichchhaya nichchhayan.
50	... 3	*for* Manjusá *read* Mañjusá
„	... 6	*for* Kammadina *read* kammádiná.
„	... 8	*for* Neruttu *read* Nerutti.
51	... 25	*for* banavára, *and elsewhere, read* bháṇavára.
52	... 8	*for* kanchena *read* kañcheva.
„	... 9	*for* pancha *read* pañcha.
„	... 16	*for* sampinḍa *read* sampiṇḍa.
„	... 17	*for* cha *read* chha.
„	... 19	*for* ñyáse *read* nyáse.
„	... 20	*for* gahetv *read* gahetvá.
„	... 21	*for* ganantá *read* gaṇantá.
„	... „	*for* sata sata *read* satta sata.
„	... 28	*for* ñyáso *read* nyáso ; *also at* p. 53.
57	... 26	*for* pakarana *read* pakaraṇa.
62	... 23	*for* ván *read* váṇ.
66	... 2	*for* pancâlâh *read* páñcâlâh.
68	.. 28	*for* Buddhagosa *read* Buddhaghosa ; *also at* pp. 69, 70, etc.
69	... 3	*for* Karanan *read* Karaṇan ; *also line* 4, 22, 27.
„	... 6	*for* Panchamí *read* Pañchamí.
71	... 15	*for* vichayohàro *read* vichayáháro ; *also at line* 16, and 74.

PAGE.		LINE.	
71	...	17	*for* vichinati *read* vichiṇati ; *also at line* 18.
"	...	19	*for* nissaranan *read* nissaraṇan.
72	...	19	*for* pánánan *read* páṇánan.
"	...	20	*for* nívaranan *read* nívaraṇan ; *also at other places.*
73	...	13	*for* cha *read* chá.
"	...	30	*for* dkkhatá *read* dukkhatá
74	...	1	*for* dhukkatá *read* dukkhatá.
78	...	16	*for* Lághu *read* Laghu etc,
81	...	12	*for* nikádi *read* ṇikádi.
"	...	13	*for* Vásettha *read* Vásiṭṭha.
82	...	11	*for* nika *read* ṇika.
83	...	16	*for* manjúsan *read* mañjúsan ; *also at line* 23.
84	...	25	*for* súvádi *read* svádi.
86	...	5	*for* mundhisú *read* muṇḍisú.
"	...	20	*for* shabdkirímehi *read* s'abdakirímehi.
88	...	12	*for* Dhátupáthas *read* Dhátupáṭhas
115	...	4	*for* sute *read* suto.
116	...	13	*for* patricide *read* parricide.
"	...	9	*for* Sanghancha *read* Saṅghañcha.
121	...	28	*for* bhikkhu *read* bhikkhú.
"	...	30	*for* chiraṭṭhittan *read* chiraṭṭhitatthan.
126	...	20	*for* Sávatti *read* Sávatthi.
133	...	26	*for* sanbuddhe *read* sambuddhe.
"	...	28	*for* nitvána *and* nitva, *read* ṇitvána *and* ṇitvá.
134	...	8	*for* Thehi *read* tehi.
"	...	11	*for* yavbayan *read* savhayan.
"	...	23	*for* garu *read* garú
"	...	30	*for* sattapanne *read* sattapaṇṇi.
135	...	4	*for* avinásanan *read* avinásayan.
"	...	22	*for* sáratto *read* sárattho.
136	...	6	*for* Kasappa *read* Kassapa.
158	...	12	*for* Tanbapaṇṇí *read* Tambapaṇṇí.
"	...	21	*for* sambhuddo *read* sambuddho.
159	...	15	*for* Tambapaṇṇa *read* Tambapaṇṇí.

PAGE.		LINE.	
159	...	21	*for* viaggan *read* vyaggan.
"	...	24	*for* deyyan *read* dheyyan.
160	...	13	*for* Mutusaivás *read* Muṭasíva's.
164	...	8	*for* sámanera *read* sámaṇera.
"	...	16	*for* Sangamitta *read* Saṅghamitta.
171	...	9	*for* kalan *read* kalaṇ.
"	...	11	*for* nayanoddhavan *read* nayanoddhavaṇ.
"	...	14	*for* s'ríghanan *read* s'ríghanaṇ.
173	...	20	*for* savu *read* sau.
174	...	12	*for* nirvana *read* nirváṇa.
177	...	18	*for* dos'a *read* dosha.
179	...	1	*for* vacanát *read* vachanát.
184	...	30	*for* siyádi *read* Syádi.
185	...	1	*for* Nádi *read* Ṇádi.
189	...	14	*for* Kavu *read* Kav.
191	...	18	*Regard last* n *as* ṇ. *See explanation at p.* 235.
201	..	6	*for* Prákkrama Bahu *read* Parákramabáhu.
"	...	12	*for* langaṭa *read* la(n)gaṭa.
"	...	17	*for* nuba *read* nu(m)ba.
211	...	8	*for* noharina *read* nohariṇa.
"	...	7	*for* situmini *read* situmiṇi.
218	...	4	*for* nodamúda *read* nodẹmúda.
220	...	6	*for* revu *read* rẹv.
222	...	10	*for* pamana *read* pamaṇa.
"	...	11	*for* pamano *read* pamaṇo.
"	...	14	*for* Dakqna *read* Dakaṇa.

www.ingramcontent.com/pod-product-compliance
Lightning Source LLC
Chambersburg PA
CBHW060612030726
47498CB00005B/1653
* 9 7 8 3 3 3 7 2 3 0 3 1 9 *